John Wentworth, Chicago Historical Society

Early Chicago. Fort Dearborn

An Address Delivered at the Unveiling of the Memorial Tablet ....

John Wentworth, Chicago Historical Society

Early Chicago. Fort Dearborn
An Address Delivered at the Unveiling of the Memorial Tablet ....

ISBN/EAN: 9783337109165

Printed in Europe, USA, Canada, Australia, Japan

Cover: Foto ©ninafisch / pixelio.de

More available books at **www.hansebooks.com**

Early Chicago.

FORT DEARBORN

AN ADDRESS,

Delivered at the Unveiling of the Memorial Tablet to Mark the Site of the Block-House,

On Saturday Afternoon, May 21st, 1881,

Under the Auspices of the

CHICAGO HISTORICAL SOCIETY,

To which have been added

NOTES AND AN APPENDIX.

BY

HON. JOHN WENTWORTH, LL.D.,

Late Editor, Publisher, and Proprietor for Twenty-Five Years of the "Chicago Democrat," the First Corporation Newspaper; Member of Congress, for the Chicago District, for Twelve Years; Two Terms Mayor; and a Settler of 1836.

CHICAGO:
FERGUS PRINTING COMPANY.
1881.

Entered according to Act of Congress, in the year 1881, by
FERGUS PRINTING COMPANY,
In the office of the Librarian of Congress, at Washington.

Revised from *The Chicago Tribune*, of Sunday, May 22, 1881.[*]

FORT DEARBORN.

The Memorial Tablet, Marking the Site of the Old
 Block-House, Unveiled—Address by Hon. John Wentworth—
 A Mass of Historical Information—Documents and Statements
 never before made Public—Capt. Heald's Own Story of the
 Circumstances Connected with the Massacre—Letter Ordering
 the Establishing of the Fort—Its Early Commanders—Prominent Officers who have been Stationed within its Walls—Gen.
 Scott and the Cholera—Noted Names in Early History—
 Remarks by Hon. Thomas Hoyne, Hon. Isaac N. Arnold, and
 Robert J. Bennett, Esq.—An Original Poem by Eugene J. Hall
 —A Son of Capt. Nathan Heald in Attendance.

THE tablet which marks the site of old Fort Dearborn was unveiled yesterday with appropriate ceremonies in the presence of the First Regiment I. N. G. (350 strong) and about 1500 citizens. As has been previously stated in *The Tribune*, the memento is on the north front of the building at the corner of River Street and Michigan Avenue, just opposite Rush-Street bridge. The idea originated in the Historical Society, and some of its officers having mentioned the subject to Mr. Wm. M. Hoyt, of the firm which occupies the structure, he fell in with it at once, and had the tablet put in at his own expense, and yesterday it was formally "presented" to the Historical Society. The fact that it would be was pretty well known, and by half-past three o'clock, when the militia were on the ground and massed on River Street, there was a large crowd of spectators in the vicinity who had assembled to take part in the proceedings. A stand had been erected on the corner for the accommodation of the speakers and others. On the front part of it was a model of the old block-house, with an American flag on the staff. The building was set off with two small oil-paintings of the fort and flags, every window on both fronts

[*] The issue of *The Tribune*, which contained the foregoing account of this interesting historical event, was indeed a remarkable one. It was made up of the regular edition, of 20 pages, and an extra of 16, containing the revised New Testament, *literatim, et verbatim, et punctuatim*. The entire paper was, therefore, made up of 36 pages, of seven columns to a page, or 252 column-

containing one of the latter, and a large flag was pendant from a rope strung across the street. Other structures in the neighborhood were similarly adorned.

Among the well-known citizens and old settlers on the stand and in the audience were the following: Gurdon S. Hubbard, Dr. Hiram Wheeler, who came to Chicago in 1831, and slept the first night on the floor of the block-house; Judge John A. Jameson, Hon. Thomas Hoyne, Hon. Isaac N. Arnold, John Bates, 1832; Thos. Rapp, Samuel D. Ward, Albert D. Hagar, James J. Richards, James Lane, E. F. C. Klokke, Rev. David Swing, Andrew J. Galloway, Walter Kimball, Hon. Wm. Bross, Mayor Carter H. Harrison, James Couch, Hon. E. M. Haines, Augustin Deodat Taylor, Michael Dulanty, Reuben J. Bennett, N. Landon; Lawrence Bauer, whose wedding reception took place in

in all. The New Testament occupied 112 columns of minion—a type two sizes larger than that used in setting up advertisements. Aside from its clear, attractive presentation of a work which the public was curious and even anxious to obtain at the earliest moment, and in all its entirety, *The Tribune* had its full complement of telegraphic and local news, editorial matter, and advertisements. Nothing was slurred over; nothing was omitted. It was a complete newspaper, in the best sense of the word. Out of the total of 252 columns, 72 were devoted to advertisements, and the remaining 180—including the 112 used in printing the New Testament—to reading matter. Of the 72 columns of advertisements, about 40 were taken up with displayed advertisements, about 31 with small advertisements, including the "Wants," and about a column with paid reading matter. Of the regular reading matter, 120 columns were set in minion, 59 in nonpareil, and 1 in agate.

The entire Testament revision was set up, corrected, placed in the forms, and stereotyped between the hours of ten in the morning and ten in the evening—a piece of work which is only a fair illustration of *The Tribune's* unsurpassed mechanical facilities. Eighty-seven compositors were employed in setting the type, and five in correcting the errors noted by the proof-readers, though neither class of workmen was continuously employed on the New Testament. A number of them were taken off the work along in the afternoon of Saturday, to set advertisements, while the remainder worked indiscriminately on the New Testament and the reading matter which went to make up the regular Sunday edition. Had the whole force been employed continuously on the New Testament, the whole revision would have been set up, corrected, locked up in the forms, and stereotyped in eight, instead of twelve hours. *The Tribune* has shown its enterprise in similar directions on several previous occasions, but on this one it excelled itself, furnishing a notable instance of what unlimited mechanical facilities, intelligently controlled, are able to accomplish.

the Fort; Hon. Elihu B. Washburne, Charles C. P. Holden, Joel C. Walter, Arthur G. Burley, Mark Kimball, Mr. —. McChesney, Thomas B. Carter, Rev. Jeremiah Porter, Benjamin F. Ayer, Charles Crosby, Capt. Darius Heald, Frank Hoyne, Col. W. H. Thompson, Gen. Philip H. Sheridan, William M. Hoyt, ex-Mayor Isaac L. Milliken, Moses J. Wentworth, Gen. A. L. Chetlain, Wm. B. H. Gray, Daniel K. Pearsons. W. H. King, Wm. K. Ackerman; Alexander, Henry, Philip, William S., Maurice D.P., and Isadore, all sons of Gen. John B. Beaubien; Saliston, David, George, Edward, Frank Gordon, and Slidell, all sons of Mark Beaubien; Frank, John, and William R., sons of Henry, and grandsons of Gen. J. B. Beaubien; Oscar Downs, son-in-law of Mark Beaubien, and Samuel S. Beach.

The gathering was called to order by the Hon. Isaac N. Arnold, President of the Historical Society, who said:

FELLOW-CITIZENS: I suppose there are many here to-day, possibly, who do not know that on the spot where we stand, and extending north, inclosed with pickets, was old Fort Dearborn, far off in the then wilderness. We have met to-day to place in position and to inaugurate a tablet that shall tell to all who shall come after us, where that Fort was located. There is present with us a gentleman who, forty-eight years ago, organized the first church in Chicago, and who preached his first sermon in the Fort. It is altogether proper that those services be opened with prayer, and that that gentleman should address the Throne of Grace on this occasion.

The Rev. Jeremiah Porter, who preached in the Fort in 1833, and was Chicago's first resident pastor, came forward and offered prayer.

Mr. Robert J. Bennett was then introduced and said:

MR. CHAIRMAN: In behalf of my respected kinsman and friend, Mr. William M. Hoyt, of this City, it is my pleasant privilege to present to you as the honorable President and representative of the Chicago Historical Society, and through you to the world, this tablet which is soon to be uncovered to the view of this audience. At the suggestion of members of your Society, this memorial stone is placed to tell the passers-by through the years to come that here stood old Fort Dearborn; that here, within the memory of men now living, stood the outmost defence of our common country; that here, on this spot, thrice consecrated by blood and fire, was planted the germ which in so short a time has budded, blossomed, and grown into this magnificent City. While we are looking over the past let it not be forgotten that we are making history for the future. We will fondly hope that the record of this generation will be as satisfactory to the next as are the events we now commemorate to us. May the Chicago of the future as far exceed the present in all that is great and glorious as does the present exceed the days of old Fort Dearborn.

Mr. Chairman, hoping this memorial stone will be as gladly received as it is cheerfully given, I ask Chicago's oldest citizen, our much esteemed Gurdon S. Hubbard, to unveil this tablet for inspection and acceptance.

The military presented arms, and, as Mr. Hubbard drew from in front of the tablet the flag which had covered it, the crowd cheered and the band played a medley of National airs.

Order being restored, Mr. Arnold requested Hon. Thomas Hoyne to respond on behalf of the Historical Society, and he did so as follows:

MR. BENNETT: I have been selected by the Historical Society to return to you their profound and grateful thanks for the very appropriate and beautiful memento which, at your own cost, you have placed on this historical corner. It is a memento which, as every one will see at a glance, recalls centuries of time, and embodies almost the whole history of events. We stand upon historical ground. We stand upon the ground where, as you have very eloquently said, was planted the original germ of the population who to-day constitute the great commercial metropolis of not only the West, where the Fort was established in advance of civilization, but the commercial centre of the country. We stand in the presence, also, of things which bring to remembrance some of the most remarkable events of National history. On yonder shore of this same river two centuries ago—in the winter of 1674—stood the first Christian missionary that ever visited this land,—the pious and humble Marquette, the discoverer of the Mississippi, who was the first white man that ever spent a winter on this river, or at this spot. And, sir, we stand upon the ground where, at the beginning of this century, a whole garrison marched out, and upon the shore of this lake, below here, were slaughtered mercilessly by the aboriginal inhabitants of this same land.

We say to you, Mr. Bennett, and your friend, Mr. Hoyt, and others whose patriotism and enterprise have secured this monument, that you have set an excellent example; for, as the events are fast passing from the memory of the generation now coming up, it is essential that such monuments as this be erected by men like yourself to perpetuate what is associated with the foundation of this great commercial metropolis, wonderful in its rise, wonderful in its advance, and wonderful in its consummation.

Eugene J. Hall next read the following original poem:

FORT DEARBORN.
Chicago, 1881.

Here, where the savage war-whoop once resounded,
    Where council-fires burned brightly years ago,
Where the red Indian from his covert bounded
        To scalp his pale-faced foe.

Here, where gray badgers had their haunts and burrows,
    Where wild wolves howled and prowled in midnight bands,
Where frontier farmers turned the virgin furrows,
        Our splendid city stands.

Here, where brave men and lovely women perished;
    Here, where in unknown graves their forms decay;
This marble, that their memory may be cherished,
        We consecrate to-day.

No more the farm-boy's call, or lowing cattle
    Frighten the timid wild-fowl from the slough;
The noisy trucks and wagons roll and rattle
        O'er miles of pavements now.

Now are our senses startled and confounded,
    By screaming whistle and by clanging bell,
Where Beaubien's merry fiddle once resounded,
        When Summer twilight fell.

Here stood the Fort, with palisades about it,
    With low log block-house, in those early hours,
The prairie fair extending far without it,
        Blooming with fragrant flowers.

About this spot the buildings quickly clustered;
    The logs decayed; the palisades went down;
Here the resistless Western spirits mustered,
        And built this wondrous town.

Here from the trackless slough its structures started,
    And, one by one, in splendor rose to view;
The white ships went and came, the years departed,
        And still she grandly grew.

Till one wild night, a night each man remembers,
    When round her homes the red fire leaped and curled,
The sky was filled with flame and flying embers
        That swept them from the world.

Men said, "Chicago's bright career is ended!"
  As by her smoldering stones they chanced to go,
While the wide world its love and pity blended
    To help us in our woe.

O where was ever human goodness greater?
  Man's love for man was never more sublime;
On the eternal scroll of our Creator
    'Tis written for all time.

Chicago lives, and many a lofty steeple
  Looks down to-day upon this Western plain;
The tireless hands of her unconquered people
    Have reared her walls again.

Long may she live, and grow in wealth and beauty,
  And may her children be in coming years
True to their trust, and faithful to their duty
    As her brave pioneers.

Mr. Arnold then asked Hon. John Wentworth to step forward, saying that Chicago was more indebted to him than any other man for the appropriations obtained from Congress for the magnificent harbor they saw before them.

"The Chicago Historical Society," began Mr. Wentworth, whose appearance was greeted with cheers, "requested me to prepare a history of Fort Dearborn. When I found that I must confine myself to history, I immediately removed from my table all my poetical works; I also laid aside my Dictionary of Eloquent Quotations, and my Compendium of Interesting Anecdotes. I have aimed not only to give a brief history of all persons ever connected with the Fort, but, when possible, to give the names of some of their descendants now living, thus connecting the past with the present. I hope thereby to receive for our Historical Society new facts for the development of Chicago's Early History." Regardless of a severe wind blowing directly in his face, and of the whistling of the tug-boats numerously passing through the Rush-Street bridge, not one hundred feet from him, Mr. Wentworth, in the open air, delivered the following address

FORT DEARBORN:

AN ADDRESS,

Delivered under the auspices of the Chicago Historical Society, on Saturday, Afternoon, May 21, 1881, on the Fort Site,

BY HON. JOHN WENTWORTH, LL.D.

THE first official recognition of an intention to construct a fort at Chicago may be found in a letter upon the records of the War Department, dated June 28th, 1804, directed to Gen. James Wilkinson, but which letter bears no signature. As the letter was dated at the War Department, and as the Secretary of War alone could give such directions, there can be no doubt but that it eminated from Gen. Henry Dearborn, Secretary of War during President Jefferson's administration, from 1801 to 1809. This letter says:

"Being of opinion that, for the general defence of our country, we ought not to rely on fortifications, but on men and steel; and that works calculated for resisting batteries of cannon are necessary only for our principal seaports, I can not conceive it to be useful or expedient to construct expensive works for our interior military posts, especially such as are intended merely to hold the Indians in check. I have, therefore, directed stockade-works, aided by block-houses, to be erected at Vincennes, at Chikago, at near the mouth of the Miami of the Lakes, and at Kaskaskias, in conformity to the sketch herewith enclosed, each calculated for a full company; the block-houses to be constructed of timber, slightly hewed, and of the most durable kind to be obtained at the respective places; the magazines for powder to be of brick of a conic figure, each capable of receiving from fifty to one hundred barrels of powder. Establishments of the kind here proposed will, I presume, be necessary for each of the military posts in Upper and Lower Louisiana, New Orleans and its immediate dependencies excepted. I will thank you to examine the enclosed sketch, and to give me your opinion on the dimensions and other proposed arrangements. You will observe the block-houses are intended to be so placed as to scour from the upper and lower stories the whole of the lines. The back part of the barracks are to have port-holes which can be opened when necessary for the use of musketry for annoying an enemy. It will, I presume, be proper, ultimately, to extend the pallisades round the block-houses."

This letter spells Chicago with a *k*. This sketch, referred to, can not be found in the archives at Washington, and, as the opinion of Gen. Wilkinson was solicited as to the dimensions and other proposed arrangements, and as he was more of a frontiersman than the Secretary of War, it is not improbable that a new plan altogether was adopted.

Gen. Henry Dearborn was a native of New Hampshire, and was a distinguished Soldier in the war of the Revolution, and in that of 1812. In times of peace, he was almost always in civil service, dying at Roxbury, Mass., June 6th, 1829, where a portion of his mansion still stands.

Henry G. R. Dearborn, his grandson, a resident of Chicago in the summer of 1838, and afterward of Winnebago County, and who married there, July 6th, 1840, Sarah M., daughter of Henry Thurston, of Harlem, of that county, one of our most respected early settlers, still lives at Roxbury. He is the son of Gen. Henry A. S. Dearborn, who lived and died there, and was a soldier of the war of 1812, and a member of Congress, and worthily filled the shoes of his father.

Gen. Wilkinson was a Marylander, and was a general in the war of the Revolution, and thereafter passed most of his time upon the frontier, being associated with Gen. Anthony Wayne in most of his campaigns against the Indians. But, whatever the plan was, it is a legitimate inference from the letter of the Secretary, that the plan was the same for all the points mentioned. It has occurred to me that, as the other forts were of longer continuance than ours, and, in all probability, much longer, we may yet find among some of the old settlers, or the Historical Societies of those localities, some kind of a picture that will give us an approximate idea of what our original Fort was. I am making efforts in this direction.

John H. Kinzie, in his Narrative, says, "Although it stood upon the same ground as the last Fort, it was differently constructed, having two block-houses on the southern side; and on the northern side, a sally-port, or subterranean passage from the parade ground to the river."

This we officially know, that on June 28th, 1804, there was no fort here, but that one was being projected. September 30, 1804, there were one captain, two second lieutenants, four sergeants, four corporals, four musicians, and fifty-four privates here. Jan. 1, 1805, Capt. John Whistler and his son, 2d-Lieut. Wm. Whistler, were reported here; also, 1st-Lieut. Moses Hooke, who was a native of Massachusetts, and resigned when captain, Jan. 20, 1808.

By the treaty of Greenville, in 1795, the Pottawatomies, Miamis, and their allies, relinquished their right to "one piece of land, six miles square, at the mouth of the Chicago River, emptying into the south-west end of Lake Michigan, *where a fort formerly stood.*" Many persons, besides myself, have endeavored to find something to give character to this Fort, thus recognized by Gen. Wayne, but there has been only one conclusion reached in relation to the matter, and that is, that it was only a French trading-post with mere temporary outside protection against Indian robberies.

THE FIRST FORT DEARBORN, ERECTED IN 1804.*

* It stood nearly on the site of the Fort erected in 1816, and finally demolished in the summer of 1856. It was somewhat different in its structure from its successor. It had two block-houses, one on the south-east corner, the other at the north-west. On the north side was a sally-port, or subterranean passage, leading from the parade ground to the river, designed as a place of escape in an emergency, or for supplying the garrison with water in time of a siege. The whole was enclosed by a strong palisade of wooden pickets. At the west of the fort, and fronting north on the river, was a two-story log building, covered with split-oak siding, which was the United-States factory, attached to the fort. On the shore of the river, between the fort and the factory, were the root-houses, or cellars of the garrison. The ground adjoining the fort on the south side, was enclosed and cultivated as a garden. The Fort was furnished with three pieces of light-artillery. A company of United States troops, about fifty in number, many of whom were invalids, constituted the garrison. It received the name of Fort Dearborn, by which it was ever after known as long as it continued a military post. Such was the old Fort previous to 1812. Through the kindness of Mrs. JOHN H. KINZIE, who furnished the sketch, we are enabled to present a view of this Fort as it appeared previous to that year.—*Chicago Magazine, Vol. 1., No. 1., March, 1857.*

FORT DEARBORN.

Official records show that the Fort was called "Fort Dearborn," in 1812, and there is nothing to indicate that it was not so called from 1804.

The Adjutant-General's official records say: "Post established, by United States forces, in 1804. Situated within a few yards of Lake Michigan, in latitude 41° 51' north; longitude 87° 15' west."

The Adjutant-General writes me that from 1804 to 1812 there are no records on file. So I must fill up this space of time from unofficial sources.

At various times after my arrival here, on the 25th of October, 1836, I was in the habit of meeting Major William Whistler of the regular army here, where he had a daughter, who is still living, the widow of Robert A. Kinzie. Major Whistler died at Newport, Ky., December 4th, 1863, in his eightieth year, or thereabouts, but his widow died more recently, and visited this City, in full possession of all her mental faculties, in 1875. He was appointed second-lieutenant, June 8th, 1801. Thus his military life would cover over sixty years of the history of Chicago; and during the most of this time he, or some descendant of his family, has been here; he claiming to have come here in 1803, as a second-lieutenant in the company of his father, and to have passed that winter here with his wife, and which statement she confirmed when last here. Two of his children were born in the old Fort, and probably the only children ever born there. Many of our old settlers remember John Harrison Whistler, who was born there October 7th, 1807, married Esther Bailly of old Baillytown, near Porter Station, Porter County, Indiana, at the house of Gen. John B. Beaubien, in Chicago, and died in Burlington, Kansas, October 23d, 1873. Another son was born there who died young.

In 1832, Major William Whistler was commandant of the Fort, having been made so June 17th, and so was here during the Black-Hawk war, and during the cholera season. In the absence of official documents, the statements of the Kinzie family and of the Whistler family are our best authority, five generations of the latter and four of the former having lived here. I quote from the *Chicago Antiquities*, by H. H. Hurlbut:

"It was a coveted pilgrimage which we sought, as any one might believe, for it was during the tremendous rain-storm of the evening of 29th October, 1875, that we sallied out to call at Mrs. Col. R. A. Kinzie's, for an introduction to that lady's mother, Mrs. Whistler. * * * Her tenacious memory ministers to a voluble tongue, and we may say briefly, she is an agreeable, intelligent, and sprightly lady, numbering only a little over 88 years.

"'To-day,' said she, 'I received my first pension on account of my husband's services.' * * * Born in Salem, Mass., July 3d, 1787, her maiden name was Julia Ferson, and her parents were John and Mary (La Dake) Ferson. In childhood she removed with her parents to Detroit, where she received most of her education. In the month of May, 1802, she was married to William Whistler, born in Hagerstown, Maryland, about 1784, a second-lieutenant in the company of his father, Captain John Whistler, U.S.A., then stationed at Detroit. In the summer of 1803, Captain Whistler's company was ordered to Chicago, to occupy the post and build the Fort. Lieut. James S. Swearingen (late Colonel Swearingen, of Chillicothe, O.) conducted the company from Detroit overland. The U. S. schooner *Tracy*, Dorr, master, was dispatched at the same time, for same destination, by the lakes, with supplies, and having also on board Captain John Whistler, Mrs. Whistler, their son George W., then three years old, (afterward the distinguished engineer in the employ of the Russian government), Lieut. Wm. Whistler, and the young wife of the last-named gentleman. The schooner stopped briefly on her route at St. Joseph's River, where the Whistlers left the vessel and took a row-boat to Chicago. The schooner on arriving at Chicago, anchored half a mile from the shore, discharging her freight by boats. Some 2,000 Indians visited the locality while the vessel was here, being attracted by so unusual an occurrence, as the appearance in these waters of 'a big canoe with wings.' Lieut. Swearingen returned with the *Tracy* to Detroit."

"There were then here, says Mrs. W., but four rude huts, or traders' cabins, occupied by white men, Canadian French, with Indian wives. * * Capt. Whistler, upon his arrival, at once set about erecting a stockade and shelter for their protection, followed by getting out the sticks for the heavier work. It is worth mentioning here, that there was not at that time, within hundreds of miles, a team of horses, or oxen, and, as a consequence, the soldiers had to don the harness, and with the aid of ropes drag home the needed timbers. * * Lieut. Whistler, after about five years sojourn here, was transferred to Fort Wayne, having previously been made a first-lieutenant. * *

"Col. Wm. Whistler's height at maturity was 6 feet 2 inches, and his weight at one time was 260 pounds. He died in Newport, Ky., Dec. 4th, 1863." Mrs. Whistler lived to be ninety years of age, dying on February 13th, 1878, at Newport, Ky., and leaving four daughters, one son, Gen. J. N. G. Whistler, now stationed at Fort Keogh, Dakota, and thirty-seven grandchildren.

according to the obituary notice published at the time. Mrs. Gen. Philip H. Sheridan is her grand-niece.

This Capt. John Whistler, father of William, according to *Gardner's Military Dictionary*, was originally a British soldier, and was made prisoner with Gen. Burgoyne, at Saratoga, October, 1777, where our Gen. Henry Dearborn was serving as Major. He afterward joined the American army, became sergeant, and by hard fighting, won his way to a captaincy in the 1st Infantry, in April, 1802. He was made Brevet-Major in 1812, and continued in that capacity until his company was disbanded after the close of the war, June, 1815. He died at Bellefontaine, Mo., in 1827, where he had been a military store-keeper several years. The United States official register says he was a native of Ireland. There is nothing to contradict the general impression that about the year 1810, he was succeeded by Capt. Nathan Heald, who commanded at the destruction of the Fort; making but two commandants in the life of the first Fort, the one being a witness of its commencement, and the other of its destruction. Heald was made Major, August 26th, 1812, eleven days after the massacre, and went into private life with the disbandment of his regiment at the close of the war, June, 1815. His wife was Rebekah, daughter of Col. Samuel Wells, of Louisville, Ky., and niece of the murdered Capt. William Wells,* for whom our Wells Street was named. Mrs. Juliette A. Kinzie, in her *Wau-bun*, says, "The Indians stole Capt. Wells, when a boy, from the family of Hon. Nathaniel Pope, of Kentucky, with whom he was living."

Some writers contend that, had Capt. Whistler been in charge of the Fort instead of Capt. Heald, the massacre would not have taken place. Capt. Heald has had no one to speak for him here. But he was appointed from Massachusetts a lieutenant, in 1799, and could not be supposed to have had that acquaintance with the characteristics of the Indians which Whistler had, who had been in his country's service ever since Burgoyne's surrender in 1777, and principally against the Indians, and frequently participating in the campaigns of Gen. Arthur St. Clair, and in one of which he was wounded.† Fault-finders say he

---

* For history of Capt. Wm. Wells and family, see Appendix A.

† In the Biographical Sketches of the Members of the Corinthian Lodge of Masons, at Concord, Mass., I find the following: "Nathan Heald, initiated in 1797, died at Stockland, [now O'Fallon], in St. Charles Co., Mo., where he had resided for some years, in 1832, aged 57 years. He was born in New Ipswich, N.H., [Sept. 29,] 1775, [was the third son of Col. Thomas and Sybel (Adams) Heald,] and in early life joined the U. S. Army." Mrs.

should have done one of two things, neither of which he did.
He should have abandoned the Fort at once upon receiving his
orders from Gen. William Hull, commanding at Detroit, which
were received here on the 7th, or else have put the Fort in a condition for permanent defence. Gen. Hull's orders were to
evacuate the post if practicable, and, in that event, to distribute
the property belonging to the United States, in the Fort and in the
factory or agency, to the Indians in the neighborhood. It was
not until eight days thereafter that Capt. Heald evacuated the
post. Yet there may have been considerations held out to him
by friendly chiefs and their friends, which they could not make
good after the news of the war with Great Britain became generally spread. Even Gen. Hull thought the Indians friendly, or he
would not have ordered the property distributed as he did. But
Mackinaw had surrendered to the British on the 17th of July, and
the Indians may have heard of it, although Capt. Nathan Heald
did not hear of it until the arrival of Gen. William Hull's message, on the 7th. As the Indians generally favored the British,
the news from Mackinaw may have excited them. Gen. Hull surrendered Detroit to Gen. Isaac Brock (who was killed at the
battle of Queenstown, on the 13th. October, ensuing) about
twenty-four hours after the Chicago massacre. And it is a
remarkable fact that our John B. Beaubien was at the surrender
of Mackinaw, whilst his brother, Mark Beaubien, was at that of
Detroit.

I now quote from the Adjutant-General's letter of April 2d,
1881, giving all that appears upon the records of the War Department, respecting the destruction of the Fort:

"August 15th, 1812, the garrison, having evacuated the post
and were *en route* for Fort Wayne, under the command of Capt.
Nathan Heald, 1st United States Infantry, composed of 54 regular
infantry, 12 militia-men, and 1 interpreter, was attacked by the
Indians to the number of between 400 and 500, of whom 15 were
reported killed. Those of the garrison killed were Ensign Geo.
Ronan, 1st Infantry, Dr. I. V. Van Voorhis, Capt. Wells, interpreter, 24 enlisted men United States Infantry, and 12 militia-men;
2 women and 12 children were also killed. The wounded were

Maria (Heald) Edwards, of this City, born at New Ipswich, N.H., in 1803,
mother of Mrs. Gen. A. L. Chetlain, was the oldest child of his brother
Hon. Thomas Heald, one of the Associate-Judges of the Supreme Court of
Alabama, who died at Mobile, Alabama, in 1821, aged 53. There was a
younger brother, Jonas Heald, who died at St. Louis, Mo., single. Mrs.
Edwards has a sister, Mrs. Eliza Heald Stone, residing at Concord, Mass.,
but no brothers.

Capt. Nathan Heald and Mrs. Heald. None others reported. The next day, August 16th, 1812, the post was destroyed by the Indians."

Ensign George Ronan was from the State of New York, and a graduate of the Military Academy, in 1811. Dr. Isaac V. Van Voorhis was also from the State of New York, and appointed surgeon's-mate in 1811. Both are supposed to have been unmarried. Capt. William Wells was a brother of Col. Samuel Wells, a prominent man in Kentucky. Lieut. Linai T. Helm, also in the Fort, who is not mentioned in the Adjutant-General's letter, but who is mentioned in the various histories of the massacre as among the wounded and prisoners, (as also is his wife), was appointed ensign in 1807, (State not given), and promoted to be captain in April, 1814, and resigned in September of the same year. He married Margaret, a daughter of Capt. McKillup, a British officer, who was killed near Fort Defiance, Ohio, in 1794, whose widow married the original John Kinzie, called by the Indians Shaw-nee-aw-kee, meaning silversmith. So she was half-sister to John H. and Robert A. Kinzie.

Capt. Helm left an only child, Wm. Edwin Helm, who lived with Gen. Hunter, until the war of the Rebellion; he then went into the army, and never being heard from, is supposed, by his relatives, to have been killed in the war. Others claim that he has since lived at St. Louis. Capt. Linai T. Helm was son of William Willis Helm, a Revolutionary soldier, of Prince-William County, Va., who married ——— Taliafero, of Caroline County, Virginia. Capt. Helm is said to have died whilst traveling at the East, about 1817, at or near Bath, Steuben County, N.Y.

Capt. and Mrs. Margaret Helm were married in Detroit, 1808, and after his death she married, at Chicago, 1836, Dr. Lucius Abbott, of Detroit, Mich., and died in 1845, at Grand Rapids, Mich. He was appointed assistant-surgeon from Connecticut, Jan. 15, 1828, and resigned, March 31, 1834. After his wife's death he returned to Connecticut, and died there.

Capt. Helm had a brother, Francis T. Helm, who was appointed lieutenant from New York, in 1814, and left the army at the close of the war, 1815; he had a son, Charles J. Helm, who was appointed first-lieutenant from Kentucky, March 8, 1847, and served in the army until the close of the Mexican war; who married Louise, daughter of Col. William Whistler, now living at Newport, Ky., and sister of Mrs. Robt. A. Kinzie. He was aid-de-camp to Gen. John S. Wool.

The details of the massacre would require more time than I have to spare on this occasion. I have given all that the

records at Washington show.* Next to them in importance are
the contemporaneous accounts† copied into *American State
Papers;* and also into *Niles' Register* of 1812, 1813, and 1814.
Next is the *Narrative of the Massacre of Chicago*, by John H.
Kinzie,‡ who was a boy here at the time, having been born in
Sandwich, Upper Canada, July 7, 1803, published in 1844. Next,
Brown's History of Illinois; and next, *Annals of the West*, published at St. Louis, in 1851; *History of the Maumee Valley*, by
H. S. Knapp; *McBride's Pioneer Biography; Lossing's Field Book
of the War of 1812; Brice's History of Fort Wayne.* Upon this
matter and many others appertaining to the early history of
Chicago, Mrs. Juliette A. Kinzie's *Wau-bun*, published in 1855,
is very instructive; but it is not properly appreciated because
it is written in the shape of leisure sketches instead of con-
secutive history. Those who think lightly of her work should
call at my office and copy a thorough index of it, which I have
made, and they will find that *Wau-bun* is a historic treasure.
Robert Fergus, of this City, is publishing a very valuable series
of pamphlets upon *Early Chicago*, in which much respecting this
massacre is given. There is also something in *Blanchard's History
of Chicago and the North-West.* After a diligent search at the various Departments, I can not find that any of the soldiers here at
the time of the massacre, nor that any of their descendants, have
applied for a land-warrant or a pension. So I have been unable
to procure for you the names of any descendants of those whose
lives were preserved, nor can I give you the names of those
whose lives were lost, except those published in the papers about
the time, nor the names of any living descendants. The com-
pany-roll can not be found. Yet I will give to whatever history this address may acquire the names of the soldiers and of
others I have found out, and perhaps some family genealogist
may yet do what I have been unable to do. The following
soldiers reached Plattsburg, New York, in 1814, after being
redeemed as British prisoners at Quebec, Canada: James Van
Horn, Joseph Knowles, Paul Grummon, (or Grummow or Grummond or Gromet), Elias Mills, James Bowen, Nathan Edson,

* See Appendix B.   † See Appendix C.

‡ The *Massacre of Chicago*, was written by Mrs. John H. Kinzie, and published by Ellis & Fergus, printers, Saloon Buildings, Chicago, in 1844. The
copy was written in a half-bound blank-book, small letter-page, of about four
quires, in Mrs. Kinzie's handwriting. Shortly after its publication, Judge
Henry Brown issued his *History of Illinois*, and he copied Mrs. Kinzie's
pamphlet, which made two chapters of his history. Mrs. K. said that "the
Judge had no right to take the *Massacre*, or to make the alterations which
he made."—R. FERGUS, June 14th, 1881.

Dyson Dyer, James Corbin, and Phelim Corbin, whose wife (Mrs. Corbin) was inhumanly massacred. Mrs. Holt, wife of Sergeant Holt, is mentioned as having afterward lived in Ohio. Sergeant Hays was killed. A soldier named Cooper* was killed, but his family was saved.

Among the soldiers who were killed, or who died from exposure after the massacre, were John Neads, Hugh Logan, August Motte, and —— Nelson from Maryland.†

During my residence in Chicago, I have made repeated efforts to trace out some descendant or relative of Capt. Nathan Heald without success. After I began to write this address, I felt more anxious than ever to learn something more of him, and addressed letters to various places seeking information. Luckily, one of my letters reached a gentleman who knew a son of his, and he lost no time in seeing him and some neighbors who also knew the family; and in hastening to me the following statements, gathered in a short interview; being remembrances of what they had heard from his parents, they having read nothing upon the subject and not thinking that there was anyone at this late day feeling any interest in it:

"Capt. Nathan Heald was married in Louisville, Kentucky, May 23d, 1811, to Rebekah Wells, a native of Kentucky, and daughter of Col. Samuel Wells, of that place. They started at once for Fort Dearborn, and went all the way on horseback. She rode a beautiful and well-trained bay mare, upon which the Indians ever looked with longing eyes. They made several attempts to steal her. She was riding her when the attack was made, and the Indians considered her one of the greatest trophies of the battle. Great, but unsuccessful efforts were made to repurchase her. Gen. Hull sent Capt. Wm. Wells, with about thirty-two friendly Indians, to escort Capt. Heald to Fort Wayne.

* See Appendix D.

† When the last Fort was taken down, in 1856, an old paper was found, reading as follows:

"Permission is hereby given for one **gill of whiskey each**: Denison, Dyer, Andrews, Keamble (may be Kimball or some other **name beginning** with K), Burnam, J Corbin, Burnett, Smith, McPherson, Hamilton, Fury [not certain], Grumond [or Grummon, or Grummow, or Grumet], Morfitt [or Marfett], Lynch, Locke [or Locker], Peterson, P. Corbin, Van Horn, Mills.
November 12th, 1811."

The most of the names had been partially erased with pen and ink, probably to show that they had received their whiskey. Therefore, some of the names may be erroneous.

Rebekah Heald.

From a portrait in possession of her son, Hon. Darius Heald.

There were in Fort Dearborn only twenty-five or thirty fighting men. The others were upon the sick-list. It was in the very hot weather of August. The order to vacate created no dissatisfaction at Fort Dearborn or vicinity, except with the sutler or storekeeper, interpreters, traders, and that whole class who felt that their occupation would be gone if the Fort should be abandoned. They are the persons who have handed down all the reflections upon Capt. Heald's conduct in leaving the Fort. When the soldiers had proceeded about one and a-half miles from the Fort, they were surprised and surrounded by about 600 Indians who had formed in a horse-shoe or semi-circular shape upon the bluff. The troops were upon the lake shore. Capt. and Mrs. Heald were riding together. Capt. Wells was somewhat in advance, dressed in Indian costume, with his Indian forces. Capt. Wells first noticed the design of the Indians and rode back and informed Capt. Heald, who at once started for the most elevated point upon the sand-hills, and endeavored to mass his wagons, baggage, women, and children, and sick soldiers, so as to make a better defence whilst the fight was going on. At the first attack, Capt. Wells' Indians made their escape. Early in the fight, Capt. Heald and his wife became separated. Capt. Wells rode up to Mrs. Heald, with blood streaming from his mouth and nostrils, and told her that he thought he had been fatally wounded, and requested her to inform his wife that he had fought bravely and knew that he had killed seven Indians before he was shot. Soon his horse was shot, and, as the horse fell, his foot was caught in the stirrup and he was held under the dead horse some time. Whilst in this position, he killed his eighth Indian. He was released from this position just in time to meet his death from a bullet in the back of his neck. The Indians immediately scalped him, cut out his heart and flourished it about upon a gun-stick, then divided it into small pieces and ate it whilst warm, Mrs. Heald being a witness. She was led back to the Fort as a prisoner.

"Capt. Heald received a wound in the hip which always troubled him, and, it is believed, caused his death in 1832. He drew a pension in consequence thereof. Having but about a half-dozen men left in a fighting condition, Capt. Heald surrendered. The Indians returned to the Fort, plundered and burned it. They then camped along the lake shore, near the Fort. The next morning, an Indian chief, named Jean Baptist Chandonais, who was a half-breed, having possession of Capt. Heald as his prisoner, sought out the captor of Mrs. Heald and purchased her. She had supposed that her husband was killed. Chandonais took

Mrs. Heald to her husband. She had received six wounds. When the Indians were leading her away as prisoner, one of the squaws attempted to take a blanket from her, when she, with her riding-whip, struck her several times; which act of bravery, under the circumstances, greatly excited the admiration of the Indians. The next day, the chief Chandonais took all the warriors with him for the purpose, it was said, of burning a prisoner, leaving Capt. Heald and wife in charge of the squaws and a young Indian boy. That evening, through the assistance of the boy who accompanied them, and probably with the assent of Chandonais, they made their escape in a birch-bark canoe to Mackinaw, and finally reached Detroit, where Capt. Heald surrendered himself as a prisoner of war. The British officer in charge was a Mason as well as Capt. Heald. This officer greatly assisted them and, when exchanged, he gave them money to take them home.

"The Indians took from Capt. Heald a large ornamental silver shawl or blanket-pin, marked R.A.M., and from Mrs. Heald a tortoise-shell comb mounted with gold, and they were finally sold at St. Louis, where Lieut. John O'Fallon, a U.S. officer from Kentucky, recognized, purchased, and sent them to Louisville, Ky., where they arrived before Capt. and Mrs. Heald.

"Capt. Heald and wife came to St. Charles County, Mo., in the spring of 1817, and settled at Stony Point, near the town of O'Fallon in that county, where they resided until his death, April 27th, 1832, aged fifty-seven years. Mrs. Heald remained there also until her death, April 23d, 1857, aged eighty-one years. She was a leading member of the Baptist Church, and was greatly respected for her great firmness and kindness. They were buried upon the home place. Mrs. Heald left a manuscript history of her horseback tour from Louisville, in 1811, to Chicago, of her life whilst at Chicago, and of the massacre, and her final return to St. Louis. But it was lost during the war of the Rebellion.

"They had two daughters, both now dead, Margaret dying single in 1836, aged twenty, and Mary (the oldest) dying in 1835, the wife of Capt. David McCausland, who still survives her. They had a son, Darius, born January 27th, 1822, and still lives upon the home place, near O'Fallon. He represented St. Charles County in the Missouri Legislature in 1856-59. Col. Samuel Wells, father of Mrs. Heald, was a noted Indian-fighter and brother of Capt. William Wells.

"Chandonais and his son visited Major Heald in the fall before his death, and passed some days with him, recounting the scenes of the massacre and calling to mind the incident of the blanket."

I find the following in *Gardner's Military Dictionary:*

Samuel Wells was from Kentucky. Major in Adair's Mounted Volunteers, in 1793; Major, and distinguished himself in battle of Tippecanoe, Nov. 7, 1811; Colonel of 17th Infantry, 1812; disbanded with regiment, May 12, 1814; Major-General of Kentucky Militia.

William Wells, brother of above, was from Kentucky, was captain commanding company of spies, under Maj.-Gen. Anthony Wayne, from July 28, to December, 1794.

William Wayne Wells, son of Capt. William, was appointed cadet at West Point from Indiana, September, 1817; second-lieutenant, 1821; first-lieutenant, 1825; resigned July 31, 1831, and died in 1832. [Died on board the Steamer *Superior*, off Erie, Pa., whilst returning home.]

All accounts agree that the massacre took place about one mile and a-half south from the Fort. It was pointed out to me in 1836, and the historic bluffs or sand-hills existed for many years thereafter.

Medore B. Beaubien, son of Gen. John B. Beaubien, sends me, by his brother, Alexander, who has just returned from a visit to him, at Silver Lake, Shawnee County, Kansas, the following to read to you:

"I was born at Grand River, Michigan, in 1809, and came to Chicago with my father, in 1813, and walked over the ruins of the old Fort that was burnt by the Indians. After me, all father's children were born in Chicago."

[At this point Mr. Wentworth caused a general commotion in his audience by saying:]

Ladies and gentlemen, I am going to give you a recess by introducing to you a gentleman who unexpectedly called upon me yesterday, and whom I believe you will all be glad to know. Hon. Darius Heald, of O'Fallon, St. Charles County, Mo., son of Capt. Nathan Heald, commandant of the Fort at the time of the massacre, who came here on purpose to witness the ceremonies of this day.

[Mr. Heald came forward amid great cheering and thanked the people for their reception. He exhibited the shawl-pin, into the rim of which the Indians had made a hole, so as to wear it in their ear or nose. It was the opinion of many that it might have been made here by our original John Kinzie, who was a silversmith at one time. He then exhibited his mother's bridal comb, which attracted great admiration from the ladies; having been well preserved. The shell was cut in the shape of an eagle, and it was plenteously studded with gold so as to represent the eagle's wings. Mr. Heald said he had heard his mother say that, whilst she was writhing in pain from her many wounds and lying upon the ground, she saw an Indian chief strutting around with that comb in his hair. Mr. Heald also exhibited a small ivory miniature of his mother's uncle, the massacred Capt. Wm. Wells, and of his own grandfather, Col. Samuel Wells.]

There is no doubt but the Indians, who resided within the immediate vicinity of the Fort, were friendly, and did their best to pacify the numerous warriors who flocked here from the more distant hunting-grounds. But they were so determined upon warfare that they proceeded, directly after the massacre, to Fort Wayne, and joined the Indians there in a continued assault upon the Fort, until relieved by Gen. Wm. H. Harrison, on the 16th September, following. Scarcely a person escaped the massacre who did not have some kind words to say of some friendly Indian whose acquaintance had been previously formed.

The Adjutant-General writes to me that his records only show that the post was reöccupied about June, 1816, Capt. Hezekiah Bradley commanding. The troops continued in occupation until October, 1823, when the post was evacuated, and left in charge of the Indian-agent. It was reöccupied, October 3d, 1828. Nothing is on file respecting the rebuilding of the Fort.

When I was in Congress, under the second term of President Tyler, in 1843 and '44, Hon. John C. Calhoun was Secretary of State, and I remember, in a conversation with me about Chicago, that he claimed that the Fort was completed under the early part of his term as Secretary of War, and he asserted that there was a disposition among the officers here to call it Fort Chicago; but he thought it would be disrespectful to Gen. Henry Dearborn, then living and standing high in the affections of the people, and having a claim upon their gratitude as a soldier and statesman. Calhoun's term commenced with the inauguration of President Monroe, March 4th, 1817. The building of the Fort in 1816, may have been the cause or the result of the treaty of that year, in which the Pottawatomies ceded to the United States all the country in this region, described as the country upon the headwaters of Lake Michigan. They were to be paid $5700 yearly, and their number was estimated at three thousand and four hundred. They remained the peaceful occupants of all they wanted until after my arrival, Oct. 25, '36. Our old settlers received a very welcome visit not long since from Col. John T. Sprague, who made himself very popular here whilst, as a second-lieutenant, collecting the scattered bands, and making arrangements to take them to their new home,* where they have ever remained

* See *Sketch of the Pottawatomies*, by J. D. Caton, No. 3, Fergus' Hist. Series.

contented, and from whom we often hear through their agent, a member of the first Board of Trustees of the Original Town of Chicago, in 1833, Medore B. Beaubien, now mayor of their commercial centre, Silver Lake, Shawnee County, Kansas. Colonel Sprague was son-in-law of Gen. Wm. J. Worth, and won honors in the Florida and Mexican wars. He has recently deceased.

Capt. John B. F. Russell was here upon detached Indian-service, when I came, and superintended the Indians' final removal. He entered West Point from Massachusetts, in 1814, was made captain in 1830, and resigned, 22d June, 1837. He built the first public hall in our City, at the south-east corner of Lake and Clark Streets, known as "The Saloon" where courts, public meetings, balls, etc., etc., were held. It was there where Stephen A. Douglass and John T. Stuart, candidates for Congress, had a public discussion in 1838. He was the first man to establish an office for the sale and purchase of real estate and payment of taxes here. He died here January 3, 1861, leaving a widow and son, both still living here.

I quote from a paper read before the Chicago Historical Society by Hon. Isaac N. Arnold, its President, upon the authority of Mr. John H. Kinzie's daughter, Mrs. Nellie Gordon, and published in the Chicago *Tribune*, July 18th, 1877:

"In 1816, the Kinzie family returned to their desolate home in Chicago. The bones of the murdered soldiers who had fallen four years before, were still lying unburied where they had fallen. The troops, who rebuilt the Fort, collected and interred the remains. The coffins which contained them were deposited near the bank of the river, which then had its outlet about at the foot of Madison Street. The cutting through the sand-bar for the harbor caused the Lake to encroach and wash away the earth, exposing the long range of coffins and their contents, which were afterward cared for and reinterred by the civil authorities."*

Among my earliest recollections of Chicago was seeing projections of coffins from the steep banks of the lake shore, south of the Fort, about Lake Street.

Capt. Bradley commanded from June, 1816, until May, 1817; Brevet-Major Daniel Baker,† until June, 1820; then Capt. Bradley again, to Jan. 1st, 1821; Maj. Alexander Cummings to Oct., 1821; Lieut.-Col. Jno. McNeil to July, 1823; Capt. Jno. Greene to Oct., 1823. They are all dead; Bradley dying in 1826; Baker in 1836; Cummings in 1842; McNeil in 1850, and Greene in 1840. None of them have descendants in this region of whom I ever heard.

* See No. 10 Fergus Historical Series, p. 21. † See Appendix E.

I never had an acquaintance with any of them, except Col. McNeil, afterward brevetted Brigadier-General. He was a native of New Hampshire, and passed his last years there. From him I received my earliest impressions of Chicago. He claimed that his daughter, now living, the widow of Hon. Chandler E. Potter, of Manchester, N.H., was the first child born in the new Fort. I met her, a few years since, walking from the site of the Fort, and she told me she had been trying to find her birthplace. Another daughter, still living, is the wife of the present Gen. Henry W. Benham. He lost his only son, Lieutenant J. Winfield Scott McNeil, in an engagement under Gen. Hernandez, with the Indians, in Florida, in 1837. Gen. McNeil was brother-in-law of President Franklin Pierce, the late Lieut. John Sullivan Pierce, and Lieut.-Col. Benjamin K. Pierce.*

Gen. McNeil was the competitor of Gen. Scott, for being the tallest and heaviest man who was ever in the American army. Both were brevetted for their gallantry at the battle of Niagara, Canada, in 1814, where McNeil was so severely wounded that

---

* Lieut. John Sullivan Pierce married Harriet Puthuff, daughter of the Indian-agent at Mackinaw, who was a Virginian, and came to Mackinaw about 1818. He was Wm. Henry Puthuff, appointed adjutant from Ohio, May 7, 1812; major, Feb. 21, 1814; and disbanded, with his regiment, at the close of the war, in 1815. He was a member of the Michigan legislative council in 1824, and died in November of that year. Lieut. Pierce died at Detroit, in 1825. After his death, and that of her father, Mrs. Pierce went to Chillicothe, Ohio, with her two children.

Lieut.-Col. Benjamin K. Pierce married Josette Lafromboise, when he was in command of Fort Mackinaw, about 1815–16, daughter of Joseph Lafromboise, who married Madeline, daughter of Jean Baptiste Marcotte, a fur-trader of Mackinaw, who married a woman of the Ottawa tribe of Indians. Mrs. Pierce died in Nov., 1821, leaving Harriet, who married Jas. Brewerton Ricketts, who graduated at West Point, in 1839, and was a captain in 1852. Mrs. Rickets did not live long, but left a daughter who married an army officer, and is still living. Lt.-Col. Pierce married again. Joseph Lafromboise had a maiden sister who taught a young ladies' school at Mackinaw, as early as 1793 or 1794. Madame Madeline Lafromboise, after she was thirty years of age, educated herself; and her husband having been killed upon the Upper Mississippi, she took charge of his business and continued a trader in the American Fur Company's employ, visiting various trading-posts and looking after the acts of the employés. Her sister, Madame Therese Schindler, was grandmother of the widow of the late Hon. H. S. Beard, now living at Green Bay, Wisconsin, and to whom I am indebted for this information.

The Lafromboise family of this City, claimed relationship to that of Mackinaw; but it is probable that our Francis, Sr., was no nearer related than cousin or second-cousin to Joseph, of Mackinaw. In 1826, Francis, Sr., voted here, with three sons, Joseph, Claude, and Francis, Jr. Gen. John Baptiste Beaubien's second wife was Josette Lafromboise, daughter of Francis, Sr. Medore B. Beaubien, of Silver Lake, Kan., son of Gen. John B., by his first wife, now has for his second wife the widow of Thomas Watkins, (a clerk in the Chicago postoffice, in 1837), and daughter of our Joseph Lafromboise.

he was incapacitated for further duty, and went into civil service, being at one time surveyor-general of the port of Boston. I have often measured with both these distinguished men, and I feel safe in saying that those who have seen me have an accurate idea of their size and height.

From October, 1823, the Fort was in charge of Dr. Alexander Wolcott, from Connecticut, the uncle of our present and long time-honored county surveyor, named for him.

There was an Indian trading-post at Chicago, on Lake Michigan, in Indiana Territory, in 1805. Charles Jouett, from Kentucky, (sometimes written Jewett), was Indian-agent at Detroit, in 1803. The Chicago agency may then have been under the supervision of the Detroit agent. He signed his name afterward as Indian-agent at Chicago. Mathew Irwin* was the Indian-

* Mathew Irwin, sometimes called Indian-agent, and sometimes Factory-agent, at Chicago, in 1810, received $1165 salary. Official reports show that there was in that year $4732 worth of merchandize and $877 worth of furs and peltries, and that the factory-building cost $500. Between 1807 and 1811 the profits on the trade at Chicago was $3725. From the 1st of March to the massacre, Charles Jouett appears to have succeeded Mr. Irwin. After the Fort was rebuilt, the Indian trade commenced again, and during the years 1817-18-19, there were 191 Deer skins, 71 Beaver skins, 1182 Raccoon skins, 27,077 Muskrat skins, and 16 Fox skins purchased. These were sold at Georgetown, D.C., on ninety days' credit. Between July, 1820, and December, 1821, Alexander Wolcott, as Indian-agent, paid out $27,600. His salary was $1300. John Kinzie received $500 as sub-agent. In 1831-32, Thomas J. V. Owen was Indian-agent, and disbursed here, during the year, $4987, and in 1832-33, $64,593. George W. Dole, (afterwards alderman), is paid for salt, and Messrs. Beeson, Winslow & Beeson for tobacco. Col. Owen's salary was $1300; Gholson Kerchival, his brother-in-law, (afterward member of the Legislature), received $524 as sub-agent. James Stewart, as sub-agent, $375. Billy Caldwell, (Sauganash) interpreter, $493. David McKee, (who died at Aurora, Ill., April 8th, 1881), blacksmith, $480, Joseph Pothier, (who married Victor Miranda, a half-breed, and was living at Milwaukee, at last dates), assistant-blacksmith, $220. Dexter Graves, (father-in-law of the late E. H. Hadduck, who died May 30, 1881), assistant in issuing provisions. John Currin, agriculturist at Carey Mission. [The Carey Mission, referred to in this note, was a few miles from Niles, Michigan, and was under charge of the Baptists. Not far from it in the same county, near where Bertram, Berrien County, now is, was the St. Joseph Mission, under charge of the Catholics.] Robert A. Kinzie, (son of John), assistant in furnishing presents to the Indians. Isaac Harmon, Justice of the Peace, fees for prosecuting John Welch for selling liquor to Indians, $2.82. [He was brother to Dr. Elijah Dewey Harmon, who died Jan. 3, 1869.*] In 1833-4, payments were made to some of the same persons, and also to John S. C. Hogan, (postmaster), Brewster, Hogan & Co., William See, (Rev.), blacksmith, John Calhoun, (publisher of *Democrat*), Ferdinand Seybold, Clemens Stose, (afterward alderman, and now living at SanFrancisco, Cal.), Joseph Bouché, or Bushy, James Smallwood, Peter Pruyne, (afterward State Senator), and J. S. W. Beeson.

* See *Early Medical Chicago*, No. 11 Fergus' Historical Series, pp. 12—18.

agent here, in 1810. Dr. Alexander Wolcott, was Indian-agent here as early as 1820, and so continued until his death, in 1830. He was succeeded by Col. Thomas J. V. Owen, of this State, who was born in Kentucky, April 5th, 1801, and was one of our first Board of Town Trustees, in 1833, who died here October 15th, 1835, whose wife (now living at East St. Louis, in this State) was daughter of Hon. Miles Hotchkiss, and niece of our United States Senator, Elias K. Kane. If you will go down to Lewiston, in Fulton County, you will find, upon the list of marriages there, the following, at Chicago precinct of that county: "By John Hamlin, J.P., July 20th, 1823, Alexander Wolcott and Ellen Marion Kinzie."

Mr. Hamlin resided at Peoria, and was on his way home from Green Bay, when he performed the ceremony. Chicago had neither clergyman nor Justice-of-the-Peace then. But this trouble was soon avoided by the appointment of her father as one of the Justices-of-the-Peace for Fulton County, upon the 2d of December following. We had to wait until we became a part of Peoria County before we had a second one, who was Billy Caldwell, (Sauganash), who was appointed April 18th, 1826. Mrs. Wolcott, remarried, in Detroit, May 26, 1836, Hon. George C. Bates, of that City, (where she died, August 1, 1860, leaving Kinzie Bates, born there April 19, 1838, now captain in U. S. Infantry,) more recently of this City, but now of Leadville, Colo. It is claimed that she was the first white child born in Chicago [1805], the place of her birth being on the North-Side, at the historic home of John and Eleanor Kinzie, and I know not why she can not be said to have been the first white person married here. The U.S. Official Register of 1826, shows that Wolcott's salary was $1300, and that he had a Sub-Agent, Alexander Doyle, born in Virginia, at a salary of $500, and that Mr. Kinzie drew a salary of $500 as Indian interpreter; and Alexander Robinson, better known as Chechepinqua, whose descendants still reside in this City, at a salary of $365; and also Peresch LeClerc, a Frenchman, well known after I came here, but having no descendants that I am aware of, at a salary of $432. In the year 1823, there appears to have been an Indian-agent or factor here from Connecticut, named A. B. Lindsley, at a salary of $1300, of whom nothing is now known. There was a Jacob B. Varnum here as factor, as early as 1817, from Massachusetts, at a salary of $1300, and who was continued here for some time after Dr. Wolcott came, of whom also nothing is known.

Mr. Alexander Beaubien informs me that, in 1866, an aged gentleman called to see him, and inquired about his father. He said he lived here in 1820, and boarded in the old John Dean house with his father, the site of which has been washed away and would now be out in the Lake, if it had not been filled up. He said his name was Varnum, and he lived then in Petersburg. Mr. Beaubien had forgotten whether in Kentucky or Virginia. John Dean was a post-sutler.

The Adjutant-General's official records show the following: Upon May 27th, 1823, Major-General Jacob Brown, General-in-Chief of the Army, issued this order:

"The Major-General, commanding the army, directs that Fort Dearborn, Chicago, be evacuated, and that the garrison thereof be withdrawn to the headquarters of the 3d Regiment of Infantry.

* * * The Commanding-General of the eastern department will give the necessary orders for carrying these movements into effect, as well as for the security of the public property at Fort Dearborn."

Thus matters stood at the Fort until, Major-General Brown being dead, his successor, as General-in-Chief of the Army, Maj.-Gen. Alexander Macomb, gave the following order under date of Washington, August 19th, 1828:

"In conformity with the directions of the Secretary of War, the following movements of the troops will be made without delay: Two companies of the 5th Regiment of Infantry to re-occupy Fort Dearborn, at the head of Lake Michigan, the remaining eight companies to proceed by the way of the Ouisconsin and Fox Rivers, to Fort Howard, Green Bay, where the headquarters of the Regiment will be established."

Mrs. John H. Kinzie, in her *Wau-bun*, thus alludes to this change of the soldiers: "The troops were removed from the garrison in 1823, but restored in 1828, after the Winnebago war. There was a disturbance between the Winnebagoes and white settlers on and near the Mississippi. After some murders had been committed, the young chief, Red Bird, was taken and imprisoned at Prairie du Chien to await his trial, where he died of chagrin and the irksomeness of confinement. It was feared that the Pottawatomies [our Indians] would make common cause with the Winnebagoes, and commence a general system of havoc and bloodshed upon the frontier. They were deterred from such a step, probably, by the exertions of Billy Caldwell [Sauganash], Robinson [Chechepinqua], and Chamblee [Shabonee], who made an expedition among the Rock-River bands to argue and persuade them into remaining tranquil."[*]

[*] See Sketch of *Caldwell and Shabonee*, by Wm. Hickling, in No. 10 Fergus' Historical Series, pp. 29—46.

I can never think of either of these three persons without being reminded of the many pleasant and instructive hours that I have passed with them individually and collectively, listening to their own experience, describing battle after battle—the massacre at Chicago and the battle of the Thames included—and narrating personal interviews with and characteristics of Tecumseh, Gen. Harrison, and Gen. Wayne, whom they always called "Old Tempest." Caldwell or Sauganash* died with his tribe at Council Bluffs, Iowa, Sept. 28, 1841, in his 60th year, childless. His wife died before he left here. His only child, Susan Caldwell, died here in 1834. Chamblee or Shabonee died near Morris, in Grundy County, in this State, July 17, 1859, aged 84 years, whilst Robinson or Chechepinqua lived to vote for me several times for Congress, and to call on me as mayor and smoke the pipe of peace. He died upon his reservation, near River Park, in this county, April 22, 1872, aged 110 years. Both of these latter have living descendants.

The Winnebago Indians occupied all that portion of Wisconsin Territory bordering on Wisconsin River, numbering about 1550, of whom 500 were warriors. Hence the importance of making headquarters at Fort Howard—Green Bay—and afterward of the construction of Fort Winnebago, under the superintendence of Lieut. Jefferson Davis.

Gen. David Hunter writes me from Washington, under date of May 18, 1881: "In October, 1829, I saw on the north side of the River, opposite the Fort, a white man, and wondering where he could have come from, I got into a small wooden canoe, intended for only one person, and paddled over to interview him. He introduced himself to me as 2d-Lieut. Jefferson Davis, of the 1st Infantry, from Fort Winnebago, in pursuit of deserters. I, of course, was very glad to see Lieut. Davis. I invited him to lie down in my canoe, and I paddled him safely to the Fort. He was my guest until refreshed and ready to return to Fort Winnebago. This, no doubt, was the first visit of Jefferson Davis to Chicago."

[At this point of his address, Mr. Wentworth asked pardon for the following digression.]

As I was starting for this assemblage, I purchased the three o'clock *Evening Journal*, and was greatly surprised to learn that Mr. Davis arrived in this City this morning. I immediately drove to his hotel and found that he was absent. I intended to have invited him to come here and address you. He could tell you many things of interest about the North-West in early times.

* See Appendix F.

And I know he would. For, when he and I were in the House of Representatives together, he was accustomed to inquire for our early families, and to narrate many pleasant incidents. I know you would have given him a cordial reception. I think we must have nearly a thousand of his soldiers, in the late war of the Rebellion, amongst us doing business, and we had rather have more than less of them. Chicago has ever been a hospitable, as well as a cosmopolitan city. She welcomes emigrants from all climes and of all sentiments. As early as 1826, we had an Indian chief, who fought against us in the war of 1812, for Justice of the Peace, and we have had officers, as well as citizens. of every diversity of sentiment and nativity ever since, and one of the great elements of our prosperity has been that we make everyone feel at home here. When I, as your Mayor, went to Montreal, in 1860, to solicit the Prince of Wales to make our City a visit, the great obstacle that I had to overcome was the fears that our numerous foreign population might give vent to their prejudices against royalty, and perpetrate some outrage. But he did come, and, after his return home, the Duke of Newcastle wrote me that nowhere was he treated so satisfactorily as in Chicago. And yet we had not an extra policeman during his stay. You remember how it was in 1864, at the time of the great National Convention, when Hon. Clement L. Vallandigham, who had been banished, by President Lincoln, for his treasonable efforts into the rebel country, addressed our citizens, in the evening, from the court-house door-steps. there was not the least disturbance, and every policeman was performing his regular routine duties. And, when he closed and I was called upon to respond to him, I was treated with the same respect by his friends that he had been by mine.* Now, would it not have created a sensation throughout the country if it could have been telegraphed that Jefferson Davis was here to-day entertaining us with his experience in Early Chicago! Such a despatch would have done us good and Mr. Davis good also. It is not my fault that he is not now here.

[Mr. Davis rode within one block of the tablet whilst Mr. Wentworth was speaking. When he read the reference to himself the next morning and learned its kind reception by the audience, he expressed his regrets at not being present, and especially when he learned that Gen. P. H. Sheridan was upon the stage.]

The companies at the Fort, from Oct. 3d, 1828, to their withdrawal, May 20th, 1831, were companies A and I of the 5th In-

* See Appendix G.

fantry. Capt. John Fowle, who commanded the Fort, was from Massachusetts, and was killed April 25th, 1838, by a steamboat explosion on the Ohio River. His 1st-lieutenant was the present Gen. David Hunter, of Washington City, whose wife, Maria H. Kinzie, daughter of John, born in 1807, is the oldest white person now living who was born in Chicago. A 2d-lieutenant was John G. Furman, from South Carolina, who died at the Fort on August 29, 1830. Another 2d-lieutenant was Abram, son of Martin Van Buren and his private-secretary when President. There was an assistant-surgeon, Clement A. Finley, from Ohio, whose last record I find as medical-director under Gen. Taylor, in Mexico, in 1846. The second company was commanded by Capt. Martin Scott, from Vermont, who was killed whilst as colonel he was leading his regiment at the battle of El Molino del Rey, in Mexico, Sept. 8, 1847. James Engle, from New Jersey, was his second-lieutenant, who resigned in 1834 and died soon after. His wife was here with him. A brevet second-lieutenant, from New Hampshire, Amos Foster, was under him also, a brother of the late Dr. John H. Foster,* of this City. He was shot by a soldier at Fort Howard, Green Bay, February 7, 1832. Engle, Foster, and Hunter voted at an election in the Chicago precinct of Peoria County, on July 24, 1830, for Justice-of-the-Peace and Constable. These were the first votes ever cast here by military officers.

On March 31, 1831, Gen. Macomb issued the following order: "The Post of Chicago will be evacuated as early as practicable, and the garrison, consisting of two companies of the 5th Regiment of Infantry, will proceed to Green Bay and occupy Fort Howard."

On Feb. 23, 1832, he issued this order: "The headquarters of the 2d Regiment of Infantry are transferred to Fort Niagara. Lieut.-Col. Cummings, with all the officers and men composing the Madison Barracks at Sacketts Harbor, will accordingly relieve the garrison of Fort Niagara, and Major Whistler, of the 2d Infantry, on being relieved by Col. Cummings, with all the troops under his command, will repair to Fort Dearborn (Chicago) and garrison that post.

"Assistant-Surgeon DeCamp, now on duty at Madison Barracks, is assigned to Fort Dearborn and will accompany the troops ordered to that post.

"These movements will take place as soon as the navigation will permit."

This brings us to the second crisis in the history of Chicago, twenty years after the massacre, when the settlers, affrighted by

* See *Early Medical Chicago*, No. 10 Fergus' Historical Series, page 30.

the depredations of Black-Hawk's warriors with their wives and children, sought refuge in the Fort.* Then the Asiatic cholera came and they fled the Fort, but dared not return to their homes, and thus they vibrated between the Indians and cholera, suffering for the necessaries of life. The War Department's records say: "Fort Dearborn having become a general hospital on July 11th, no returns were received until its reöccupation; companies G and I, 2d Infantry returned to the Fort, on Oct. 1st, from campaign." This refers to the march of Gen. Scott to Rock Island in pursuit of Black Hawk. Our Esquire Sauganash with his two friends, Shabonee and Chechepinqua, successfully used their influence to keep the Indians in this vicinity in amity. Some recent writers have asserted that the coffins, which I have heretofore noticed, contained the bodies of soldiers who died of the cholera at that time. But I served in Congress with Gen. Humphrey Marshall, of Kentucky, who came here with Gen. Scott, as a second-lieutenant, and helped bury the dead, among them a classmate, Second-Lieutenant Franklin McDuffie, of Rochester, New Hampshire, who died July 15th, and he said the dead were thrown unceremoniously into a pit, and oftentimes those helping to carry a body there in a very few hours had to be thrown in themselves, and the soldiers and citizens afterward were afraid to remove them. Luther Nichols, who died May 2d, 1881, in this City, was, at the time, a regularly enlisted soldier, the last to reside in our City, and helped bury the dead. He described the pit as at the north-west corner of Lake Street and Wabash Avenue. Mr. Nichols was born at Gilbertsville, Otsego County, New York, in 1805, and enlisted as a United-States soldier in 1828; came to Chicago under Major Whistler, and was honorably discharged in 1833.

Major Whistler arrived here on June 17th, 1832, and kept command until May 14, 1833. Surgeon Samuel G. I. DeCamp, from New Jersey, of whom I can learn nothing, was succeeded in 1833 by Surgeon Philip Maxwell,† who after residing here for several

* See Appendix II. Also, *Gurdon S. Hubbard's Narrative*, in No. 10, Fergus' Historical Series, p. 41.

† Among the valuable documents which fell into my hands whilst collecting material for the history of Fort Dearborn was a book, presented by I. L. Usher, Esq., of La Crosse, Wis., which I have deposited with the Chicago Historical Society. It is entitled "Medical Prescription Book of U. S. Army used at Fort Dearborn." Some leaves have been torn therefrom. But is in a good condition from November, 1832, until the evacuation of the Fort, December 29, 1836. Dr. Philip Maxwell came to the Fort as surgeon, February 3, 1833, and left at the evacuation. So the prescriptions entered in the book are undoubtedly his, and are interesting as showing the great change in medical practice. The name of Luther Nichols is upon the sick-list,

years, died upon his farm at Geneva Lake, Wisconsin, November 5th, 1859, aged sixty years. He was a member of our Legislature, in 1848, and father-in-law of Joel C. Walter, of this City. His bust is one of those upon the block fronting the Court House, on the east side of Clark Street. He was a very social and popular man, and whenever you see a Chicago boy write his name Philip M., you can tell for whom he was named. The captain was Seth Johnson, who resigned in 1836, and ended his days in this city, leaving descendants, his daughter Harriet having married Josiah E. McClure, of this City, Jan. 8, 1837. In 1840, he was Alderman of the old 4th ward, when there were but six wards in the City and only two upon the West Side, his ward comprising all territory north of Lake Street, his residence being in old Waubansia. He was also deputy-collector of the port of Chicago when it belonged to the Detroit district. The first-lieutenant was Julius J. B. Kingsbury, who distinguished himself in the Mexican war and was Major when he resigned. He passed much of his time in this City when not on duty, and, by judicious investment, accumulated a large fortune, which with the aid of lawyers is likely to share the fate of most large fortunes before it passes through the third generation. His son, inheriting his father's love of the good old flag, was killed in the war of the Rebellion, leaving an infant son. His daughter married Capt. Simon Bolivar Buckner, from Kentucky, who, after winning great honor in the Mexican war, became a general in the rebel army. He has been reconstructed now and has the devout sympathies of the numerous friends of Major Kingsbury, in his efforts to save for the grandchildren a good share of the Kingsbury estate. I was quite intimate with Major Kingsbury and I will give him the credit of having the most exalted appreciation of a soldier's duty to his wife and children. His investments here were not a matter of speculation but a sense of duty. However diminutive his salary and wherever stationed, his anxiety for the future of his family would have induced savings and investments.

There were three second-lieutenants here who left with Major Whistler, in 1833, and never returned to have any status with our Chicago people. Hannibal Day, of Vermont, who was a captain in 1838; James W. Penrose, of Missouri, who distinguished him-

---

March 10, 1833; and Sergeant Joseph Adams, aged eighty-six years, now living at South Evanston, in this county, and present at the Calumet Club's reception to the Old Settlers on the 19th inst., was prescribed for on the 15th of March, 1835. The book was taken to Fort Howard, Green Bay, Wis., where it was no longer used for its original purpose.

See also Nos. 5 and 11, Fergus' Historical Series, *Sketches of Dr. Maxwell.*

self in the Mexican War, and was brevetted major, and died at Plattsburg, New York, in 1848; and Edwin R. Long, of North Carolina, who died a first-lieutenant at Detroit, Mich., in 1846.

In May, 1833, Capt. John Fowle was again placed in command of the post as the successor of Maj. Whistler, and with him came Brevet-Major De Lafayette Wilcox, who was afterwards, at two periods in command of the post, ending with August 1st, 1836. Maj. Wilcox distinguished himself, was wounded in war of 1812, and died at Pilatka, Florida, in 1842. His name will be perpetuated through our legal reports as representing the United States in the celebrated suit of Gen. John B. Beaubien's grantees or lessees to gain possession of the land upon which the Fort was situated under the preëmption and other laws.

Major Wilcox, and a second-lieutenant, James L. Thompson, were elected members of the Executive Committee of The Chicago Temperance Society, January 30th, 1834. And Che-che-pin-qua (Alexander Robinson) joined it. He created a sensation by pulling a whisky-bottle from his pocket and smashing it with his tomahawk. Philo Carpenter, still living here, was secretary, and can probably tell how long before they had to erase the Indian Chief's name. Yet there was such a society before this, of which John Watkins, now living near Joliet, our first public school-master, was secretary, in 1833, and he may know whether Sauganash and Shabonee had not preceeded Che-che-pin-qua, in the good cause.

With Major Wilcox also came 1st-Lieut. Louis T. Jamison, from Virginia, who, as captain, resigned in 1838. He remained here some time, and will be remembered by all our old settlers, marrying for his second wife, (having lost his first one here, who was from the Chippewa tribe of Indians), a daughter of Gen. Geo. W. McClure, from New York, who distinguished himself in the war of 1812, was an early settler near Dundee, in this State, and died there August 16th, 1851, aged eighty.

Capt. Jamison became a sutler at camp Ringgold, in Texas, near the close of the Mexican war, and died in that region. There was a second-lieutenant, John T. Collinsworth, from Tennessee, who resigned in 1836, went to Texas, where he was made inspector-general, and died there January 28th, 1837. There was also a second-lieutenant, James Allen, from Ohio, uncle of Hon. B. F. Allen, of Des Moines, Iowa, and he was the second man in charge of our Harbor Works. Among the young officers ever stationed at our Fort, he is the most favorably remembered, and was the most of a society man. He took naturally to the company of which our promiscuous population was composed. There could be no social gathering without an invitation to him. He was one of the people all the time. When he went away to join his company the citizens unanimously and successfully petitioned to have him sent back to be placed in charge of our Harbor-Works. The present Chief of Engineers, Gen. A. A. Humphreys, at Washington, writes me, "I went to Chicago in the latter part of Sept., 1838, and relieved Capt. James Allen." Mr. A. V. Knickerbocker, of this City, has presented me, for the Historical Society, some very interesting letters of his, showing the genial character of the man, written to his father, of the same name, who was for many years clerk of the Harbor Department. Lieut. Allen was made captain of dragoons in 1837, raised a brigade of Mormon volunteers, in the region of his command, for the Mexican war, and died, unmarried, at Fort Leavenworth, Aug. 23, 1846, on his route to New Mexico, then a part of the enemy's territory. The first steamboat built in our City was named for him. It was built near the forks of the river, on the North-Side, and run from here to St. Joseph, Captain Pickering. There were lively times on its deck in the evening, after our young folks began to sing,

> "Come, Uncle Mark,* tune your old violin,
> And give us a dance on the Jim Al-*lin*."

On the 19th of June, 1833, our Fort had a new commandant, Major George Bender, from Massachusetts, who resigned his position in the army on the 31st of October, thereafter, and died in Washington City, without additional military service, Aug. 21st, 1865. He commenced the work upon our harbor, the first appropriation therefor, of $25,000, having been made in 1833, the year after the Black-Hawk war, its importance not having been appreciated until Gen. Scott was compelled to send his soldiers on shore from steamboats, one-half of a mile out in the Lake.

Chicago has celebrated many occasions, all considered great at the time. But the commencement of the harbor was the first one. There are several now living who remember it. Capt. Morgan L. Shapley, of Meridian, Texas, one of the first employés, writes me:

"There were two or three stores on South-Water Street. Mark Beaubien, the noted fiddler, had a hotel at the head of Lake Street. There were less than a dozen dwelling shanties in the entire town. The first stone was procured about three miles up the south branch of the river. The work was commenced on the south side of the river. The ties and timber were procured upon

---

* See Appendix I.

the Calumet River, and were rafted into the Lake. The next year, 1834, the work was commenced upon the north side of the river, Lieut. James Allen, superintending."

With Major Bender came Capt. Joseph Baxley, from Maryland, who continued at the Fort until he resigned from the army on April 1st, 1836. He lived with us some years thereafter, but his subsequent history is unknown to me. There was a first-lieutenant, Ephraim Kirby Smith, from Connecticut, who was here until December, 1836. He became Major, distinguished himself in the Mexican war, and was mortally wounded at the battle of El Molino del Rey, dying September 11th, 1847, near City of Mexico. And there was a second-lieutenant, from Tennessee, James L. Thompson, until December, 1836, who resigned from the army, May 18th, 1846, and was drowned soon after in the St. Clair River. He was son-in-law of Gen. Hugh Brady.

December 18th, 1833, Major John Greene, heretofore alluded to, was sent back as successor of Major George Bender, in command of the post, who continued here until September 16, 1835. There came here, October 15th, 1835, a second-lieutenant, Alexander H. Tappan, from Ohio, who continued until September, 1836, and resigned from the army, July 31st, 1838. He resided here until the Mexican war, when he joined Capt. T. B. Kenny's company of the 5th Regiment of Illinois Volunteers, Col. E. W. B. Newby. He was honorably discharged at the close of the war, at Alton, Ill., and has not since been heard from.

Capt. St. Clair Denny, from Pennsylvania, came in August, 1836, and remained until the Fort was abandoned. He resigned from the army, April 30th, 1839, and was afterward made paymaster. I know nothing further of him.

The last commandant of the post was Brevet-Major Joseph Plympton,* from Massachusetts, arriving on August 1st, 1836. He remained at the Fort until June or July, 1837, although the soldiers were withdrawn on December 29th, 1836,† in accordance with the following order of Major-General Alexander Macomb, dated November 30th, 1836:

"The troops stationed at Fort Dearborn, Chicago, will immediately proceed to Fort Howard and join the garrison at that post. Such public property as may be left at Fort Dearborn will remain in charge of Brevet-Major Plympton, of the 5th Infantry, who will continue in command of the post until otherwise instructed."

I saw the last sentinel withdrawn from the entrance, and the last soldier march out, and I heard the last salute fired from Fort

* See Appendix Q.   † See Appendix K.

Dearborn.* For a while we missed the cannon's discharge at sunrise and sunset. And soon sunrise and sunset lost their significance in the measurement of Chicago time.

Major Plympton made many friends here, and frequently visited us. His wife was a Livingston, from New York. He was brevetted a colonel for his meritorious services in the Mexican war, after having distinguished himself in the Florida war. He was promoted to colonel in 1853, and died June 5, 1860. He had a son, Peter William Livingston Plympton, who graduated at West Point, in 1847, and was a brevet-major when he died, at Galveston, Texas, August 10, 1866, aged thirty-nine, and he had a brother, Joseph R. Plympton, now living at Lake City, Florida, and a sister Emily, who married Capt. Mansfield Lovell, a graduate of West Point, in 1842, who distinguished himself in the Mexican war.

The Fort was afterward taken charge of by the superintendent of the harbor-works. Lieut. A. A. Humphreys, (now general), from Pennsylvania, succeeded Capt. Allen, and he was succeeded by 2nd-Lieut. Jesse H. Leavenworth, from Vermont, who resigned, October 31st, 1836, to become civil-engineer, but was retained in government employ; and, at last dates, was Indian-agent at some of our western posts. He and Mrs. Leavenworth are favorably remembered for the manner in which they made the Fort lively with their frequent elegant entertainments. They were liberal in their invitations, and if their guests did not desire to mingle generally, there were apartments enough in the Fort to gratify all distinctive nationalities, conditions, or tastes; all amusements being in order from psalm-singing to dancing to the music of Mark Beaubien's violin.

Next came Capt. John McClellan, from Pennsylvania, brother of Gov. Robert McClellan, of Michigan, who remained until the harbor appropriation was expended, and then he went to the Mexican war, where he was brevetted lieutenant-colonel for meritorious services, and died soon after, unmarried.

Then came the late Gen. Joseph D. Webster, from New Hampshire, as 1st-lieutenant, who constructed the first Marine Hospital, and remained in charge until the Illinois Central Railroad took possession of all there was left of the Fort-Dearborn Reservation.

I have taken no account of the officers who came here with Gen. Scott, July 10th, 1832. He left Buffalo with four steamers,

---

* Opposite the name Fort Dearborn, in the Army Returns for the year 1837, is printed, "Garrison withdrawn May 10, 1837, and Capt. Louis T. Jamison is the only person connected with the army in the Fort."
See letter of Sergeant Joseph Adams, Appendix K.

the *Henry Clay, Superior, Sheldon Thompson,* and *William Penn.* But owing to the breaking out of the cholera, the steamers *Henry Clay* and *Superior* were sent back from Fort Gratiot. I have a letter from Captain A. Walker,* who commanded the *Sheldon Thompson* at that time, saying:

"The disease became so alarming on the *Henry Clay* that nothing like discipline could be preserved. Everything in the way of subordination ceased. As soon as the steamer came to the dock, each man sprang on shore, hoping to escape from a scene so terrible and appalling. Some fled to the fields, some to the woods, whilst others lay down in the streets and under the cover of the river bank, where most of them died unwept and alone. * * * Fort Dearborn was evacuated for the accommodation of sick troops. Major Wm. Whistler and Capt. Seth Johnson, and many others, with their families, who had previously occupied the barracks, took shelter wherever they could, some under boards, placed obliquely across fences, and others in tents.

* * The Chicago River, at that time, was but a mere creek, easily forded at its mouth, whilst it wended its way along the beach, flowing into the lake a short distance south of the present locality of Lake Street. * * * The only means of obtaining anything for fuel was to purchase the useless log-building used as a stable. That, together with the rail-fence enclosing a field of some three acres near by, was sufficient to enable our boats to reach Mackinaw on our return trip."

Gen. Winfield Scott, sometime after the Mexican war, told me that he had often been in great danger, and that he had witnessed a great deal of suffering, but he had never felt his entire helplessness and need of Divine Providence as he did upon the lakes in the midst of the Asiatic cholera. Sentinels were of no use in warning of the enemy's approach. He could not storm his works, fortify against him, nor cut his own way out, nor make terms of capitulation. There was no respect for a flag of truce, and his men were falling upon all sides from an enemy in his very midst. And his responsibilities were never greater. Indian massacres were demanding his utmost haste, and there were with him the most of the class of West-Point graduates, to obtain their first lesson in Indian warfare. There were forty-five in the class of 1832. Twenty-nine of them left Buffalo for the Black-Hawk war, but were nearly all sent back from Fort Gratiot. I have their names and official record.† Six only now belong to the army, and of these six, five are upon the retired list, leaving only Col. John N. Macomb, of the Engineers, in active service.

* See Appendix L. † See Appendix J.

Gen. Ward B. Burnett, a member of that class, from Pennsylvania, one of the few now remaining, and the only one known to me, visited this City last August, and, with fresh memory gave me a full description of the scenes of those times. He was one of those sent back in the steamer *Henry Clay*, from Fort Gratiot. He afterward returned here, and, under the direction of Capt. James Allen, he superintended the first harbor-works at Michigan City and St. Joseph. He resigned, July 31st, 1836, and became an engineer upon the Illinois-and-Michigan Canal, and so continued until the suspension of the work thereon, in 1840. He afterward went into the Mexican war, and so distinguished himself that the gold snuff-box was presented to him, which had originally been presented by the corporation of the city of New York to Gen. Jackson, and was bequeathed in Gen. Jackson's will to the corporation of New York again, in trust, for the best soldier among its residents in the next war. Gen. Burnett also distinguished himself in the war of the Rebellion.

On the 28th of May, 1835, Chicago had a sensation, and I am sorry that I was not here to enjoy it. But many now living were here. I have enjoyed almost every one since. Chicago has ever been noted for its sensations, and that is one of the reasons why I have never liked to leave it. You can not find any other place that has so many of them. Why travel about when there is so much of interest transpiring at home? On that day, Gen. John B. Beaubien went to the public land-office and purchased, for ninety-four dollars and sixty-one cents, the entire Fort-Dearborn Reservation. He derived his military title from an election by the people, not from any conspicuous military talents, but because he had the most friends of any one in town, and he kept them to the day of his death. The State, at that time, was divided into military districts, and the people elected the generals. He had lived upon the reservation many years, and he had found some law, which satisfied our land-officers that he was entitled to make the purchase, the same as many others have found laws under which they could purchase our Lake-Front ever since. The news spread. Everybody was a daily paper in those days. We had but two newspapers then, and both were weeklies. The people assembled in squads and discussed the situation. The question was raised: did Gen. Beaubien buy the Fort with the land? What were the officers to do? There was no telegraph in those days. Gen. Beaubien was congratulated. He had an entire Fort of his own. A conflict between the United States' troops and the State militia might ensue. Gen. Beaubien, himself, was in command of the militia. Would he use them to dispossess the United States' forces? Fancy yourselves here at that time, and remember that the men of that day were the substratum of our present society, and you can appreciate how great a day that of May 28th, 1835, was. The Receiver of Public Moneys, at that time, was Hon. Edmund D. Taylor, now residing at Mendota, in this State, and for many years a resident of this City.

Nothing serious happened, however, as a case was agreed upon and submitted, in 1836, to Judge Thomas Ford, of the Cook County Circuit Court, at the October term, in the shape of an action of ejectment, and entitled John Jackson *ex dem.* Murray McConnell *v.* De Lafayette Wilcox.

The first time I ever saw Thos. Ford, who afterward gained such a splendid reputation as our Canal-Governor, and as historian of our State, was when, in Nov., 1836, he called at my office and left his written opinion to be published in my *Chicago Democrat*. His opinion was very elaborate, and just as favorable to the plaintiff as it could possibly be, whilst he decided against him. He thought Gen. Beaubien's purchase was entirely legal, but that his title could not be enforced until he had procured his patent from Washington; which one thing needful he was never to procure. The suit was appealed to the State supreme court, where Justice Theophilus W. Smith, in behalf of a majority of the court, gave a long and exhaustive opinion, very valuable to this day as a historical document, reversing the decision of the Court below.* Justice Smith was a resident of this City, father-in-law of ex-Mayor Levi D. Boone. He was a warm, personal friend of Gen. Beaubien, and his learned opinion was the work of both heart and head. I have often met him at the General's entertainments. The suit was then taken to the United States Supreme Court, where another very elaborate opinion, and one very valuable as a historical document to this day, was given; which effectually wiped out every pretence to a claim that Gen. Beaubien had. On December 18th, 1840, he was glad to call at the land-office and receive his money back, without interest.†

Upon April 23d, 1839, Hon. Joel R. Poinsett, Secretary of War, appointed Hon. Matthew Burchard, then Solicitor of the General Land-Office, the agent of the Department, to come to Chicago and sell the reservation. Judge Burchard caused the land to be surveyed and platted as Fort-Dearborn Addition to Chicago. His survey made the reservation contain 53¼ acres; being 3¼ acres less than the quantity marked upon the original official plat, the quantity having been diminished, it was sup-

* See *Scammon's Reports*, vol. i.   † See *Peters' United States Reports*, vol. viii.

posed, by abrasions caused by the action of the water of the Lake. All was sold except what was needed for the occupants of the public buildings, and there was realized from the sale what was considered at that time the great sum of $106,042.*

At this time, Chicago had another sensation. Gen. Beaubien had subdivided the land and sold, or given away, his interest in a great many lots. The owners of such rights undertook to shape a public sentiment so as to prevent any one from bidding against them at the time of the sale. The very numerous friends of Gen. Beaubien and his family, sympathized with such a movement. It would be difficult to mention any man of any official prominence or aspirations, from the Judge of our Supreme Court to the humblest citizen, who did not favor non-intervention. Politics also were running very high. The next year, President Martin VanBuren would seek a reëlection, and many interested and sympathizing were his political supporters, and they argued that it would injure the party if the poor people of the West were to be outbid by Eastern speculators. Threats of personal violence were not unfrequently made. Out of the party clamor grew the dedication of Dearborn Park. It was thought a great thing to give so large a tract for a public park. We had nothing of the kind then. It was thought, by the Democratic-party leaders, a measure that would greatly benefit the administration in this region. Yet Judge Burchard dared not have an open sale; and resolved to advertise for sealed bids for a portion of the lots daily, with a determination to reject bids which he thought too low, and to stop the sale if he found the people were influenced by intimidation. Everything proceeded satisfactorily until the lots upon which Gen. Beaubien lived were to be offered. He was expected to procure his homestead for a nominal sum merely, and violent threats were made against any man who dared bid against him. But there was one man, James H. Collins, and I think the only man in the City who dared do this; who had denounced the whole transaction from the beginning in every place he had an opportunity. He had denounced the land-officers and the Judges of the Courts. He was one of the earliest Abolitionists in our State, and would shelter fugitive slaves, and would travel any distance to defend one when captured, or defend a man who was arrested for assisting one to his freedom. He was a man of ability and integrity, and took great delight in defying popular clamor. He took an average of the price at previous sales and put in his sealed bid, thereby securing

* A detailed account of this sale, with names of purchasers, may be found in No. 2 of Fergus' Historical Series—*Chicago Directory for 1839*, page 47.

all the land which Gen. Beaubien desired, being the land upon the east side of Michigan Avenue, in Block 5, between South-Water Street and the lots reserved, where the Marine Hospital afterward was, except the corner lot, known as lot 11, for which Gen. Beaubien paid $225. Mr. Collins bid $1049 for the next five lots, 10, 9, 8, 7, and 6, where Beaubien's house, out-buildings, and garden were. His life was threatened. He was burnt in effigy. Many indignities were put upon him. To all this he bid defiance, asserting that the friends of Gen. Beaubien might possibly take his life, but they could never have his land. He was one of Chicago's ablest lawyers, the candidate of the early Abolitionists for Congress, and far the ablest man in their organization. Had he lived a few years longer, he, unquestionably, would have been assigned to some one of the highest positions in the country. Thus Gen. Beaubien lost his old homestead, except this one lot which he soon sold as insufficient for him; and not one who claimed under him was successful in procuring a lot. If you wish to find the traditional residence of Gen. Jean Baptiste Beaubien, after he moved from what was before known as the John-Dean house, go east upon South-Water Street until you come to the north-east corner of South-Water Street and Michigan Ave., and you will find it. Gen. Beaubien subsequently moved to near what is now River Park, on the Desplaines River, in this county, near the reservation of Alex. Robinson, the Indian chief. The General died at Naperville, DuPage Co., Jan. 5, 1863.

At the session of Congress, in 1848, I succeeded in procuring an amendment to the Naval Appropriation Bill, appropriating $10,000 for the construction of a Marine Hospital on such site as should be selected by the Secretary of the Treasury on the lands owned by the United States. It was one of my best arguments, for the appropriation, that the Government already owned the land for the site. This took up another portion of the Reservation, it being upon the northern portion of block 5, fronting Michigan Avenue and being upon the east side thereof, and adjoining and north of the lots Mr. Collins bought. It was not until September 17, 1850, that I was enabled to telegraph to you, from Congress, that we had secured the Illinois-Central-Railroad grant.*
And it was not until the 14th day of October, 1852, that Hon. Charles M. Conrad, Secretary of War, in consideration of $45,000, made the deed of what was unoccupied of the Reservation to that company, in which was the following preamble: "Whereas the military site of Fort Dearborn, commonly known as the Fort-Dearborn Reservation, at Chicago, Illinois, has become useless

* See Appendix M.

for military purposes, and the tract thereof not being used or necessary for the site of a fort or for any other authorized purposes, has been sold," etc., etc. The railroad company, complaining that it paid this sum of $45,000 from necessity and under protest in order to expedite their road into the City and insisting that the land was included in the grant made by Congress, which I, who took an active part in framing and passing the law, could not endorse, brought suit in the Court of Claims,* at Washington, for refunding the money. The court decided against the claim.

I have thus shown you how the entire Reservation was disposed of, except what would make about eight full lots, upon which the old light-house was located, or near it. They were not needed for light-house purposes; and were lots 1 to 6 in block 4, fractional lots 8 and 9 in block 2, and the north 34 feet of lot 1 in block 5, all near the Rush-Street bridge.† James F. Joy bought for the Railroad Company (Michigan Central or Illinois Central, or both jointly) the land occupied by the Marine-Hospital building, being the south ten feet of lot 1 and lots 2, 3, 4, and 5 in block 5. The hospital was burned in the great fire of 1871.

The Government had erected a new light-house at the end of the North Pier. I was in Congress, and the thought occurred to me that the best way to dispose of the remaining land upon which the old light-house and other necessary Government buildings had been located was to present it to that kind-hearted and popular old pioneer, Gen. Jean Baptiste Beaubien. And it was so done by an act approved Aug. 1, 1854. And there was not a citizen of Chicago who knew him who ever questioned its propriety, to my knowledge. The last man in charge of the old light-house was that genial old settler, his brother Mark, who passed away on the 11th of April, 1881, aged 81 years. He came here, from Detroit, in 1826, where he resided at the time of Gen. Hull's surrender and he witnessed it. He brought a violin with him and

---

* See U.S. Senate Miscel. Doc., No. 145, 1st Session of 35th Congress.

† EXTRACT FROM THE REPORT OF HON. MATHEW BURCHARD, AGENT OF THE WAR DEPARTMENT, DATED NOV. 21, 1840.—"By the official plat herewith enclosed, it will be seen that block 1, and lots 8, 9, and 10 in block 2, lots 1, 2, 3, 4, 5, and 6 in block 4, and lots 1, 2, 3, 4, and 5 in block 5 are colored blue. These were reserved from sale, and embrace all the grounds occupied by the light-house, keeper's dwelling, and fortress of Fort Dearborn within the pickets, including the officers' quarters and barracks. This ground is very valuable. My object in reserving so much property was to secure and protect the Light, which is situated on lot 8 of block 2, from obstruction by private buildings which otherwise might have been erected between its present position and Lake Michigan, also to afford room and shops for the superintendent of the public works." [By such officers it was occupied for some fifteen years.]

U. S. Marine Hospital.	Big Locust Tree.
Storehouse,	Magazine. Block-house.
Soldier's Barracks.	Officer's Quarters. Light-house.
Stables, Artillery.	Commandant's Quarters. Light-keeper's House.
	Ferry Slip.

FORT DEARBORN IN 1850.*

* The above is a very good representation of the Fort, in 1850, from a daguerrotype, by Polycarpus von Schneidau, a Swedish nobleman, taken from the south front of the Lake House, which was situated on the east side of Rush Street, extending from Michigan to Kinzie (now called North-Water) Streets. The ferry, shown in the foreground, landed on the North-Side, about where the "Empire Warehouse" now is. The building faintly shown between the block-house and the light-keeper's, is the residence of the late "Judge" Henry Fuller, and was just outside of the Fort enclosure, and the ground is now covered by Spaulding & Merrick's tobacco works. There was another building in the Fort enclosure, not shown in this view, just east of the block-house; were the officers' quarters in this view removed, it would appear as if in front of the large locust-tree, and was the quartermaster's or sutler's quarters. The parade-ground was between the commandant's, officers', and sutler's quarters on the west, and the building where the artillery was housed, the soldier's barracks, and the storehouse on the east; and was about 80 feet wide, and extended from the river bank south, the full length of the enclosure—say 400 feet; near its southern extremity was a gentle rise of ground or knoll, in the centre of which was an 8-inch piece of square timber, imbedded in the earth, placed upright, about 2 feet high, upon the top of which was a brass plate on which had been a sun-dial. South of this sun-dial, say 100 feet, was a turn-style through which you entered the Fort enclosure from the centre of Michigan Avenue, which then commenced at this point. The whole Fort enclosure was surrounded by a rough-board fence, white-washed, about 6 feet high; the pickets having been removed at an earlier date. The kitchen-garden was in the south-west corner of the enclos-

and with it made more hearts merry than any man who ever lived
in Chicago. He requested that it be given to me upon his death-
bed, and upon the evening of the 19th of May, 1881, I presented
it to the Calumet Club, whose members ever delighted to enter-
tain him.* He was Mark Beaubien, a brother of Gen. John B.
Beaubien, who claimed to have brought the first piano to our City,
which is yet in good tune with his granddaughter, Mrs. Sophia
Ogee, daughter of the late Chas. Beaubien, now living in Silver
Lake, Kansas. When I came here, on October 25th, 1836, there
was no other piano on the South-Side and none on the West. So
much has been said and written of these two brothers in connection with early Chicago, and all in kindness and commendation,
that I will forego the promptings of my heart at this time respecting them. Yet the Beaubiens and that piano and that fiddle are
inseparably connected with the history of the Fort-Dearborn
Reservation. For years, John B. was the only resident upon it
outside the Fort; and, when the light which had so long illumi-
nated our Lake, under the superintendence of his brother Mark,
was extinguished, Congress gave to him what was left of its foundation and surroundings, after widening the river.

A light-house† was established here, by an Act of Congress,
March 3, 1831. It fell‡ soon after completion, in October of
that year; but it was soon rebuilt. Samuel C. Lasby was the
first keeper. When I came here, in 1836, William M. Stevens
was keeper; then John C. Gibson; then William M. Stevens
again. President Harrison appointed Silas Meacham; President
Polk, James Long; President Taylor, Chas. Douglass; President
Pierce, Henry Fuller; and President Buchanan, Mark Beaubien.
The annual salary was all the while $350. These men are all
numbered with the dead. And so are nearly all those who ever
occupied the Fort, some falling in the War of 1812, some in subsequent Indian wars, some in the Mexican war, and some in the
war to protect and perpetuate a union in defence of which the
others had fallen. We have marked the site and written the history of old Fort Dearborn. All else has given way to the march
of commerce. But the name remains, a name associated with all
the thrilling scenes of the American Revolution, from Bunker Hill
to Yorktown, from the capture of Burgoyne to that of Cornwallis.

ure. The street or road shown in above view between the block-house and
the light-keeper's is River Street. The piles, upon which the turn-table of
the present bridge at Rush Street was built, were driven (at about the spot,
indicated in the above view, where the boat is partly drawn ashore) part in
the bank of the River and part in the water; and the channel south of this
turn-table has since been excavated.—F.

* See Appendix N.   † See Appendix O.   ‡ See Appendix P.

From an Ivory Minature in the possession of his grand-nephew, Hon. Darius Heald.

APPENDIX.

A.
THE WELLS FAMILY.

The descendants of Col. Samuel Wells and Capt. William Wells claim that their parents were Virginians, and some say that both Samuel and William were born there. *Gardner's Army Dictionary* states that both came into the U.S. service from Kentucky. Mrs. Capt. Heald, the daughter of Col. Samuel, was married at Louisville, Ky. Capt. William was stolen when about twelve years of age, from the residence of the Hon. Nathaniel Pope, of Kentucky, by the Miami Indians, and was adopted as a son by Me-che-kau-nah-qua or Little Turtle, one of the most distinguished warriors and leaders of his day, who was half-Mohican and half-Miami. Capt. Wells fought upon the side of the Indians and distinguished himself in their defeat of Gen. Josiah Harmar, in 1790, and in their defeat of Gen. Arthur St. Clair, in 1791. They had great admiration for his dash and courage. About the time that Gen. Anthony Wayne was appointed to take command of the Western army, Capt. Wells began to realize that he was fighting against his own kindred and might kill some of them in battle, and resolved to sever his connection with the Indians. He invited the chief of Miamis, Little Turtle, to accompany him to a point on the Maumee, about two miles east of Fort Wayne, long known as the "Big Elm," where he thus addressed him: "Father, we have long been friends. I now leave you to go to my own people. We will be friends until the sun reaches its mid-day height. From that time, we will be enemies; and, if you want to kill me then, you may. And, if I want to kill you, I may." He set out immediately for Gen. Wayne's army, was made captain of a company of spies, and fought with him until the treaty of peace at Greenville, in 1795. After that, he was joined by his wife, who was a daughter of Little Turtle, and his children. He lived with Little Turtle, at Fort Wayne; they were always fast friends; and after the peace of Greenville, in 1795, was declared under Wayne's treaty, Capt. Wells accompanied Little Turtle to Washington, and they together visited nearly all the Eastern Cities. Little Turtle died at Fort Wayne, Ind., 14 July, 1812. Capt. Wells settled upon a farm and was afterward made Indian-agent and Justice-of-the-Peace. His Indian name signified Black-Snake. His correspondence preserved in the *American State Papers*, as well as many manuscripts still in existence, (some of which being now in my possession), show that he was a good scholar for his times. He had one other Indian wife, a Weah woman, and one American wife who survived him. His children were all well educated. The most of them were by Wa-nan-ga-peth, the daughter of Little Turtle, and they all were as follows:

Ah-pez-zah-quah—Ann Wells married Dr. Wm. Turner, of Fort Wayne, Indiana, died childless, July 26, 1834.

Pe-me-sah-quah—Rebekah Wells married Capt. Hackley, of Fort Wayne, and died June 14, 1835, leaving Ann and John.

Ah-mah-quau-zah-quah—(a sweet breeze)—Mary Wells, born at Fort Wayne, Indiana, May 10, 1800, married Judge James Wolcott, (who was from Torrington, Connecticut, and is said to have been cousin of our original Dr. Alexander Wolcott), at St. Louis, Mo., March 8, 1821. She died at Maumee City, (now South Toledo), Ohio, February 19, 1843. He died there January

5, 1873, having remarried and having children by his second wife. He lived at Fort Wayne (which had ever been the home of the Wells family) until 1826, when he removed to South Toledo, O. Frederick Allen Wolcott was killed before Atlanta, Ga., July 22d, 1864.

Wa-pe-mong-gah—William Wayne Wells, graduated at West Point, in 1821, and is alluded to in the Address.

Jane Wells married Mathew or Samuel Griggs, and now lives at Peru, Indiana, and has children.

Samuel G. Wells died childless.

Yelberton P. Wells died, leaving one child, at St. Louis, Mo.

Juliana Wells, died childless.

All those having Indian names claimed that their names were given them by their grandfather, Little Turtle.

Hon. J. L. Williams, in his *History of the First Presbyterian Church of Fort Wayne*, says: "Of the first members of this church, two were half-breed Indians, Mrs. Turner and Mrs. Hackley, who had before (in 1820) joined the Baptist Church, under the labors of Rev. Mr. McCoy, missionary to the Indians at Fort Wayne. They were educated in Kentucky, and are yet kindly remembered as ladies of refinement and intelligent piety." Mrs. Wolcott, was a zealous Episcopalian, having united herself with the first church of that order upon the Maumee River, east of Fort Wayne.

The following children of Judge James and Ah-mah-quau-zah-quuah (Wells) Wolcott are now living: William Wells Wolcott, Toledo, Ohio; Mary Ann Wolcott, now Mrs. Gilbert, South Toledo, Ohio; Henry Clay Wolcott, South Toledo, Ohio; James Madison Wolcott, South Toledo, Ohio. The latter writes: "We are proud of our Indian (Little Turtle) blood, and of our Capt. Wells blood. We try to keep up the customs of our ancestors, and dress occasionally in Indian costumes. We take no exceptions when people speak of our Indian parentage. We take pleasure in sending to you the tomahawk which Capt. William Wells had at the time of his death, and which was brought to his family by an Indian who was in the battle. We also have a dress-sword, which was presented to him by Gen. William H. Harrison, and a great many books which he had; showing that, even when he lived among the Indians, he was trying to improve himself. He did all he could to educate his children." Capt. Wells, in the year of his death, sent to President Madison, at Little Turtle's request, the interpretation of the speech that that chief made to Gen. W. H. Harrison, January 25, 1812.

B.

STATEMENT COMPILED FROM THE RECORDS OF THE ADJUTANT-GENERAL'S OFFICE, IN THE CASE OF FORT DEARBORN, WITH COPIES OF ORDERS:

STATEMENT:

Fort Dearborn, situated at Chicago, Ill., within a few yards of Lake Michigan; Latitude 41° 51' North; Longitude 87° 15' West. Post established by the United States forces in 1804. [From 1804-12, no records are on file.]

August 15th, 1812, the garrison having evacuated the post and were *en route* for Ft. Wayne, under the command of Capt. Nathan Heald, 1st U. S. Infantry, composed of 54 Regular Infantry, 12 Militia-men, and 1 Interpreter, was attacked by Indians, to the number of between 400 and 500, of whom 15 were reported killed. Those of the garrison killed were Ensign George Ronan, 1st Infantry, Dr. Isaac V. VanVoorhis, Capt. Wells, Interpreter, 24 enlisted men U. S. Infantry, and 12 militia-men; 2 women and 12 children were also killed.

The wounded were Capt. Nathan Heald and Mrs. Heald. None others reported. The next day, August 16, 1812, the post was destroyed by the Indians, Re-occupied about June, 1816, Capt. Hezekiah Bradley, 3d Infantry, commanding; the troops continued in occupation until October, 1823, when the post was evacuated and left in charge of the Indian agent; it was re-occupied October 3, 1828.

Capt. Hezekiah Bradley, 3d Infantry, commanded the post from June, 1816, to May, 1817; Brevet-Major D. Baker, 3d Infantry, to June, 1820; Capt. Hezekiah Bradley, 3d Infantry, to January, 1821; Major Alex. Cummings, 3d Infantry, to October, 1821; Lieut.-Col. J. McNeal, 3d Infantry, to July, 1823; Capt. John Greene, 3d Infantry; to October, 1823; post not garrisoned from October, 1823, to October, 1828. No returns of post on file prior to 1828.

COPIES OF ORDERS:

Order No. 35.   Adjutant-General's Office, Washington, 27 May, 1823.

The Major-General, commanding the army, directs that Fort Dearborn, Chicago, be evacuated, and that the garrison thereof be withdrawn to the headquarters of the 3d Regiment of Infantry.

One company of the 3d Regiment of Infantry will proceed to Mackinac and relieve the company of Artillery now stationed there, which, with the company of Artillery at Fort Shelby, Detroit, will be withdrawn and ordered to the Harbor of New York.

The Commanding-General of the Eastern Department will give the necessary orders for carrying these movements into effect as well as for the security of the public property at Forts Dearborn and Shelby.

By order of MAJOR-GENERAL BROWN,
(Signed) CHAS. J. NOURSE, *Act'g Adjutant-General*.

Order No. 44.   Adjutant-General's Office, Washington, 19 Aug., 1828.

[EXTRACT.] In conformity with the directions of the Secretary of War, the following movements of the troops will be made without delay:

1. Two companies of the 5th Regiment of Infantry to re-occupy Fort Dearborn, at the head of Lake Michigan; the remaining eight companies to proceed, by the way of the Ouisconsin and Fox Rivers, to Fort Howard, Green Bay, where the headquarters of the Regiment will be established.

Four Co's of this Reg't to constitute the garrison of Ft. Howard; two Co's, the garrison for Michilimackinac, and two for that of Ft. Brady.   *   *

4. The Quartermaster-General's Department to furnish the necessary transportation and supplies for the movement and accommodation of the troops.

The Subsistence department to furnish the necessary surplus of provisions.

The Surgeon-General to provide Medical Officers and suitable Hospital supplies for the posts to be established and re-occupied.

5. The Commanding-Generals of the Eastern and Western Departments are respectively charged with the execution of this Order, as far as relates to their respective commands.

By order of MAJOR-GENERAL MACOMB,
(Signed) R. JONES, *Adjutant-General*.

Order No. 5.   Adjutant-General's Office, Washington, 31 March, 1831.

[EXTRACT.] 1. The Post of Chicago will be evacuated as early as practicable, and the garrison, consisting of two companies of the 5th Regiment of Infantry, will proceed to Green Bay, and occupy Fort Howard.   *   *

By order of ALEXANDER MACOMB,
Major-General, Commanding the Army,
(Signed) R. JONES, *Adjutant-General*.

48   FORT DEARBORN.

The following Statement shows the Companies composing the Garrison of the Post, at different periods, after Oct. 3D, 1828, until its Abandonment; also, the Commanding Officers and other Officers on duty at the Post, from time to time:

GARRISON.	OFFICERS.	RANK.	ON DUTY, FROM	TO	REMARKS.
Companies "A" and "I," (5th Infantry) from October 3, 1828, to May 29, 1831.	John Fowle, Jr.,	Capt. & Bvt-Maj. 5th Inf.,	Oct. 3, 1828,	Dec. 14, 1830.	Commanding Post. [May 20, 1831.
	David Hunter,	1st-Lieut.	Oct. 3, 1828,		Commanding post from Dec. 14, 1830, to Aug. 29, 1830.
	John G. Furman,	2d-Lieut. "	Oct. 3, 1828,	Aug. 29, 1830.	A.-A.C.S. and A.-A.Q.-M. d. Aug. 29, 30
	Abram VanBuren,	Bvt 2d-Lieut. "	Oct. 3, 1828,	March, 1829.	[Son of President Van Buren.]
	C. A. Finley,	Assistant-Surgeon,	Oct. 3, 1828,	Dec. 14, 1830.	
	James Engle,	2d-Lieut. 5th Infantry.	Oct. 3, 1828,	May 20, 1831.	
Troops withdrawn, May 20, 1831.	Amos R. Foster,	Bvt 2d-Lieut. 5th "	June 20, 1829.	May 20, 1831.	
	Martin Scott,	Captain, " "	Nov. 4, 1829.	Aug. 20, 1830.	
Re-occupied, June 17, 32.	Wm. Whistler,	Major, 2d Infantry,	June 17, 1832.	May 14, 1833.	Commanding Post.
Companies "G" and "I," (2d Infantry) from June 17, 1832; "I" to May 15, 1833; "G" to May 31, 1833.	S. G. I. DeCamp,	Assistant-Surgeon,	June 17, 1832,	Nov. 23, 1832.	No returns between June and Oct., 32.
	Seth Johnston,	Captain, 2d Infantry,	June 17, 1832.	May 15, 1833.	"Fort Dearborn having become a General Hospital, on the 11 July last, no returns were rendered until its re-occupation. "G" and "I," 2d Inf., returned to post on 1st of Oct. from campaign. [Vide return of Post for October, 1832.]
	J. J. B. Kingsbury,	1st-Lieut. "	June 17, 1832.	May 31, 1833.	
	Hannibal Day,	2d-Lieut. "	June 17, 1832.	May 15, 1833.	
	J. W. Penrose,	Bvt 2d-Lieut. 2d Inf'y,	June 17, 1832.	May 31, 1833.	
	F. R. Long,	"	June 17, 1832.	May 15, 1833.	
	P. Maxwell,	Assistant-Surgeon,	Feb. 3, 1833.	Dec., 1836.	
Companies "A" and "B," (5th Infantry) from May 14th, 1833, to Dec. 29th, 1836, when the garrison was withdrawn.	John Fowle, Jr.,	Capt. & Bvt-Maj. 5 Inf.,	May 14, 1833.	June 19, 1833.	Commanding Post.
	H. Wilcox,	"	May 14, 1833.	Aug. 1, 1836.	Com'd'g post from Oct. 31 to Dec. 28, 33, and from Sept. 16, 35, to Aug. 1, 36.
	I.- T. Jamison,	1st-Lieut. "	May 14, 1833.	Dec., 1836.	
	J. Allen,	Bvt 2d-Lieut. "	May 14, 1833.	Jan., 1834.	
	J. T. Collinsworth,	"	May 14, 1833.	June 20, 1833.	
	George Bender,	Major "	June 19, 1833.	Oct. 31, 1833.	Commanding Post.
	J. M. Baxley,	Captain "	June 20, 1833.	April, 1836.	
			(May 29, 1833,	July, 1834.	
	E. K. Smith,	1st-Lieut. "	(Oct. 23, 1836.	Dec., 1836.	
	J. L. Thompson,	2d-Lieut. "	June 20, 1833.	Dec., 1836.	
	John Greene,	Major "	Dec. 18, 1833.	Sept. 16, 1835.	Commanding Post.
	A. H. Tappren,	Bvt 2d-Lieut. "	Oct. 15, 1835.	Sept., 1836.	
No Returns on file subsequent to May, 1837.	St. Clair Denny,	Captain "	August, 1, 1836.	Dec., 1836.	(thereof till June or July, 1837.
	J. Plympton,	Capt. & Bvt-Maj. "	Aug. 1, 1836.	Dec. 29, 1836.	Com'd'g Post, and remained in charge

Order No. 17. Adjutant-General's Office, Washington, 23 Feb., 1832.
(COPY.) The head-quarters of the 2d Regiment of Infantry are transferred to Fort Niagara. Lieut.-Col. Cummings, with all the officers and men composing the garrison of Madison Barracks, Sacketts' Harbor, will accordingly relieve the garrison of Fort Niagara; and Major Whistler, of the 2d Infantry, on being relieved by Lieut.-Col. Cummings, with all the troops under his command, will repair to Fort Dearborn (Chicago, Illinois) and garrison that post.

Assistant-Surgeon DeCamp, now on duty at Madison Barracks, is assigned to duty at Fort Dearborn, and will accompany the troops ordered to that post.

These movements will take place as soon as the navigation will permit.

By order of MAJOR-GENERAL MACOMB,
(Signed) R. JONES, *Adjutant-General.*

General Order, Head-quarters of the Army,
No. 80. Adjutant-General's Office, Washington, Nov. 30, 1836.
[EXTRACT.] 1. The troops stationed at Fort Dearborn, Chicago, will immediately proceed to Fort Howard and join the garrison at that post. Such public property as may be left at Fort Dearborn will remain in charge of Brevet-Major Plympton, of the 5th Infantry, who will continue in command of the post until otherwise instructed. * * * *

By order of ALEXANDER MACOMB, Maj.-Gen. Com'd'g-in-Chief,
(Signed) R. JONES, *Adjutant-General.*

Adjutant's-General's Office,
Washington, April 2, 1881.
OFFICIAL, (Signed) C. McKEEVER,
Assistant-Adjutant General in charge.

C.

CONTEMPORANEOUS ACCOUNTS.

Mathew Irwin, [or Irvine], Indian agent, writes from Chicago, May 13th, 1811, to the Secretary of War:

"An assemblage of the Indians is to take place on a branch of the Illinois, by the influence of the Prophet. The result will be hostile in the event of war with Great Britain."

Salienne, Indian interpreter at Chicago, writes under date of June 2, 1811:
"Several horses have been stolen. The Indians in this quarter are inclined to hostility."

John Johnston, [who was U.S. factor at Fort Wayne], writes from Piqua-Town, Ohio, under date of May 1, 1812:
"The Indians have recently murdered two men at Fort Dearborn."

Mathew Irwin [or Irvine] writes, Chicago, 10th March, 1812:
"The Chippewa and Ottawa nations, hearing that the Winnebagoes and Pottawatomies are hostilely inclined toward the whites, sent speeches among them, desiring them to change their sentiments, and live in peace with the whites." April 16, 1812: "On the 6th, a party of ten or eleven Indians surrounded a small farm-house, on Chicago River, and killed two men. The Indians are of the Winnebago tribe."

EXTRACTS FROM LETTERS FROM CAPTAIN HEALD:

CHICAGO, 7th February, 1812.

An express arrived at the post on the 1st instant, from Gen. [William, afterward Governor of Missouri,] Clark. He was sent for the purpose of finding out the disposition of the Indians; he was a Frenchman, and well acquainted with the Indians. He told me, that the Indians on the Illinois were hostile disposed towards the United States, and that the war between the Indians and the white people had just commenced, alluding to the late battle on the Wabash, [Tippecanoe.]

An express arrived here on the first of the month from St. Louis, sent by Gen. Clark, Indian-agent of that place, for the purpose of finding out the disposition of the Indians, between here and there. This express is a Frenchman, who is well acquainted with the Indians, and he is of opinion that there are many of them determined to continue the war against the whites.

CHICAGO, March 11, 1812.

I have been informed, and believe it to be true, that the Winnebagoes have lately attacked some traders on the Mississippi, near the lead mines; it is said they killed two Americans and eat them up, and took all their goods; there are two French traders whom they robbed of all their goods and suffered them to go off alive. This news came to me from a Frenchman, at Millwaike, who has been to the Winnebago nation. The Winnebagoes who escaped from the Prophet's town, are still in the neighborhood.

CHICAGO, April 15th, 1812.

The Indians have commenced hostilities in this quarter. On the 6th inst., a little before sunset, a party of eleven Indians, supposed to be Winnebagoes, came to Messrs. Russel and See's cabin, in a field on the Portage branch of the Chicago River, about three miles from the garrison, where they murdered two men, one by the name of Liberty White, an American, and the other a Canadian Frenchman, whose name I do not know. White received two balls through his body; nine stabs with a knife in his breast, and one in his hip, his throat was cut from ear to ear, his nose and lips were taken off in one piece, and his head skinned almost as far round as they could find any hair. The Frenchman was only shot through the neck and scalped. Since the murder of these two men, one or two other parties of Indians have been lurking about us, but we have been so much on our guard that they have not been able to get any scalps.

[See Mrs. Kinzie's *Wau-bun*, pp. 203-47, for a fuller account of this affair.]

From Niles' *Weekly Register*, Vol. iii., p. 79, October 3d, 1812.

FALL OF FORT DEARBORN AT CHICAWGO. — Yesterday afternoon the *Queen Charlotte* arrived at Fort Erie, seven days from Detroit. A flag of truce soon landed at Buffalo Creek, Major Atwater and Lieut. J. L. Eastman, who gave the following account of the fall of Fort Dearborn. On the 1st of September, a Pottawatomie chief arrived at Detroit, and stated, that about the middle of August, Capt. Wells, from Fort Wayne, (an interpreter) arrived at Fort Dearborn to advise the commandant of that Fort to evacuate it and retreat. In the meantime a large body of Indians of different nations had collected and menaced the garrison. A council was held with the Indians, in which it was agreed that the party in the garrison should be spared on condition that all property in the Fort should be given up. The Americans marched out but were fired upon and nearly all killed. There were about fifty men in the Fort besides women and children, and probably not more than ten or twelve taken prisoners. Capt. Wells and Heald (the commandant) were killed.—*Buffalo Gazette*, [date not given].

From Niles' *Weekly Register*, May 8th, 1813, Vol. iv., p. 160.

EXTRACT OF A LETTER FROM WALTER JORDAN, A NON-COMMISSIONED OFFICER OF THE REGULARS AT FORT WAYNE, TO HIS WIFE IN ALLEGHENY COUNTY, DATED FORT WAYNE, OCTOBER 19, 1812:—I take my pen to inform you that I am well, after a long a perilous journey through the Indian country. Capt. Wells, myself, and an hundred friendly Indians, left Fort Wayne on the 1st of August, to escort Captain Heald from Fort Chicauga as he was in danger of being captured by the British. Orders had been given to abandon that Fort and retreat to Fort Wayne, a distance of 150 miles. We reached Chicauga on the 10th of August, and on the 15th we prepared for an immediate march, burning all that we could not fetch with us. On the 15th, at 8 o'clock, we commenced our march with our small force, which consisted of Capt. Wells, myself, and 100 Confute Indians, Capt. Heald's 100 men, 10 women, and 20 children—in all 232. We had marched half a mile when we were attacked by 600 Kickapoo and Wynbago Indians. In the moment of trial our Confute savages joined the savage enemy. Our contest lasted ten minutes, when every man, woman, and child was killed except fifteen. Thanks be to God I was one of those who escaped. First they shot the feather off my cap, next the epaulet from my shoulder, and then the handle from my sword. I then surrendered to four savage rascals. The Confute chief, taking me by the hand and speaking English said, "Jordan, I know you; you gave me tobacco at Fort Wayne. We won't kill you, but come and see what we will do with your captain." So leading me to where Wells lay, they cut off his head and put it on a long pole, while another took out his heart and divided it among the chiefs and ate it up raw. Then they scalped the slain and stripped the prisoners, and gathered in a ring with us fifteen poor wretches in the middle. They had nearly all fallen out about the divide, but my old chief, the White Raccoon, holding me fast, they made the divide and departed to their towns. They tied me hard and fast that night, and placed a guard over me.———I lay down and slept soundly until morning, for I was tired. In the morning they untied me and set me parching corn, at which I worked attentively until night. They said that if I would stay and not run away, that they would make a chief of me; but if I would attempt to run away they would catch me and burn me alive. I amused them with a fine story in order to gain their confidence, and, fortunately, made my escape from them on the 19th of August, and took one of their best horses to carry me, being seven days in the wilderness. I was joyfully received at Wayne on the 26th. On the 28th they attacked the Fort and blockaded us until the 16th of September, when we were relieved by Gen. Harrison.

From Niles' *Weekly Register*, Vol. 3, p. 155, Nov. 7th, 1812-13.

EXTRACT OF A LETTER FROM CAPT. HEALD, LATE COMMANDANT AT FORT CHICAGO, DATED AT PITTSBURGH, OCTOBER 23, 1812:—On the 9th of August, I received orders from Gen. Hull, to evacuate the post, and proceed, with my command, to Detroit by land, leaving it at my discretion to dispose of the public property as I thought proper. The neighboring Indians got the information as early as I did, and came in from all quarters in order to receive the goods in the factory-store, which they understood were to be given them. On the 13th, Capt. Wells, of Fort Wayne, arrived with about thirty Miamies, for the purpose of escorting us in by request of Gen. Hull. On the 14th, I delivered the Indians all the goods in the factory-store, and a considerable quantity of provisions, which we could not take with us. The surplus arms and ammunition, I thought proper to destroy, fearing they would make bad use of it, if put in their possession. I also destroyed all liquor on hand, soon after they began to collect. The collection was usually large for that place, but they conducted with the strictest propriety until after I left the Fort. On the 15th, at 9 a. m., we commenced our march, a part of the Miamies were detached in front, the remainder in our rear, as guards, under the direction of Capt. Wells. The situation of the country rendered it necessary for us to take the beach, with the lake on our left, and a high sand-bank on our right, at about one hundred yards distance. We had proceeded about a mile and a-half, when it was discovered that the Indians were prepared to attack us from behind the bank. I immediately marched up, with the company, to the top of the bank, when the action commenced; after firing one round, we charged, and the Indians gave way in front and joined those on our flanks. In about fifteen minutes, they got possession of all our horses, provisions, and baggage of every description, and finding the Miamies did not assist us, I drew off the few men I had left, and took possession of a small elevation in the open prairie, out of shot of the bank or any other cover. The Indians did not follow me, but assembled in a body on the top of the bank, and, after some consultation among themselves, made signs for me to approach them. I advanced toward them alone, and was met by one of the Pottawatomie chiefs, called Black-Bird, with an interpreter. After shaking hands, he requested me to surrender, promising to spare the lives of all the prisoners. On a few moments consideration, I concluded it would be most prudent to comply with his request, although I did not put entire confidence in his promise.

After delivering up our arms, we were taken back to their encampment near the Fort, and distributed among the different tribes. The next morning they set fire to the Fort, and left the place, taking the prisoners with them. Their number of warriors was between 400 and 500, mostly of the Pottawatomie nation, and their loss, from the best information I could get, was about fifteen. Our strength was about fifty-four regulars and twelve militia, out of which, twenty-six regulars and all the militia were killed in the action, with two women and twelve children. Ensign George Ronan and Dr. Isaac V. VanVoorhis, of my company, with Capt. Wells, of Fort Wayne, to my great sorrow, are numbered among the dead. Lieut. Linai T. Helm, with twenty-five non-commissioned officers and privates, and eleven women and children, were prisoners when we separated. Mrs. Heald and myself were taken to the mouth of the river St. Joseph, and, being both badly wounded, were permitted to reside with Mr. Burnett, an Indian trader. In a few days after our arrival there, the Indians went off to take Fort Wayne, and in their absence, I engaged a Frenchman to take us to Michilimackinac, by water, where I gave myself up as a prisoner of war, with one of my serjeants. The commanding officer, Capt. Roberts, offered me every assistance in his power to render our situation comfortable while we remained there, and to enable us to proceed on our journey. To him I gave my parole of honor, and came on to Detroit, and reported myself to Col. Proctor, who gave us a passage to Buffaloe; from that place, I came by the way of Presque-Isle, and arrived here yesterday.

Nathan Heald

From Niles' *Weekly Register*, Saturday, April 3, 1813. Vol. iv., p. 83.

SAVAGE BARBARITY.—Mrs. Helm, the wife Lieut. Helm, who escaped from the butchery of the garrison of Chicauga, by the assistance of a humane Indian, has arrived at this place [*Buffaloe*]; the account of her sufferings during three months' slavery among the Indians, and three months' imprisonment amongst their allies, would make a most interesting volume; one circumstance alone I will mention. During five days after she was taken prisoner, she had not the least sustenance, and was compelled to drag a canoe, (barefooted and wading along the stream), in which there were some squaws, and when she demanded food, some flesh of her murdered countrymen and a piece of Col. Wells' heart was offered her. She knows the fact, that Col. Proctor, the British commander at Malden, bought the scalps of our murdered garrison of Chicauga, and thanks to her noble spirit, she boldly charged him with his infamy in his own house. She knows further, from the tribe with whom she was a prisoner, and who were perpetrators of those murders, that they intended to remain true, but that they received orders, from the British, to cut off our garrison whom they were to escort.

Oh! spirits of the murdered Americans, can ye not rouse your countrymen, your friends, your relations, to take ample vengeance on those worse than savage blood-hounds?   March 8, 1813.   AN OFFICER.

From Niles' *Weekly Register*, 4th June, 1814, Vol. vi., p. 221.

CHICAGO.—Among the persons who have recently arrived at this place (says the Plattsburg [N.Y.] paper of the 21st ultimo) from Quebec are—

James Van Horn,	Elias Mills,	Dyson Dyer,
Joseph Knowles,	Joseph Bowen,	James Corbin, and
Paul Grummow,	Nathan Edson,	Phelim Corbin,

of the 1st Regiment of U.S. Infantry, who survived the massacre at Fort Dearborn or Chicago, on the 15th of Aug., 1812. It will be recollected that the commandant at Fort Chicago, Capt. Heald, was ordered, by Gen. Hull, to evacuate the Fort, and proceed with his command to Detroit; that having proceeded about a mile and a-half the troops were attacked by a body of Indians, to whom they were compelled to capitulate. Capt. Heald, in his report of this affair, dated October 23rd., 1812, says: "Our strength was fifty-four regulars and twelve militia, out of which twenty-six regulars and all the militia were killed in the action, with two women and twelve children. Lieut. Linai T. Helm, with twenty-five non-commissioned officers and privates, and eleven women and children, were prisoners when we separated." Lieut. Helm was ransomed. Of the twenty-five non-commissioned officers and privates, and the eleven women and children, the nine persons above mentioned, are believed to be the only survivors. They state that the prisoners who were not put to death on the march, were taken to the Fox River, in the Illinois Territory, where they were distributed among the Indians as servants. Those who survived remained in this situation about nine months, during which time they were allowed scarcely a sufficiency of sustenance to support nature, and were then brought to Fort Chicago, where they were purchased by a French trader, agreeable to the directions of Gen. Proctor, and sent to Amherstburg, and from thence to Quebec, where they arrived Nov. 8th, 1813.

John Neads, who was one of the prisoners, formerly of Virginia, died among the Indians between the 15th and 20th of January, 1813.

Hugh Logan, an Irishman, was tomahawked and put to death, he not being able to walk, from excessive fatigue.

August Mott, a German, was killed in the same manner for the like reason.

A man by the name of Nelson was frozen to death while a captive with the Indians. He was formerly from Maryland.

A child of Mrs. Neads, the wife of John Neads, was tied to a tree to prevent its following and crying after its mother for victuals. Mrs. Neads afterwards perished with hunger and cold.

The officers who were killed on the 15th of August had their heads cut off and their hearts taken out and broiled in the presence of the prisoners.

Eleven children were massacred and scalped in one wagon.

Mrs. Corbin, wife of Phelim Corbin, in an advanced stage of pregnancy, was tomahawked, scalped, cut open, and had the child taken out and its head cut off.

[From *American State Papers*, Indian affairs, Vol. II., p. 59.]

ESTIMATE OF LOSSES SUSTAINED BY THE INDIAN-FACTORY DEPARTMENT DURING THE LATE WAR BY DESTRUCTION OF BUILDINGS, ETC., BY THE ENEMY, VIZ:

1812. LATE FACTORY AT CHICAGO:

Amount Merchandise on hand at this Factory on its evacuation, which was delivered to the Indians by the commanding officer, Captain Heald,	$6,122.03½	
Amount Furs and Peltries shipped to Mackinac, and there taken by the British,	5,781.91	
Amount Soldier's due-bills on hand, most of whom, it is believed were murdered by the Indians,	33.01	
Amount debts due from officers and soldiers of the Fort,	355.27	
Amount debts due from Indians,	134.31	
Amount household furniture left in the Factory,	119.94	
Amount Factory buildings, estimated,	500.00	$13,074.47½

D.

IMPORTANT REMINISCENSES OF AN OLD SETTLER.

SHEBOYGAN, WIS., May 24th, 1881.

HON. JOHN WENTWORTH,

Dear Sir: I have had the pleasure of reading your account, and also the remarks of others in regard to Chicago and Illinois history. I am acquainted with some facts, derived from conversations with one who was there and witnessed the fight and killing of many of those who lost their lives, on that memorable day. She was a daughter of one of the soldiers, and was one of the children who, with her mother and sister, occupied one of the wagons or conveyances that was to convey them from the Fort. She told me she saw her father when he fell, and also saw many others; she with her mother and sister were prisoners among the Indians for nearly two years, and were finally taken to Mackinac and sold to the traders and sent to Detroit. On our arrival in Detroit, in 1816, after the war, this girl was taken into our family, and was then about thirteen years old and had been scalped. She said a young Indian came to the wagon where she was, and grabbed her by the hair and pulled her out of the wagon, and she fought him the best she knew how, scratching and biting, until finally he threw her down and scalped her. She was so frightened she was not aware of it until the blood ran down her face. An old squaw interfered and prevented her from being tomahawked by the Indian, she going with the squaw to her wigwam and was taken care of and her head cured,—this squaw was the one that often came to their house—the bare spot on top of her head was about the size of a silver dollar. She saw Capt. Wells killed, and told the same story as related in your pamphlet.

My father was well acquainted with Capt. Wells; was stationed with him at Fort Wayne, Indiana, where I was born, in 1807; and he was surgeon of the post. My mother was a daughter of Col. Thomas Hunt, of the 5th Inf'y.

I think there must be a mistake as to the year the Kinzies returned to Chicago. My father and family arrived in Detroit, in June, 1816; the Kinzies were there then, and I was a schoolmate of John, Robert, Ellen, and Maria during that year, and I think they returned to Chicago in 1817. Old Mr. Kinzie went in fall of 1816, and family in spring of 1817.

Capt. Wells after being captured by the Indians, when a boy, remained with them until the treaty with the Miamis. Somewhere about the year 1795, he was a chief and an adopted brother of the celebrated chief Little Turtle. Capt. Wells signed the marriage certificate, as officiating magistrate, of my father and mother at Fort Wayne, June, 1805. The certificate is now in my possession.* I was in Chicago in 1832, in the Black-Hawk-war time, as 1st lieutenant of a company of cavalry from Michigan. The regiment was commanded by Gen. Hart L. Stewart, now living in Chicago.

During the Black-Hawk war, and when in Chicago, we heard of the killing of the Hall family and the carrying off of the two girls. Our company camped that night at the mouth of the Little Calumet, and next morning went into Chicago and the Fort, was occupied by women and children from the surrounding country. Then I saw for the last time my schoolmate, R. A. Kinzie. My brother, Col. T. A. H. Edwards, was in command of the Fort after we left, and had a Cass-County regiment of militia from Michigan. We met him on our return at Door Prairie. He remained there until the arrival of Maj. Whistler, in June, 1832; he retired from the Fort before the landing of any of the U.S. troops on account of the cholera being among them, and he wished to avoid any contact with them on that account. His command camped on the prairie, about a mile from the Fort, and remained only a day or two. Fearing that the cholera might get among his men, he left for home, as he saw they were not needed any longer, and was so informed by Major Whistler.

Capt. Anderson, Ensign Wallace, and myself camped under the hospitable roof of Gen. Beaubien, on the bank of the Lake not very far from the Fort, who had kept the only house there. Mark Beaubien, Jr., went into Chicago with us, he having joined us at Niles, on his way home from school. He was the son of the one called the fiddler.

Our family lived in Detroit, and were well acquainted with the Whistlers. My father, Major Edwards, was in Detroit at the surrender of Hull, as Surgeon-General of the Northwestern Army; he went from Ohio and arriving in Detroit received his appointment; our family then living at Dayton, Ohio; at the close of the war resigned, and in 1816 removed to Detroit, and was appointed sutler to all the northwestern posts:—Fort Gratiot, Mackinac, Green Bay, [Fort Howard], and Chicago, [Fort Dearborn]; his books, now in my possession, showing his dealings with each of these stores, and all the officers mentioned in your paper.

Capt. Wells urged Major Heald not to leave the Fort, as he did not like the way the Indians acted, and was well acquainted with all their movements as learned from his Indian allies, who deserted him the moment the firing commenced. Capt. N. Heald's story is as I heard it from the mouth of the one who saw it all, the girl and her mother, the one living in our family for many years, and the mother in Detroit. Their name was Cooper.

Capt. Wells, soon after leaving the Indians, was appointed, at the request of Gen. Wayne, and was with him in his campaign against the Indians, as captain of a company of spies, and many thrilling accounts were given me of his daring and remarkable adventures as such, related by one who received them from his own lips, and in confirmation of one of his adventures pointed at an Indian present, and said, "That Indian," says he, "belongs to me, and sticks to me like a brother," and then told how he captured him with his rifle on his shoulder. This Indian was the one who gave Mrs. Wells the first intimation of his death and then disappeared; supposed to have returned to his people.

A. H. EDWARDS.

FORT WAYNE, 4th June, 1805.
I do hereby certify that I joined Doctor Abraham Edwards and Ruthy Hunt in the Holy Bonds of Matrimony on the third instant, according to law.
Given under my Hand and Seal, the day and year above written.
WILLIAM WELLS, Esq.

Further Statement of Mr. Edwards.

SHEBOYGAN, WIS., June 10, 1881.

Your letter of the 5th came to hand to-day. The person I named as being present at the massacre was Isabella Cooper, daughter of ———— Cooper, one of the soldiers who was killed during the fight. Her account, as given to me, as also her mother's, was that, as soon as all the soldiers were disposed of, the Indians made a rush for the wagons, where the women and children were. Her mother and sister, younger than herself, were taken from the wagons and carried away. A young Indian boy, about fourteen or fifteen years old, dragged her by the hair out of the wagon; and she bit and scratched him so badly that he finally scalped her, and would have killed her if an old squaw had not prevented him. I think she married a man by the name of Farnum, and lived many years in Detroit. Her mother died there about the year 1823. The sisters were living in Detroit, in 1828. I have since heard they were living in Mackinaw. I do not know the first name of Cooper. He was killed, and the girl said she saw her father's scalp in the hands of one of the Indians afterward. He had sandy hair. I think she said they were Scotch. Isabella had children. The girl said she saw Wells when he fell from his horse, and that his face was painted. What became of her sister I do not know, as I left Detroit, in 1823, but my father and mother remained there until 1828. You will receive with this a statement written by my father, [see following "Reminiscences of Abraham Edwards"], regarding himself, a short time before his death, which occurred in October, 1860, at Kalamazoo, Mich., where he had resided for many years. The statement will give you all the information in regard to himself, as well as who my mother was. Her father [Thomas Hunt] was appointed a surgeon in the army directly after the battle of Bunker Hill, where he was brought into notice by an act of gallantry, then only a boy of fifteen. He remained in the army until his death, in 1808, in command of his regiment, at Bellefontaine, Missouri. His sons and grandsons have been his representatives in the army ever since. Capt. Thomas Hunt, named in your letter, was a son, and the present Gen. Henry J. Hunt, of the Artillery, and Gen. Lewis C. Hunt, commanding the 4th Infantry, grandsons; whose father (my mother's brother) was Capt. Samuel W. Hunt, of the army.

My grandfather, Thomas Hunt, was a captain under Lafayette, and was wounded at Yorktown in storming a redoubt of the British. Afterward he was with Gen. Anthony Wayne, in his campaign against the Indians, and was left in command of Fort Wayne as its first commander after the subjugation of the Indians.

Capt. Wm. Wells was acting Indian-agent and Justice-of-the-Peace at Fort Wayne at the time he married my father and mother, and was considered a remarkably brave and resolute man. I will give you a sketch of one of his feats, as told me by my mother who was present and witnessed it all. The Indians were collected at Fort Wayne on their way for the purpose of meeting the Miamis and other Indians in council. While camped there, they invited the officers of the Fort to come out to witness a grand dance and other performances, previous to their departure for the Indian conference. Wells advised the commander of the Fort not to go, as he did not like the actions of the Indians; but his advice was overruled, and all hands went out, including the officers' ladies. But the troops in the Fort were on the alert, their guns were loaded and the sentries were doubled, as it was in the evening. A very large tent was provided for the purpose of the grand dance. After many preliminary dances and talks, a large and powerful chief arose and commenced his dance around the ring, and made many flourishes of his tomahawk. Then he came up to Wells, who stood next to my mother, and spoke in Indian, and made demonstrations with his axe that looked dangerous, and then took his seat. But no sooner than he did so, Wells gave one of the most unearthly war-whoops she ever heard, and sprang up into the air as high as her head, and picked up the jaw-bone of a horse or ox that lay near by, and went around the ring in a more vigorous and artistic Indian style than had been seen that evening; and wound up by going up to the big Indian and flourished his jaw-bone, and told him that he had killed more Indians than he had white men, and had killed one that looked just like him, and he believed it was his brother, only a much better looking and better brave than he was. The Indians were perfectly taken by surprise. Wells turned to the officers and told them to be going. He hurried them off to the Fort, and had all hands on the alert during the night. When questioned as to his actions and what he said, he replied that he told the Indians what I have related. Then he enquired of those who were present if they did not see that the Indians standing on the opposite side of the tent had their rifles wrapped up in their blankets. If I had not done just as I did, and talked to that Indian as I did, we would all have been shot in five minutes; but my actions required a council as their plans were (as they supposed) frustrated, and that the troops would be down on them at the first hostile move they made. He saw the game when he first went in, as his Indian training taught him, and he waited just for the demonstration that was made as the signal for action. Wells saw no time was to be lost and made good his resolves, and the big Indian cowed under the demonstrations of Wells. My mother said he looked as if he expected Wells to make an end of him for what he had said to Wells in his dance. "I had to meet bravado with bravado, and I think I beat," said Wells. You could see it in the countenances of all the Indians. The same advice given to Heald, if listened to, would have saved the massacre of Fort Dearborn.

My brother's full name (who was at the Fort in Chicago, in 1832) was Thomas Aaron Hunt Edwards, named after both grandfathers. He was partially educated at West Point, and had the military experience of that institution. He died at Yankton, Dakota, about ten years since.

In Wayne's campaigns, he penetrated the Indian country as far as Fort Wayne, built the Fort, and left my grandfather, Thomas Hunt, in command, as I have before stated.

The Capt. Anderson I was with, at Chicago, lived and died in Monroe, Michigan, and was a brother-in-law of Mrs. Robert Clark, of Chicago, whose son was the Republican candidate for mayor of Chicago this spring.

The Capt. Thomas Hunt, who died in Detroit, February 16, 1838, had been in the army; and, on account of a wound received in the battle of Niagara, in the war of 1812, was assigned to duty in Washington until after 1830. He then resigned and was appointed Register of land-office, at Detroit.

You will see by my father's statement, that he was the Abraham Edwards that was appointed surgeon, in 1804, and resigned in June 1, 1810.

I send a commission issued to my father to be a Justice-of-the-Peace by William H. Harrison, while Governor of Indiana, in 1805. Endorsed on this is his authority for Capt. Wm. Wells to administer the necessary oath.

I could inform you as to all the circumstances attending the abandonment by Capt. Wells of his Indian life, as related to me by my father, and coming direct from Capt. Wells himself, being very interesting to me. I have laid it up in my memory's store-house as something to tell some day to those who might wish to hear it. [See *Knapp's History of Maumee Valley.*]

I notice in No. 7 of Fergus' Historical Series something said about the first steamboat arriving at Chicago. The first boat built and run on the lakes was the *Walk-in-the-Water*, in 1818, and wrecked in the fall of the same year. The *Superior* came out next spring, and had a delegation of Oneida Indians for Green Bay on board. I think she landed them there; but am not certain if she went to Chicago. We lived in Detroit then.

You say *Walk-in-the-Water* came up to Green Bay, in 1821. Was it not the *Superior?* My impression is that the former boat was wrecked the same season or the next after her coming out, and that she did not come into the upper lakes any further than Mackinaw. But I may be mistaken.

The description you give in your reminiscences of *Early Chicago*, No. 8 Fergus' Historical Series, pp. 22 and 23, relative to the death of Tecumseh, at the battle of the Thames, as related by Shabonee, is a very correct one. I have heard my father and Gen. Lewis Cass talk over all the circumstances attending Tecumseh's death. My father arrived in Detroit soon after the battle, and had charge of some of the captured British officers, and also became acquainted with some of the Kentucky soldiers of Johnson's Regiment, who gave him a full account of the fight, and the wounding of their colonel, and the death of Tecumseh. It was Tecumseh that wounded Johnson. His ball first passed through the neck of Johnson's horse and into Col. Johnson's arm; and, as the horse plunged forward, Col. Johnson fell. Tecumseh sprang out with his tomahawk and knife. At the same moment Johnson fired and the chief fell, pierced in the breast, the ball passing downward, as was afterward ascertained by those sent from Detroit the next day after the battle, to examine the body of the chief and to identify it. As the Indians denied that Tecumseh was killed, Gen. Cass sent an old Frenchman, by the name of Schien, who was well acquainted with Tecumseh; and, upon looking on the face, he pronounced it Tecumseh, and said he has a scar on his back plainly to be seen, and turned the body over, and (sure enough) there it was. Then the question arose; did Col. Johnson kill him? Which was answered affirmatively by the Kentuckians present, who were in the fight, and who rushed forward when their colonel fell, as did also the Indians to protect their chief. The Kentuckians clubbed their rifles and brained many of the Indians who laid around their chief as well as some of the whites, who fell defending their colonel. Gen. Cass said he had not the least doubt but that Col. Johnson was the one who killed Tecumseh. The Prophet, Tecumseh's brother, was in a canoe with Gen. Cass, Col. Geo. Croghan, Col. Johnson, and my father, going to Mackinaw to attend a conference with the Indians. The colonel was pointed out to the Prophet as the man who killed Tecumseh; but the Prophet replied that the man was not living who killed his brother, for Tecumseh had killed the man who shot him at the same time. Col. J. told my father about the time, or soon after, that he did not know whether he had killed Tecumseh or not; but he was sure he had killed a big chief from his dress. The fact of the ball entering Tecumseh's breast and ranging downward, showed that he was hit from some place above him. The battle-cry of the Kentuckians was "Remember the Massacre at River Raisin." [Gen. James Winchester was defeated, January 22, 1813, at Frenchtown on the River Raisin, and his troops massacred by the Indians.] The great chief killed by their colonel lost some of his skin to sharpen the razors of his enemies, as some of them had razor-straps taken from his legs. Had they known at the time that it was Tecumseh they said they would not have done it. They considered him a better man than Gen. Henry A. Proctor, who commanded at the River Raisin. They would have skinned him alive if they had caught him.

Indeed it was not entirely safe for an Indian to visit Detroit as late as 1816, on account of the massacre at the River Raisin, if a Kentuckian was about. The celebrated chief Red Jacket came very near being a victim to this rage.

APPENDIX—SKETCH OF ABRAHAM EDWARDS. 59

A young man, brought to Detroit by my father to act as clerk in the store, whose father was one of the victims of Winchester's defeat at River Raisin, happened to get sight of Red Jacket while in Detroit. He loaded a gun and laid in wait to shoot him as he went out of town. My father, missing the young man, went in pursuit of him, as he was told by some one that had seen him going out of town with a gun. He was found secreted in a barn very near to the road, where the chief would have to travel. On being asked what he was going to do, he replied that he had seen an Indian chief in town with his father's vest on, and he was going to kill him and take it off from him. It took a good deal of persuasion to induce him to give up his gun and return to the store, and by the first opportunity he was sent home.

I saw a Kentuckian knock an Indian down with his fist and stamp him, and he would have killed him had he not been stopped. This happened in the street of Detroit some years after. A. H. EDWARDS.

[Mr. Edwards sends with this a Book which was the Ledger of his father, kept at Detroit, from 1817 to 1824. In it there is an account against "The Chicago Trading House," commencing August 12, 1817, and ending June 6, 1821.]

REMINISCENCES OF THE LIFE OF ABRAHAM EDWARDS.

"Abraham Edwards (eldest son of the late Capt. Aaron Edwards) was born at Springfield, New Jersey, November 17th, 1781; and was licensed to practise medicine in the autumn of 1803. In June, 1804, he was appointed, by President Jefferson, garrison-surgeon, and by the Secretary of War, Gen. Dearborn, he was ordered to Fort Wayne, (Indiana), where, in the month of June, 1805, he was married to Ruthy Hunt, eldest daughter of the late Col. Thomas Hunt, then commanding the 1st regiment of United States Infantry at Fort Wayne. Their three eldest children were born there—Thomas, Alexander, and Henry. In 1810, on account of the sickness of Mrs. Edwards, the doctor resigned his commission in the army, in the spring of 1810, and removed to Dayton, Ohio, and engaged in the practice of his profession. In the autumn of 1811, he was elected a member of the Ohio Legislature from the County of Montgomery, of which Dayton was the county-seat; and in March, 1812, he was appointed captain, by President Madison, in the 19th Regiment U.S. Infantry. As the prospects of a war with Great Britain were apparent, Gen. Hull was ordered to Dayton, Ohio, to organize an army, with which he was to proceed to Detroit to protect that frontier. Three regiments of Ohio volunteers were at Dayton when the General arrived. The regiments were commanded by Cols. Duncan McArthur, Lewis Cass, and James Findlay. The 4th Regiment U.S. Infantry, commanded by Col. James Miller, joined the volunteer regiments at Urbana, to which place they had marched a few days previously. Gen. Wm. Hull had been authorized by the President (Mr. Madison) to organize his army staff, and, as a vacancy in the office of surgeon existed in the 4th Regiment U.S. Infantry, Dr. Edwards was appointed to fill the vacancy during the campaign, and was also ordered to take charge of the medical department of the army as hospital-surgeon, in which capacity he served until the inglorious surrender of the army at Detroit, August 16th, 1812. Here he was paroled by Gen. Isaac Brock, and permitted to return to his residence in Ohio. After being exchanged, he was ordered to Chillicothe, as a captain in the line of the army, to superintend the recruiting service of that State. In November, 1813, he received an order from Gen. Lewis Cass, who was then in command of Detroit, to proceed to that place to take command of about 200 men belonging to the 19th Regiment. During the same month he arrived at Detroit, and assumed the command as before mentioned. In December, of the same year, he received an order from the War Department to accompany Gen. Cass, and other officers, to Albany, as witnesses in the court-martial about to assemble for the trial of Gen. Hull. During the winter of 1814 and '15, he visited Washington, and was appointed, by the President, department quartermaster-deputy, with the rank of major, and ordered to Pittsburg to take charge of the U.S. stores at that place, where he remained until the close of the war, in 1815. It was then left at his option to be retained in the army, on the peace establishment, as a captain in the line; but he chose the walks of private life. He retired from the army in October, 1815, and removed to Detroit. When President Monroe made his tour of the United States, in 1816 and 1817, and visited Detroit, Major Edwards was President of the Board of Trustees, and with the corporate authorities of Detroit, visited the President at Gov. Cass' residence, and tendered him the hospitalities of the town. A few days after, when he was about to leave for Ohio, he made him another visit, and in the name of the corporation presented him with a pair of horses and wagon to convey his baggage to Ohio.

In 1818, Gov. Cass organized the militia, and made appointments in the same. Major Edwards was appointed first Aid to the Commander-in-Chief with the rank of colonel.

In 1823, the first Legislative Council for Michigan Territory was elected, and in 1824, the first Legislative Session was held at Detroit, and Major Edwards was unanimously elected President of the Council, which place he filled for eight years.

In the month of March, 1831, he was appointed Register of the U.S. land-office for the Western District of Michigan, by President Jackson. Previous to this appointment he had held the office of sub-Indian agent for the Indians residing in the St. Joseph Country of Michigan and Northern Indiana. The office of Register of U.S. lands was held by him until after the election of Gen. Taylor, when he was removed from office for being a Democrat.

Major Edwards was one of the Presidential electors for the State of Michigan, and cast his vote for Franklin Pierce, for President, and W. R. King, for Vice-President."

My father was nearly eighty years old when he wrote the foregoing. A. H. E.

E.

CULTIVATION OF LAND BY THE SOLDIERS.

Under the head of General Regulations of the Army, September 11, 1818, is the following:

"A more extensive cultivation will be commenced at Chicago and other posts. * * * This cultivation of any public land, not otherwise appropriated, in the vicinity of the garrisons and posts, shall be carried on by the troops, under the direction of the several commanding officers of the posts, and will embrace the bread and other substantial vegetable parts of the ration."—*American State Papers*, Military Aff's, Vol. ii., p. 265.

F.

LETTER FROM SHABONEE AND SAUGANASH.

[The following letter, written in the midst of an excited political contest, by some friend, for the chiefs to sign, is inserted to show their personal history and experience. Caldwell could read and write English. Shabonee could not.] From the *Chicago Daily American*, 9th June, 1840.

COUNCIL BLUFFS, March 23d, 1840.

TO GEN. HARRISON'S FRIENDS:

The other day, several newspapers were brought to us; and, peeping over them, to our astonishment, we found that the hero of the late war was called a coward. This would have surprised the tall braves, Tecumseh of the Shawnees, and Round Head and Walk-in-the-Water of the Wyandotts. If the departed could rise again, they would say to the white man that Gen. Harrison was the terror of the late tomahawkers. The first time we got acquainted with General Harrison, it was at the council-fire of the late Old Tempest, Gen. Wayne, on the headquarters of the Wabash, at Greenville, 1796. From that time until 1811, we had many friendly smokes with him; but from 1812 we changed our tobacco smoke into powder smoke. Then we found Gen. Harrison was a brave warrior and humane to his prisoners, as reported to us by two of Tecumseh's young men, who were taken in the fleet with Capt. Barclay on the 10th of September, 1813, and on the Thames where he routed both the red men and the British, and where he showed his courage and his humanity to his prisoners, both white and red. See report of Adam Brown and family, taken on the morning of the battle October 5th, 1813. We are the only two surviving of that day in this country. We hope the good white men will protect the name of Gen. Harrison. We remain your friends forever.

CHAMBLEE, [SHABONEE], Aid to Tecumseh.
B. CALDWELL, [SAUGANASH], Captain.

G.

REPLY OF HON. JOHN WENTWORTH TO HON. CLEMENT L. VALLANDIGHAM.

From the *Chicago Tribune*, August 28th, 1864.

The following report of the reply of the Hon. John Wentworth, to Vallandigham, made at the gathering in the Court-House Square, on Friday evening, was inadvertently omitted from our report in Saturday's issue:

On the retirement of Vallandigham from the steps, the crowd called for "Long John," "Wentworth," the two names being synonymous in Chicago for our last appointed Police Commissioner. Mr. Wentworth appeared upon the stand, and said:

I am pleased with the opportunity, which your call affords me, to lay my own views of public policy and public affairs before you, and in so doing, I trust I shall not be deemed an intruder, for I would not thrust myself before you, nor press my views upon unwilling ears.

It has long been a part of my political ethics, that the true method of discussing public affairs was, for the *pros* and *cons* to go together before the people. In every public address for the past years of my life, I have enforced the correctness of this understanding. I, therefore, request the attention of all, for I am no party man. I am chained to the partizan car of no class, no interest, no organization. To my country, and my country alone, do I owe fealty and render homage. I love my country. It nurtured me in my youth, it honored me in my manhood, and now, when I have passed the meridian of life, I love to respond to any call to plead in her behalf. As we cast our eyes over the land, and witness the tears that everywhere prevail, and the dangers that now environ the republic, the heart of the patriot sinks with doubt and dread. War, with all its dread calamities following in its train, is convulsing the nation. The art of arms has succeeded the pursuits of peace, and nearly a million of men confront each other in battle array. Amid the horrors of war, we naturally look and long for peace. The fathers and mothers of Chicago, whose sons are braving the hazards of battle and the perils of disease, long for peace. The wives of Illinois, whose husbands have perished, or are perishing, in the terrible struggle, send up their daily prayers for the cessation of the strife. My own wish and hope is for peace. My regret, when the maddened traitors of South Carolina fired upon the national ensign, and forced the Federal authority into a conflict, was not more keen and poignant than my joy will be deep and sweet when they lay down their arms and cease the warfare they then so wickedly, foolishly, and devilishly inaugurated. This is the peace for which we hope, for which we pray, for which we fight.

The struggle is like every conflict that has ever existed since Time began, and if we would have a termination of the struggle we must conquer. The road to victory is the road to peace. It is to this alternative that we are driven—a shameful surrender or a certain triumphant lasting victory, and consequently peace.

I have listened, with great interest, to the eloquent and well-considered remarks of that peculiar Democratic champion who has just addressed you from the stand. I have heard him bewail in feeling, touching terms the existence and continuance of this accursed war. In terms of indignation he has inveighed against the Federal administration for the part it has had to act in the bloody drama. But, while he was thus depricating war and violence, I listened, in vain, for one single breath of censure, for one word of reproof from his lips of those who first madly unchained the ugly demon, and let loose the storm of deadly hate. Why were not the vials of his wrath poured upon the head of the infamous Beauregard, and the insurgent government of Montgomery, who basely trained their cannon upon a citidel floating the national flag, and shed the first blood in this fraternal fight? Not a Federal gun had been fired, not an act of hostility committed, when the rebellious chief, acting as Secretary of War for a rebel government, telegraphed the fatal order—"Open fire upon Fort Sumpter." Then the strife began. But this denunciator of war, this deprecator of strife, this messenger of peace, in his speech to-night, running through nearly an hour and a-half, had not a word of denunciation and reproof for those who, before God and man, are guilty of its commencement. Why this omission? Why this studied silence on the part of Mr. Vallandigham? Why are his invectives directed solely to the general government which, when assailed, only then attacked? Does Mr. Vallandigham wish to be understood that the acts of the traitors, in opening the strife, is not worthy of censure, while the act of the government in opposing force to force, is entitled to an hour's temperate denunciations? I draw no uncharitable inferences. I arraign not the purity or honesty of his motives, but I submit that these things are worthy of remembrance. If you, my friends, are quietly marching along the street and are brutally assaulted, and fight back, as becomes a man, would you not say to the man who denounced you for striking back, but had no word of censure for your assailant, would you not say to him, I ask, that he was your enemy, and would have tossed up his hat at your defeat? Nor would the inference be unjust. My Peace Friends, if the Republicans should assail your gathering here to-night and fire on your assembly, would you be responsible for the fight which might ensue? And how would you obtain peace? By vacating the square, or by enforcing respect for the laws?

But Mr. Vallandigham tells us to accept peace, to stop fighting and negotiate for a reconstruction. Sir, we want no "reconstruction." The old Constitution, the Union as it was, and the Constitution as it is, the Constitution of Washington, Jefferson, and Madison is all we desire. Under that Government we lived and prospered, and were happy. Under it the West grew up, expanded, peopled with millions of men, and under it Chicago rose to be the pride of the North-West and glory of the continent; and when a man talks to me about reconstruction, or prates of a new Union, I mark him as an enemy of my country and the robber of my children. The old Union with its glorious memories, its unfulfilled hopes, its history blazing upon every page with words and deeds of deathless glory, all bind me to the old Union, and cause me to abhor the name of reconstruction. I would say to the gentleman from Ohio, and those who think with him: "In God's name say no more of reconstruction." But, sinking every other consideration, forgetting all other motives, moved by no other impulse, let your zeal, your efforts, and your energies, all be directed to the maintenance of the old Constitution. That is hallowed by the memory of Washington, the glorious history of our revolutionary struggle, and dearer, by far, is it to us and our children, than any newfangled combination that can be hatched by any convention.

It is rarely that any good comes out of a convention, and the proposed convention of the States, both rebel and loyal, is the most unpromising of the entire brood. If we want peace then, let us conquer. If the South want peace, let them lay down their arms and cease war. Then will I be willing to deal with them justly and generously. Then will I try to forget the rivers of Northern blood they have shed in their unholy struggle for slavery. Then will I try to forget the thousands they have slain, the homes they have bereaved, the hopes they have crushed, and the hearts they have broken. But while an arm wields a sabre, while the Constitution is defied and the laws laughed to scorn, I will uphold the authority whose solemn oath was, that the Constitution should be preserved and the laws maintained.

But Mr. Vallandigham told you that the government could never be held together by coercive force, that power, brought to apply upon the unruly, could never reduce them to obedience. Was there ever a greater heresy uttered by the mouth of man? No coercion! Why, gentlemen, the coercive power of government is the only safety and salvation of society. No government, no community can exist an hour without it. It was the weakness of the articles of the old Confederation that they conferred no coercive power, and the statesman of that day saw the pressing necessity of the new Constitution. Take to-day, from municipal and governmental organization, the power of coercion, and society goes at once into anarchy and chaos. The weak would become the modern prey of the strong, and might would, indeed, become right. I have been told that there are those who would disturb the quiet of gathering in this City. We, the authorities of the City, coerce them into respect of law. Surely you should not denounce coercion. That glorious old war-horse of Democracy, Gen. Jackson, from whose lips I inhaled the pure inspiration of Democracy, and at whose feet I received the first lessons of political and governmental duty, was gloriously free from this modern heresy. His celebrated proclamation against the nullifiers, in which coercion gleamed and glistened in every line, will give him a name and an immortality in history when the maligners and denunciators of this policy shall have been forgotten. I, therefore, stand for Gen. Jackson, and against Mr. Vallandigham. Will you stand for Mr. Vallandigham, and against Gen. Jackson?

But I will not press the matter further. The attention you have given me fills me with gratitude, and leads me to hope that the canvass will not be marked by such bigotry and intolerance as usually attend political campaigns. Our interests are one, our hopes are identical. Let us, therefore, meet and discuss this matter in a spirit of fraternal love, and good will flow from the interchange of opinions, and, together, we will reap the rich harvest of wealth and glory that awaits our country. As the children of a common destiny, the pathway of our progress should be marked by no shameful bickerings, no jadings, no discord. Differ we may, differ we must. But the difference may be honest and the association not unfriendly, but arm in arm, two by two, let us push on in the race of civilization and progress, and reach the summit of greatness and glory, a proud example of a free, enlightened, and tolerant people who love Union, Liberty, and Law; who, when their country was assailed, defended it, and when treason reared its bloody banner, beat it back, and handed down to posterity the rich legacy of their fathers.

H.
CHICAGO'S EARLY DEFENDERS.

In my pursuit of the names of the early settlers of Chicago, a friend has presented me with the following, which he assures me was copied, some years ago, from the original. The officers are all dead. Captain Kerchival, once a prominent man in this city, and who represented it in the Legislature in 1838, died within a year or two in California, leaving a son who is a printer in this city. His widow resides at East St. Louis, Ill., with her sister, the widow of Colonel Thomas J. V. Owen, once Indian Agent here. The two Lieutenants, having been Postmasters in this city, are well remembered. Of the soldiers, I know of but one living, David McKee, of Aurora, Ill. If there is another living, he is wanted at the Chicago Historical Society's rooms, corner of Dearborn Avenue and Ontario Street.

After this organization, Governor John Reynolds sent Major Daniel Bailey to Chicago, and he raised a battalion of four companies from the citizens of Northern Illinois. The pay-roll of these four companies of volunteers, I am told, is still preserved at Washington, D. C., where it was sent for the purpose of procuring land-warrants. It is hoped that a copy of it will soon be in the Chicago Historical Society's library. I doubt not but the names of many persons now living are upon it.

I am inclined to think the paper was drawn up by Colonel Richard J. Hamilton, the stepfather of our present Judge Murry F. Tuley. Thirty-seven is the number capable and willing to bear arms at that date. There was no clergymen here to be their chaplain, if they had wanted one.

Chicago, Oct. 17, 1879.   JOHN WENTWORTH.

MUSTER-ROLL.

MAY 2, 1832.—We, the undersigned, agree to submit ourselves, for the time being, to Gholson Kerchival, Captain, and George W. Dole and John S. C. Hogan, First and Second Lieutenants, as commanders of the militia of the town of Chicago, until all apprehension of danger from the Indians may have subsided:

APPENDIX—SOLDIERS OF THE BLACK-HAWK WAR. 65

Richard J. Hamilton,
Jesse B. Brown,
Isaac Harmon,
Samuel Miller,
John F. Herndon,
Benjamin Harris,
S. T. Gage,
Rufus Brown,
Jeremiah Smith,
Heman S. Bond,
William Smith,
Isaac D. Harmon,
Joseph Lafromboise,
Henry Boucha,
Claude Lafromboise,
J. W. Zarley,
David Wade,
William Bond,
Samuel Ellis,
Jeddiah Woolley,
George H. Walker,
A. W. Taylor,
James Kinzie,
David Pemeton,
James Ginsday,
Samuel Debaif,
John Wellmaker,
Wm. H. Adams,
James T. Osborne,
E. D. Harmon,
Charles Moselle,
Francis Labaque,
Michael Ouilmette,
Christopher Shedaker,
David McKee,
Ezra Bond,
Robert Thompson.

COOK COUNTY'S SOLDIERS IN THE BLACKHAWK WAR.

To the Editor of the Chicago Evening Journal:

I send you a list of the soldiers who volunteered from this County to go with General Scott in pursuit of Blackhawk. The most of these gentlemen are dead, but they have left descendants who constitute some of our most valuable citizens. There are many citizens of Chicago now living who had a personal acquaintance with nearly all of them. I have given the residence of those whom I know are now living. Probably others are living whose residence I do not know. This list has been sent to Washington and compared with the original. Many of them resided in that part of Cook County which is now DuPage Co.

The Fourth Corporal is now the County Judge of Dupage County, and would be a good man for gentlemen of historical tastes to interview. JOHN WENTWORTH.

Chicago, March 2, 1880.

Muster-Roll of a Company of Mounted Volunteers, in the Service of the United States, in defence of the Northern frontier of the State of Illinois, against the Sac and Fox Indians, from the County of Cook, in said State, in the year 1832, under the command of Captain Joseph Naper:

JOSEPH NAPER, Captain, afterward member of legislature.
ALANSON SWEET, First-Lieutenant, now living at Evanston, Ill.
SHERMAN KING, Second-Lieutenant, lived at Brush Hill, Ill.
S. M. SALISBURY, First-Sergeant, afterward Cook Co. Commissioner, at Wheeling, Ill.
JOHN MANNING, Second-Sergeant.
WALTER STOWELL, Third-Sergeant, afterward Post-Master, at Newark, Ill.
JOHN NAPER, Fourth-Sergeant, lived at Naperville, brother to Joseph.
T. E. PARSONS, First-Corporal.
LYMAN BUTTERFIELD, Second-Corporal.
I. P. BLODGETT, Third-Corporal, father of Judge H. W. Blodgett.
ROBERT NELSON MURRAY (Naperville), Fourth-Corporal, now County judge.

Privates:

P. F. W. PECK, died at Chicago,
WILLIAM BARBER,
RICHARD M. SWEET,
JOHN STEVENS, Jr.,
CALVIN M. STOWELL,
JOHN FOX,
DENIS CLARK,
CALEB FOSTER,
AUGUSTINE STOWELL,
GEORGE FOX,
T. PARSONS,
DANIEL LANGDON,
WILLIAM GAULT,
URIAH PAINE,
JOHN STEVENS,
SETH WESTCOTT,
HENRY T. WILSON (Wheaton),
CHRISTOPHER PAINE,
BASLEY HOBSON,
JOSIAH H. GIDDINGS,
ANSON AMENT,
CALVIN AMENT,
EDMUND HARRISON,
WILLIARD SCOTT (Naperville),
PEREZ HAWLEY,
PETER WICOFFE.

1.

MARK BEAUBIEN.

Private telegrams received here yesterday, from Kankakee, announced that Mark Beaubien was in a dying condition, the result of enlargement of the liver. Mr. Beaubien was one of the most interesting of the "old settlers" of Chicago. He was first brought into recent prominent notice in the newspaper reports of the first of the old settlers' receptions, which are now an annual institution of the Calumet Club. At that reception, he was present, with the identical fiddle with which he was wont, nearly fifty years before, to supply the essential harmony for the social events of the Chicago of that day. He was the lion of the evening, and before the reception closed, his old associates of half a century previous, danced the same old dances to the same old tunes which had enlivened the evenings of their youth.

Nearly every speech that evening contained an allusion to the old gentleman. Gen. Henry Strong characterized him as "the Apollo of the early settlers"; ex-Chief-Justice John Dean Caton told facetiously the story of how old Mark won a horse-race from Robert A. Kinzie, and of how, to use his (Mark's) own expression, he kept tavern "like hell"; the Hon. John Wentworth called to memory several of the festive occasions upon which the veteran settler had employed his musical power to good effect; and ex-Lieut.-Gov. Bross reminded his hearers of the way in which the ancient tavern-keeper divided his time between "keeping tavern vigorously," working the ferry at Wolf Point, and running pony-races with his Indian neighbors.

Mr. Beaubien was also present at the second reception given by the Calumet Club last year, at which he received hardly less attention than on the previous occasion. The Hon. John Wentworth, telling a *Tribune* reporter yesterday his recollections of the deceased, said:

"When I came to Chicago, in 1836, Mr. Beaubien was a prominent citizen here, as well known among all classes as probably any man in the City. He was considered an indispensable requisite upon all social occasions, on account of his ability as a fiddler. In case of a party, if for any reasons the regular musicians were absent, we could always send for "old Mark," who was always ready with his fiddle. If, where he was playing, one of his strings broke, he could play on the remaining three; if two broke, the other two would do, and if they all gave way, he could hum any dancing tune that we needed in those days. He was celebrated for his good nature. I never knew him to speak unkindly of anyone, or anyone to speak unkindly of him.

"I have been more or less intimate with him from the time of my arrival in Chicago to the present, and he seldom visited the City without calling upon me. His last prominent appearances were at the receptions given by the Calumet Club to old settlers, in 1879 and 1880, where it was observed by all present that he had, mentally, all the vivacity of youth, and played the fiddle as well as ever. Another time that he distinguished himself was when, in 1876, he introduced me to an audience and created a great deal of amusement by his broken French and English.

"He claimed to have been born in 1800, but many persons thought that he was much older. He was present, in 1812, when Detroit was surrendered by Gen. Hull, and was very fond of singing songs in derision of Hull, which were sung in those days.

He and his father before him were born in Detroit, but his grandfather was an emigrant from France. He came here in 1826, and voted in the Chicago precinct, in the County of Peoria, in 1830.* The last time I looked over the poll-list of 1830, there were but two voters of that year besides himself living. These were David McKee, of Aurora, and Medore B. Beaubien, of Silver Lake, Kas., a nephew of the deceased.

"When he came to Chicago, he built a log-house at the forking of the river, on what is known as the old wigwam lot, on the corner of Lake and Market Streets. It was, at the time, the only dwelling-house on the South Side, except that of his brother, Col. John B. Beaubien. When he was building the house the Indian Chief Sauganash told him he supposed he would name his hotel after some big man, as that was the way the Americans did. 'Yes,' said Beaubien, 'I will name it after a big man. It shall be the Sauganash Hotel,'" and so it was. A few years afterward he built a frame addition to it, and in it I took, in 1836, my first meal in Chicago. He established the first ferry at the forks of the river, not far from the present Lake-Street bridge, at which time there were no bridges across the river.

"Mark had twenty-three children; he counted them over to me as I took down their names. He had fifty-three living grandchildren at the time, but he said that a great many of them had died; and a large number of great-grandchildren, whom he said he could not count over, as they came on so fast. Of late years he has lived around among his relatives in the country, occasionally visiting Chicago.

"He never held any office, and never was a candidate for one. When Chicago was incorporated as a town, August 10, 1833, the first election of Trustees was held at his house. His memory was very good until within about ten years, and his forgetfulness of late has been a great source of mortification to him, as he took great delight in telling stories of olden times.

"He never had but one fiddle that I know of, and he promised, when he died, to bequeath it to the Calumet Club, or to some of the other public institutions of this City. I think the Calumet Club will get it, as he was ever welcome there."

"Mark Beaubien died on the 11th of April, 1881, at the house of Geo. Matthews, Kankakee, Ill., who married his daughter, Mary. He married for second and last wife, Elizabeth Matthews, of Aurora, and had seven children by her; his first wife had sixteen children.—See *Tribune*, Mar. 25, 1881.

* See No. 7, Fergus' Historical Series, *Early Chicago*, by Hon. John Wentworth, p. 54.

J.

GRADUATES OF THE MILITARY ACADEMY, CLASS OF 1832, WITH REGIMENT TO WHICH ASSIGNED, FROM JULY 1, 1832.

NO.	NAME.	REGIMENT.	REMARKS.
1	*George W. Ward,	2d Artillery,	Died, October 13, 1851, at Centreville, Cal.
2	Robert P. Smith,	2d Artillery,	Resigned, December 31, 1836.
3	Benjamin S. Ewell,	4th Artillery,	Resigned, September 30, 1836.
4	George W. Cass,	7th Infantry,	Resigned, October 26, 1836.
5	Jacob W. Bailey,	1st Artillery,	Died, February 26, 1857, at West Point, N.Y.
6	Philip St. George Cocke,	2d Artillery,	Resigned, April 1, 1834.
7	*Henry G Sill,	1st Artillery,	Died, December 1, 1835, at Washington, D.C.
8	*Joseph C. Vance,	2d Artillery,	Resigned, October 31, 1835.
9	*George Watson,	1st Artillery,	Resigned, October 31, 1838.
10	Erasmus D. Keyes,	3d Artillery,	Resigned, May 6, 1864.
11	*Franklin McDuffee,	4th Artillery,	Died, July 15, 1832, at Fort Dearborn, Ill.
12	*Lewis Howell,	7th Infantry,	Resigned October 31, 1833.
13	*William Wall,	3d Artillery,	Died, August 13, 1847, at Puebla, Mexico.
14	*John M. Macomb,	4th Artillery,	Still in service as Col. Corps of Engin'rs, stationed at No. 1125 Girard St., Phila, Pa.
15	*Edward Deas,	4th Artillery,	Drowned, May 16, 1849, in Rio Grande River.
16	John E. Brackett,	2d Artillery,	Resigned, August 31, 1833.
17	*Ward B. Burnett,	2d Artillery,	Resigned, July 31, 1836.
18	James H. Simpson,	3d Artillery,	Now Col. U.S.A., retired, residing at No. 2 Monroe Place, St. Paul, Minn.
19	Alfred Brush,	4th Artillery,	Resigned, July 28, 1836.
20	*Richard G. Fain,	1st Artillery,	Resigned, December 31, 1832.
21	*Henderson K. Yoakum,	3d Artillery,	Resigned, March 31, 1833.
22	*Tench Tilghman,	4th Artillery,	Resigned, November 30, 1833.
23	William H. Pettes,	1st Artillery,	Resigned, September 11, 1836.
24	Theophilus F. J. Wilkinson,	2d Artillery,	Resigned, February 28, 1835.
25	*Lorenzo Sitgreaves,	1st Artillery,	Now Lieut.-Col. U.S.A., retired, residing at No. 1226 F Street, N.-W., Washington, D.C.
26	*George B. Crittenden,	4th Infantry,	Resigned, April 30, 1833.
27	*Jacob Brown,	2d Infantry,	Resigned, July 31, 1836.
28	Daniel P. Whiting,	7th Infantry,	Now Lieut.-Col. U.S.A., retired, residing at No. 1311 Riggs St., N.-W., Washington, D.C.
29	*Randolph B. Marcy,	5th Infantry,	Now Brig.-Gen. U.S.A., retired, residing at Orange, New Jersey.
30	*James P. Hardin,	4th Infantry,	Resigned, December 15, 1832.
31	Thomas M. Hill,	1st Infantry,	Died, July 10, 1838, at Bath, Maine.
32	*Roger S. Dix,	7th Infantry,	Died, January 7, 1849, at Hillsborough, Pa.
33	Robert H. Archer,	3d Infantry,	Resigned, December 31, 1837.
34	*James V. Bomford,	2d Infantry,	Now Col. U.S.A., retired, residing at No. 116 West Jersey Street, Elizabeth, N.J.
35	*Richard C. Gatlin,	7th Infantry,	Resigned, May 20, 1861.
36	William H. Storer,	1st Infantry,	Resigned, November 15, 1833.
37	*George H. Griffin,	6th Infantry,	Died, October 8, 1839, at Tampa, Florida.
38	John Beach,	1st Infantry,	Resigned, June 30, 1838.
39	*William O. Kello,	3d Infantry,	Died, Jan. 27, 1848, in Southampton Co., Va.
40	*Henry Swartwout,	3d Infantry,	Died, July 1, 1851, at Fort Meade, Florida.
41	*Gaines P. Kingsbury,	Mt'd Rang's,	Resigned, October 15, 1836.
42	*Humphrey Marshall,	Mt'd Rang's,	Resigned, April 30, 1833.
43	*James M. Bowman,	Mt'd Rang's,	Died, July 21, 1839, at Ft. Wayne, Indian Ter.
44	*Ashburn Ury,	Mt'd Rang's,	Died, April 14, 1838, at Matanzas, Cuba.
45	*Albert G. Edwards,	Mt'd Rang's,	Resigned, May 2, 1835.

Those to whose name this mark * is prefixed, participated in some manner in the Black-Hawk expedition of 1832. (Signed) RICHARD C. DRUM,

Adjutant-General's Office, Washington, May 6, 1881. *Adjutant-General.*

K.

LETTERS FROM THE LAST SOLDIER IN FORT DEARBORN.

SOUTH EVANSTON, COOK CO., ILL., June 17, 1881.

HON. JOHN WENTWORTH.—*Dear Sir:* I enlisted October, 1819, at Philadelphia, Pa., in the 5th Regt. U.S. Infantry, being then 23 years of age. I started with a detachment of recruits May, 1820, to join the regiment, then stationed about seven miles below the Falls of St. Anthony, near where Fort Snelling now stands. The regiment was then commanded by Lieut.-Col. Henry Leavenworth, father of Lieut. Jesse H. Leavenworth. We joined the regiment about the last of July, and work was begun on the Fort the same fall. We remained at Fort Snelling till May, 1828, when we were ordered to Jefferson Barracks, St. Louis. I remained there till September of the same year, when we were ordered to Fort Brady, near the outlet of Lake Superior. Here we remained till May, 1833, when we were ordered to Fort Dearborn, Chicago. Soon after our arrival at the Fort, I received from Washington my appointment as ordnance-sergeant of the post, and thenceforward I had nothing more to do with garrison duty. Previous to my appointment as ordnance-sergeant, I was orderly-sergeant of B company. Capt. (Brevet-Major) DeLafayette Wilcox, was captain of B company from the time we left Jefferson Barracks till he left Chicago; but, being away on a leave of absence, when A and B companies were ordered to Fort Dearborn, Lieut. Louis T. Jamison had temporary command of the company B to which I belonged. When the two companies left Fort Dearborn for Fort Howard, Major Joseph Plympton and myself were left behind. He was in charge of the Government property, and I as ordnance-sergeant of the post, to await a vacancy at some other post. I remained at Fort Dearborn till the latter end of May when, my term of enlistment having expired, I quit the army and went to farming in the town of Northfield, in Cook County. The late Edward H. Hadduck, who died 30 May, 1881, with his team, hauled my traps from the City to my claim.

Capt. John B. F. Russell did *not* come to Chicago with the company, nor did he *ever* do garrison duty in Fort Dearborn. When he came to Chicago he was on detached service in the Indian Department, and superintended the removal of the Indians to their reservation out West. The first I knew of Bernard Ward* was, I think, in 1823, when he joined the regiment at Fort Snelling with a detachment of recruits, I think, from Boston. There he was discharged from the army by reason of his term of enlistment having expired. Whereupon he went East and enlisted in the 4th Artillery; but not liking that arm of the service he got transferred to his old regiment, and rejoined us at Fort Brady, I think, in 1830. He accompanied the troops to Fort Dearborn, and was honorably discharged at the expiration of his term of enlistment. None of *my* children† were born *in* Fort Dearborn, although two

---

* Bernard or "Barney" Ward will be remembered as the first alderman ever elected from the old fifth ward, embracing all the territory on the North Side, between Clark Street and the River. There were then but six wards in the City, two on each side of the River; but the third (represented by John Dean Caton) and the fifth (by Bernard Ward) had but one each. Mr. Ward lived upon an island, since cut away, near the forks of the River, approachable from the North Side by a foot-bridge. Mr. Ward has been dead about forty years, leaving a son, now living, Henry A. Ward, born on the island, 28 March, 1834, and a daughter, who married Ralph, a deceased son of this Sergeant Joseph Adams, of South Evanston, Ill.

† Mr. Adams has two children now living, *viz.*: Henry Adams, now living at South Evanston, Cook County, Ill., and the wife of Dr. Allen W. Gray, (son of ex-Sheriff John Gray), of Chicago. He had a son, Ralph Adams, now dead, who married a daughter of ex-alderman Bernard Ward.

were born in Chicago while I was stationed there as a soldier. My family did not live in the Fort till after the troops left, when we moved in for the winter. In looking over your Fort Dearborn address, you mention of having lost track of Lieut. J. L. Thompson. He was with the Army of Observation, on the Rio Grande, and he resigned just before hostilities broke out in the Mexican war; for which his father-in-law, Gen. Hugh Brady, was much displeased. Soon after his resignation, I read in a newspaper, (your *Chicago Democrat*, perhaps?), an account of his death by drowning in the St. Clair River, near Detroit, Mich.

The Rev. Jeremiah Porter came to Chicago on the same boat that I did, and I attended the first services he held in Chicago, May, 1833.

JOSEPH ADAMS.

SOUTH EVANSTON, COOK CO., ILL., June 16, 1881.

HON. JOHN WENTWORTH,—*Dear Sir:* I am positive that the troops left Chicago late in December, 1836, but the exact date I do not know, but I *do* know that it was close upon the New Year of 1837. As to what the printed *Army Returns* show, I presume they allude to the public property, ordnance and quartermaster stores being removed to headquarters of the regiment. I do not recollect when Major Joseph Plympton left, but think he would have left when the public property was withdrawn. Capt. Louis T. Jamison remained in the garrison till late in the fall of 1837, being detailed on recruiting-service. I do not know how much longer he remained; but I saw him on some business late in the fall. I should think you would remember the fuss that occurred between Capt. Jamison and his recruits on one side, and Col. Beaubien and a number of citizens, favorable to him, on the side. The latter hauled some lumber upon the "Reservation," and Capt. James Allen brought his men from the harbor-works and conquered the aggressive party. [See *Scammon's Illinois Reports*, vol. iii., Louis T. Jamison *v.* John Doe *ex dem.* John B. Beaubien. Also De Lafayette Wilcox *v.* James Kinzie.]

I was born in the county of Stafford or Staffordshire, England, December 24th, 1794. I know I came to Chicago in May, 1833. I heard Rev. Jeremiah Porter preach frequently in an old log-building which I can not locate; but I know that it was somewhere near the junction of the two branches of the River. I think he preached his *first* sermon *there;* but I am not positive. Father Jesse Walker [Methodist] preached in the same building. There was a room fitted up for Rev. Jeremiah Porter in the garrison, after we had been there sometime. Thinking of Major Joseph Plympton and family reminds me that just sixty years ago this coming "Fourth of July," he was then a lieutenant, and in command of the company to which I belonged. He was detailed to take charge of the party to fire the *first* Fourth-of-July salute that was ever fired at Fort Snelling. I was the non-commissioned officer of the party. That was in 1821; there were then barracks built for two or three companies. Major Plympton was not married at *that time.* He left Fort Snelling about 1822, and returned (a short time before we left for Jefferson Barracks) with a wife and *perhaps one* child. I know there was *one there.* After we left the Fort, I never saw him again till he came to Chicago to take command of Fort Dearborn.

There had been salutes fired near Fort Snelling, but *not* on the *site* of the Fort itself. I remember one given for Gov. Cass, in 1820, on his return from a north-west tour among the Indians.

JOSEPH ADAMS.

L.

From the *Chicago Democrat*, March 23d, 1861.

EXTRACTS FROM LETTER OF CAPT. A. WALKER.—CHICAGO IN 1832.—ARRIVAL OF FIRST STEAMBOAT.—THE CHOLERA AND ITS FATALITY AMONG THE U.S. TROOPS AND SAILORS.—GEN. SCOTT'S ARRIVAL.—EARLY STEAMBOAT ITEMS.

BUFFALO, October 30th, 1860.

CAPT. R. C. BRISTOL,

Dear Sir: On my arrival home from New York, a few days since, from our annual meeting, I found your favor of the 3d inst., in which you speak of my former communication.

And now, in compliance with your request, I will enter more fully into detail, as you inform me many of the leading points and incidents connected with that pioneer voyage, will form a part of the recorded history of Chicago, as kept by the Historical Society. * * * It will be borne in mind that at that time but few traces of civilization could be seem, after passing the Straits of Mackinaw; nothing like light-houses, or beacon-lights, artificial harbors, or but few natural ones, were in existence; no piers, wood or coal yards were established; and not a single village, town or city on the whole distance, where now all are conspicuous along the western shores of Lake Michigan, showing a strange contrast indeed.

It will also be remembered, as stated in my former communication, that four steamers, the *Henry Clay, Superior, Sheldon Thompson*, and *William Penn*, were chartered by the United States Government for the purpose of transporting troops, equipments, and provisions to Chicago, during the Black-Hawk war, but, owing to the fearful ravages, made by the breaking out of the Asiatic cholera among the troops and crews on board, two of those boats were compelled to abandon their voyage, proceeding no further than Fort Gratiot. The disease became so violent and alarming on board the *Henry Clay* that nothing like discipline could be observed, everything in the way of subordination ceased. As soon as the steamer came to the dock, each man sprang on shore, hoping to escape from a scene so terrifying and appalling. Some fled to the fields, some to the woods, while others lay down in the streets, and under the cover of the river bank, where most of them died unwept and alone.

There were no cases of cholera causing death on board my boat until we passed the Manitou Islands, (Lake Michigan). The first person attacked died about four o'clock in the afternoon, some thirty hours before reaching Chicago. As soon as it was ascertained, by the surgeon, that life was extinct, the deceased was wrapped closely in his blanket, placing within some weights secured by lashing of small cordage around the ankles, knees, waist, and neck, and then committed, with but little ceremony, to the deep.

This unpleasant though imperative duty was performed by the Orderly Sergeant, with a few privates detailed for that purpose. In like manner twelve others, including this same noble sergeant, who sickened and died in a few hours, were also thrown overboard before the balance of the troops were landed at Chicago.

The sudden and untimely death of this veteran sergeant and his committal to a watery grave, caused a deep sensation on board among the soldiers and crews, which I will not here attempt to describe. The effect produced upon Gen. Scott and the other officers, in witnessing the scene, was too visible to be misunderstood, for the dead soldier had been a very valuable man, and evidently a favorite among the officers and soldiers of the regiment. * * *

Some very interesting and appropriate memoranda were made by the steward of the boat at the time, on one of the leaves of his account-book (which is still in my possession) by quotations from one of the poets, such as, "Sleep, soldier, sleep; thy warfare's o'er," etc.   *   *   *

On another leaf is a graphic representation of a coffin, made by pen and ink, placed opposite the account on the credit side of one of the volunteer officers, who died after reaching Chicago, with this singular and concise device or inscription written upon the lid of the coffin:

"Account settled by Death.
(Signed)   H. Bradley, clerk and steward,
Steamer *Sheldon Thompson*.

Chicago, Ill., July 11th, 1832."

There was one singular fact—not one of the officers of the army was attacked by the disease, while on board my boat, with such violence as to result in death, or any of the officers belonging to the boat, though nearly one-fourth of the crew fell a prey to the disease on a subsequent trip, while on the passage from Detroit to Buffalo.

We arrived at Chicago (as stated in the former communication) on the evening of the 10th of July, 1832. I sent the yawl-boat on shore soon after with Gen. Scott and a number of the volunteer officers, who accompanied him on his expedition against the hostile tribes, who, with Black Hawk, had committed many depredations, (though, perhaps, not without some provocation), compelling the whites to abandon their homes in the country and flee to Chicago, taking refuge in the Fort for the time being. Before landing the troops next morning, we were under the painful necessity of committing three more to the deep, who died during the night, making, in all, sixteen who were thus consigned to a watery grave. These three were anchored to the bottom in two and a-half fathoms, the water being so clear that their forms could be plainly seen from our decks. This unwelcome sight created such excitement, working upon the superstitious fears of some of the crew, that prudence dictated that we weigh anchor and move a distance, sufficient to shut from sight a scene which seemed to haunt the imagination, and influence the mind with thoughts of some portentious evil.

In the course of the day and night following, eighteen others died and were interred not far from the spot where the American Temperance House*

* N.-W. corner Lake Street and Wabash Avenue.

has since been erected. The earth that was removed to cover one made a grave to receive the next that died. All were buried without coffins or shrouds, except their blankets, which served for a winding-sheet, there left, as it were, without remembrance or a stone to mark their resting-place. During the four days we remained at Chicago, fifty-four more died, making an aggregate of eighty-eight who paid the debt of nature.   *   *   *

On approaching Chicago, I found quite a fleet of sail vessels, at anchor in the offing, where we also came to, near them. As soon as it was ascertained that cholera was on board, no time was lost in communicating from one vessel to the other the intelligence, which induced them to weigh anchor at once, and stand out to sea, hoping to escape the pestilence, which, at that time, was considered contagious. In the morning some of them were nearly lost in the distance, though in the course of the day they mostly returned and reanchored near by, in hailing distance. Among the fleet were some vessels belonging to Oliver Newberry, Esq., of Detroit, that were employed in transporting provisions and stores from the Government to that port.

The number of buildings at that time, where your populous City now stands, was but five, three of which were log-tenements; one of them without a roof, was used as a stable, and one small frame dwelling-house, besides the light-house and barracks (better known as Fort Dearborn) which was evacuated for the accommodation of the sick troops. Major Whistler, Capt. Johnson, and many others, with their families, who had previously occupied the barracks, took shelter wherever they could, some under boards placed obliquely across the fence, others in tents, etc.

It is proper in this connection to state that all the mattresess and bedding belonging to my boat, except sufficient for the crew, were taken by order of Gen. Scott for the use of the sick, giving his draft for the purchase of new bedding, which was not only a deed of mercy to those suffering ones, but a matter of favor to me, in procuring a fresh out-fit, so necessary after that disastrous voyage. There was no harbor accessible to any craft drawing more than two feet of water, hardly sufficient to admit the bateau in which the troops were landed. But little else was seen besides the broad expanse of prairie, with its gentle undulated surface, covered with grass and variegated flowers, stretching out far in the distance, resembling a great carpet interwoven with green, purple, and gold; in one direction bounded only by the blue horizon, with no intervening woodland to obstruct the vision. The view in looking through the spy-glass from the upper deck of our steamer, while laying in the offing, was a most picturesque one, presenting a landscape interspersed with small groves of underwood, making the picture complete; combining the grand and beautiful in nature, far beyond anything I had before seen.

The Chicago River, at that time, was but a mere creek, easily forded at its mouth, while it wended its way along the beach, flowing into the Lake a small distance south of the present locality of Lake Street.

The provisions and stores brought by the sail-vessels were landed on the beach of the Lake, near the mouth of the River, where now are seen the extensive railroad improvements. * * *

We remained four days after landing the troops, procuring fuel for the homeward voyage, etc. The only means of obtaining anything for fuel was to purchase the roofless log-building used as a stable. That, together with the rail fence enclosing a field of some three acres near by, was sufficient to enable us to reach Mackinaw. Being drawn to the beach and prepared for use, it was boated on board by the crew, which operation occupied the most of four days to accomplish.

There was one circumstance connected with this transaction, which, with other things, deserves to be mentioned. A youngerly man by the name of Burnham, if my memory serves, rendered a special service in aiding me in negotiating for the fuel and assisting in getting it drawn to the shore, he having the only team that could be procured. He had come in from the country but a few days before, with a yoke of oxen and a wagon, bringing with him a family, I think not his own, who had fled from the country for refuge. His services, so timely and unabating, and the kindly disposition he manifested to assist in every way in his power, together with the moderate price charged for the services, under the circumstances, went far to strengthen my faith in human nature, that all mankind are not entirely selfish, that there are some who can and do act disinterestedly. This, I verily believe, was the case, in a very large degree, with this generous-hearted young man. He, too, fell a prey to the cholera. He was attacked and died a few days after I sailed from your Fort.

After getting the fuel on board, I was detained some six hours, waiting the arrival of a gentleman whose name I think was Chamberlain. I had dispatched a messenger for him, he residing some fifteen miles in the country. At length he arrived, and engaged to accompany me as far as Detroit and act in the capacity of physician, having some knowledge in preparing medicine, being a druggist by profession.

During this protracted stay, in waiting for the doctor, the crew became quite uneasy to get under way, and leave behind them a scene fraught with associations of the dead and the dying, which they had witnessed so frequently, until they became almost mutinous. But as soon as orders were given to get under way, the celerity with which the yawl was hoisted to the stern, was a scene of exciting interest, as the duty was performed with a will and a spirit of cheerfulness, accompanied with a hearty song of "Yo-heave-ho." As they hove at the windlass, they seemed almost frantic with joy when the anchor came in sight and her prow turned homeward.

We had no cases of cholera on our passage to Detroit. The physician returned across the country, after receiving the stipulated sum for his services, which I think was some two hundred dollars, besides the stage-fare, which was one of the items in the stipulation.

In 1832, as before stated, but two steamers visited Chicago, the *Sheldon Thompson* being the first ever at that port. The *William Penn* arrived some eight days later, laden with troops, stores, etc., belonging to the Government. From the year 1832, different steamers made occasional trips to Chicago—the *Daniel Webster, Monroe, Columbus, Anthony Wayne, Bunker Hill*, and others. The most noted among them was the steamer *Michigan*, (the first), built and owned by Oliver Newberry, Esq., late of Detroit, who for many years was associated with and largely engaged in the commerce of the lakes. This boat made one or more annual trips of pleasure, generally making the circuit of Lake Michigan. She was a fine specimen of a steamer, far in advance of most boats of her time. Though her model was by no means comely, her speed was quite equal to others, having two powerful low-pressure beam-engines, and withal a staunch sea-boat. Her fine finish, splendid fixtures, and furniture, which were quite superior to any other in that day, together with her veteran commander, Capt. Blake, on board, rendered her a favorite with the traveling public.

A few years later a large class of steamers commenced making regular trips from Buffalo touching most of the intermediate ports. Among the number was the *James Madison*, owned by Charles M. Reed, Esq., of Erie, built with particular reference to the upper-lake trade. Her capacity for freight and passengers was the largest upon the Lake at that time. She was first commanded by Capt. R. C. Bristol, afterwards, and for many years, by Capt. McFadyen. Still later, in the year 1837, came the steamer *Illinois*, (the first), owned and built by O. Newberry, Esq. She was also designed for the Chicago trade. In this boat was combined many qualities, both in her size, symmetry, beauty of model, style of finish, speed, and seaworthiness, which placed her in the foremost rank of steamboats and enabled her for many years to receive a most liberal patronage. She was also brought out under the command of Capt. Blake.

From year to year emigration to Illinois and Wisconsin continued to increase, until a daily line of boats was established between Buffalo and Chicago, while at the same time the public demands were such as to require a still further advance, and a different class and style of boat with better accommodations and increased facilities, suited to the condition and circumstances of a large class of the more refined and wealthy, who were then emigrating and settling throughout your and the adjoining States. And hence the necessity of introducing the upper-cabin boat. When the *Great Western* first made her appearance upon the lakes, and during the two years in which she was being built, many, who claimed to be judges, expressed doubts of the practicability and seaworthiness of that class of boats. But in a few trips she became a favorite with the public, and, notwithstanding the opinions and prejudices of the few, was the means of bringing about an entire revolution in the construction of our steam marine upon the lakes, causing all the boats in commission and contemporary with her, to convert their lower cabins in steerages and freight-holds, and substitute the upper-cabin. * * * It is proper here to say that the *Great Western* was built expressly for the upper-lake trade, and continued to make regular trips for ten successive years. Of the estimation placed upon her during those years, it is not my province here to speak, more than to say that she was designed, modeled by, and under my command during that period. At that time (1838) the principal forwarding houses in the City were Kinzie & Hunter, Newberry & Dole, Gurdon S. Hubbard, Esq., Bristol & Porter, the latter of whom was then agents and consignees for the above-named boats, Mr. Hubbard being the agent for the *Great Western*. Subsequently she ran to the dock of Messrs. Walker, Smith and others as her agents and consignees.

The population of Chicago, if I remember rightly, did not exceed four or five thousand souls.

Your friend and obedient servant,
A. WALKER.

M.

THE OLD RAILROADS OF ILLINOIS.

OMAHA, NEB., June 15, 1881.

HON. JOHN WENTWORTH,—*Dear Sir:* I have to thank you for the receipt of copies of your lectures, and proceedings of the Calumet Club, all which bring up many familiar and departed names and faces.

I arrived at Chicago, February 11, 1837, and one of the first forms and faces, was your own, that I met. And I soon became a reader of your *Chicago Democrat*, and a visitor at your sanctum. I boarded with Mark Beaubien, at his "Illinois Exchange," and my room was on the opposite corner, a small, yellow building, which had been used by some physician whose name has escaped me.

I went to Chicago, under the promise of a situation under James Seymour, then just from the Erie road, who had been selected by Col. Edmund D. Taylor and W. B. Ogden, to survey and locate the old Galena and Chicago Union Railroad, now grown into the gigantic *North-Western*. It is not easy, after the lapse of forty-four years, and the absence of a daily journal, to recall with much exactness, the operations and incidents of that period. We began our survey at the foot of Dearborn Street, and ran three lines, nearly due west, to the DesPlaines River. Much of the time we waded in water, waist deep, and were glad, at night, to reach the *hotel* at Barry's Point, kept by Jocelyn & Chamberlin, and dry ourselves by the large fire-place.

The "hard times," following the Land Speculation, made short work of the projected railroad. We were paid off, and, June 1st, left for *Peru*, then a promising city on paper and prairie bluffs, to enter upon the surveys north and south of the Illinois River, under the old Illinois Internal Improvement system.

I can scarcely recall the names, even of our corps of engineers. James Seymour, was chief; his brother, Wm. H. Seymour, was assistant; P. H. Ogilvie, draughtsman, a lively little Scot, and a graduate of Edinboro'; H. V. Mooris, assistant-draughtsman; Geo. Howel, rodman, and myself axeman and chainman. It was my lot to drive, under the immediate superintendence of the chief, the first stake, as we understood at the time, ever driven in your City, for a railroad line. The high grass, where the fire had not swept over it, required four-foot stakes, which we *backed* for miles, using 400 feet stations. Of all our company, I have no knowledge of any other survivor.

We boarded, for some weeks, with a most pleasant gentleman, up the north-branch, in a new brick-house. I believe he was a Virginian, Archibald Clybourn perhaps. An active business man, named James A. Marshal, also boarded there. This was more than forty years ago. I left Chicago, Feb., 1841, and seven years later passed through it. I spent the winter of 1837-38 in Chicago, our office being on what was then the outskirts of the City, but now quite central, at the residence of Hiram P. Woodworth, who was our new chief-engineer. From Peru, or LaSalle, our surveys extended up the Vermillion to Dixon and Galena, from the south side of the River in the direction of Bloomington, running sixty miles without a tree or any stream to check our progress. We also surveyed a portion of the Illinois River, and run a line from Meridosia to Quincy. In 1840, Ogilvie, myself, and others listened to a four-hour speech from Stephen A. Douglas, at Dixon's Ferry, and to a shorter and spicy address from "Long John" Wentworth, then in the bloom of manhood. In 1840, I was junior assistant-engineer, and had charge of construction from LaSalle to the Bureau River, near Inlet Grove, Lee County, and a small prairie town called Greenfield, in Bureau County. In passing through Peru last week, I recalled the fact that in June, 1837, Daniel Webster was there and addressed the people upon the future of Illinois, etc., followed by toasts, etc. [He came from Peru directly to Chicago and addressed the people here.] And I wondered how many there were left in that region who then listened to the great "Expounder and Defender."

The glorious Fourth of 1837 we celebrated at Greenfield, on the banks of the dark and muddy waters of the Bureau River. Fletcher Webster, [son of Daniel], his wife, Theron D. Brewster, and pretty much all the people thereabouts, were present.

Thanking you for bringing back to mind long-buried memories of my early days, and pleasant remembrances of old friends and familiar faces, and hoping you and yours may long live to enjoy prosperity, I am,

Yours as ever,   FRED'K A. NASH.

N.

REMARKS OF MR. WENTWORTH AT THE OLD SETTLERS' REUNION UPON THE PRESENTATION OF MARK BEAUBIEN'S FIDDLE TO THE CALUMET CLUB, 19 MAY, 1881: I am a little embarassed in my position to-night, as I have to act the double part of guest and host. I am a member of this, the Calumet Club, and I am entertaining myself whilst the Club entertains the old settlers of Chicago. But in either capacity I can not but give expression to my pleasure. I am grateful to my colleagues in the Club for their hospitalities, and to Divine Providence for giving to so many of Chicago's pioneers life and strength to attend this our third annual reception. As a host, I welcome you in veneration for old associations, and as a guest I thank my colleagues of the Club for their appreciation.

I have ever felt an interest in the history of Chicago, but more especially since the fire of 1871. At that time, I was engaged in preparing an index to the *Chicago Democrat* which I published for a quarter of a century, from 1836 to 1861; such an index being a labor-saving institution to newspaper reporters and all others who might wish to refer to the events of my Chicago life. If people were desirous of information, I could then place my index before them, and they could obtain their ends without disturbing my avocations. But the fire came and destroyed both papers and index. I was saved; but there was no index to my memory, and I felt that I and all of the early settlers must soon pass away. What then was to be done to gather up and perpetuate our history? The old settlers were the landmarks; but they were scattered, and many of them outside of the reach of the Chicago Directory. The members of the Calumet Club comprehended the situation, and resolved to bring the old settlers together in an annual entertainment, the first of which took place two years ago, and many here to-night were present upon that occasion and the succeeding one; and I hope they will live to attend many others. We registered our names with the date of our arrival here, with the place of our birth, and with our ages. And we also gave to the secretary of the Club the names of all whom we knew who had not been invited, in order that they might be invited upon future occasions. The result has been that it is believed that there lives not anywhere a resident of Chicago, prior to 1840, who was of age, who has not been invited to these annual receptions. And, when they can not come, they generally write an interesting letter. And, when from the infirmities of age, they are incapacitated from writing, we are glad to know that some friend writes for them. Thus our proceedings are looked upon as a part of the history of the North-West. Our Chicago editors inform me that no one of their daily issues is so extensively called for as that next succeeding the evening of these anniversaries. The proceedings of our first reception were published in a pamphlet; and that pamphlet now has a place in all the Historical Societies of the United States; and in most of those of the Old World. I ever have that pamphlet upon my table, and, when people call upon me for information about early times, if I can not impart it, I look over the registry of names, and point out some persons who I think can do so. Thus, between us all, we can impart a great deal of valuable information, and especially to those desirous of perfecting their land-titles. What else can compare with these Calumet-Club receptions in restoring our history? I have regretted the non-attendance of the widows of our early settlers. This is to be provided for hereafter, as the Club House is to be enlarged to a capacity that will accommodate them. I know, personally, over one hundred widows of early settlers, whose presence upon these occasions would be both pleasurable and profitable. Their memories are as good as ours and they have information as valuable as ours. Besides, many of them have letters and papers that would settle many disputed points, which we have not! The history of Chicago must be written, and it must be written accurately, and these widows and ourselves must furnish the material.

I have been requested by the Chicago Historical Society, next Saturday, to match my voice in the open air against the whistle of the tug-boats that run up and down the Chicago River, at the junction of the streets at the Rush-Street bridge, and recite the history of Fort Dearborn from its construction, in 1804, to its abandonment, in 1837. In looking up material for that occasion, I have felt the advantages of these reunions as all persons will who seek knowledge of the past. If any of you have any old papers upon that subject, or any knowledge that has never been published, you will subserve the cause of history by letting me know it. If, after I have delivered my address, you notice any mistakes, I will thank you to inform me respecting them. As matters now are, on the disappearance of official records, we are much dependant upon each other for the verity of history. In the enterprise and competition of our daily papers, Chicago's history has been much mystified. Interesting events are sought after and commented upon without particularity as to dates, or the persons concerned in them. As men become old they too often become garrulous, and where they can not procure an audience, they often write letters and sign their names to them, or make statements to reporters, and such go to the world as the veritable remembrances of old settlers. They generally get their events right, but they too often make mistakes in dates and in parties to them. Hence the importance of reëstablishing the old landmarks, which it is the mission of the old settlers who meet here at these receptions to do. Many often compliment me upon the accuracy of my memory. But it is no better than the most of yours. And I dare not trust it in important matters unless backed by old papers and experiences which I am ever upon the look out to gather up and have at hand for reference.

My fellow old settlers! I miss several faces here to-night that I have been in the habit of meeting. Some are unavoidably detained, whilst others have gone to the general reunion beyond the grave. One we all miss more than any other who always has been with us. We miss him for the peculiar kind of music that he always furnished us. We miss him because, when speaking of any Chicago event, he was never the man to say, as many of us are compelled to say: "That happened before I came to Chicago." He came here in 1826, and was a voter when this City was a part of Peoria County. But he had seen much of interest before he came to Chicago. Never again shall we behold a man who was present at the surrender of Gen. Hull, at Detroit. I allude to Mark Beaubien, who died at the residence of his daughter, Mrs. George Mathews, at Kankakee, in this State, on the 11th April, of this year. Upon his death-bed, he requested that his fiddle be given to me. At every other reunion of Chicago's old settlers, Mr. Beaubien has been present and played upon it. The fiddle is here now, but the arm that wielded the bow is palsied in death. I labored among his descendants, among the old French pioneers, and among you, old settlers, to find some one to play a dirge upon it to his memory here to-night. But I was unsuccessful. And now I present it to the Calumet Club, as he was ever honored here. All its members were ever glad to see him, and he ever felt at home here. And as he has passed away, I take pleasure in presenting to you his oldest son, Frank Gordon Beaubien, now present. But he has not inherited the musical taste of his father. He was born in Chicago, and so is younger than the fiddle which his father brought here from Detroit, in 1826.* How long he had it before he came here I can not say. It has done service enough in Chicago to entitle it to honor, however. Three generations have listened to its music here. I also take pleasure in introducing you to his cousin, Alexander Beaubien, son of the late Gen. Jean Baptiste Beaubien, who was at Mackinaw in 1812, and saw the surrender of that place to the British as his brother Mark did that of Detroit. The General was a little higher toned than Mark, and brought the first piano to Chicago. And like the fiddle, that piano has been well preserved; and, after long use in Chicago, it is now doing service in the family of his granddaughter, Mrs. Sophia (Beaubien) Ogee, at Silver Lake, Kansas, daughter of the late Charles Beaubien.

And now, gentlemen, permit me to say that in this crowded room, crowded with liberal hosts to do us honor, and crowded with grateful guests to receive that honor, I want to shake hands with every old settler here to-night if I have not already done so. There is no probability that we shall ever all meet here again. Yet some will meet here. For these annual receptions are to be continuous and in a larger hall. I want you all to be enabled to say when you return to your homes and you are asked whom you met, that you have once more shaken hands with "Long John" Wentworth. And, if you live until next year, and I live, I want you to come here, see our new hall, and give then another shake.

* Mark Beaubien was not the last survivor of the settlers of 1826. Edward Ament, who voted here in that year, now lives at Newark, Kendall County, Ill., and has a son, John Ament, now living in this City. He had four brothers once living here, viz.: Hiram, now living at San Jose, California; Justus died at Big Rock, Kane County, Ill.; Calvin died at Warsaw, Hancock County, Ill.; John died at Princeton, Bureau County, Ill.; and Ansen died at La Prairie, Adams County Ill.—See No. 7 of Fergus' Historical Series, page 16.

On occasions of this kind we want sociability rather than speech-making. Refreshments await you and will be at your pleasure as long as you stay. Let us now waive all ceremony and resolve ourselves into an old-fashioned Love Feast, where we can eat drink and be merry, shouting Glory Hallelujah and praising the Lord for extending our lives to the present time.

O.
HISTORY OF THE CHICAGO LIGHT-HOUSE.

TREASURY DEPARTMENT, OFFICE OF LIGHT-HOUSE BOARD,
WASHINGTON, June 6th, 1881.

Sir: Your letter of May 27th, relative to the old Chicago light-house, within the precincts of Fort Dearborn, has been received.

In reply, I have to say that the structure in question was built, served its purpose, was discontinued and removed, prior to the organization of the Light-House Board, and that the only information this office can obtain, with regard to it, is from the imperfect records which have come down from those who, from time to time, previously had charge of the light-house service. Such of the information which you ask, as the Board is able to furnish, is herein given.

The first appropriation known to the Board for the erection of the structure in question was made by the Act, approved March 3, 1831, and is as follows: "$5000 for building a light-house at the mouth of Chicago River, Lake Michigan."

The next appropriation known to the Board, was made by the Act, approved March 3, 1847, and is: "For a light-house at Chicago, $3500."

It appears from the various light-house lists, published by the Treasury Department from 1838 to 1857, that the Chicago light-house was erected in 1831-2, but the precise date upon which it was commenced, and upon which it was finished, is not given.

In the light-house list for 1838, the building is described as follows:—
"Chicago light-house, south side of Chicago River; fixed light; tower forty feet high; fourteen inch reflector; four lamps; built in 1831-2."

The records of the office show nothing with regard to the tradition you mention, relative to the destruction of a light-house in 1831, and the erection of a new one upon the same spot. There appears, thus far, no evidence that there was any light-house at Fort Dearborn prior to 1831.

The first keeper of the light, of whom the Board has any record, was Samuel C. Lasby, who received $350 per year.

There is sent to your address, to-day, a copy of the book entitled *Documents Relating to Light-Houses, 1789 to 1871*, and you are referred to pages 88, 245, and 254, where mention is made the of several light-houses at and near Chicago. There is, also, sent you a book entitled *Laws and Appropriations from 1789 to 1855*, and you are referred to pages 93 and 132 for the appropriations for the erection of the old Chicago light-house, and to pages 144, 154, and 193, for appropriations relative to other aids to navigation in the neighborhood of Chicago; also to the index on page 227, relative to the appropriations made within the above-mentioned dates for aids to navigation in the State of Illinois.

There is also sent you, for the use of the Historical Society, a copy of the last report of the Light-House Board, and of the last issued list of lights on the lakes, in which you will find mention of the present condition of the lights near Chicago. Very respectfully, GEO. DEWEY,
Hon. JOHN WENTWORTH, Chicago.   Commander U.S.N., Naval Sec'y.

P.

FALL OF THE ORIGINAL LIGHT-HOUSE AT CHICAGO.
LETTER FROM ISAAC D. HARMON, (AGED 17), TO HIS ELDER BROTHER, CHARLES L. HARMON, DECEASED.

CHICAGO, October 31st, 1831.

Dear Brother: We have had a flattener pass over the face of our prospects in *Chicago*. The light-house, that the day before yesterday, stood in all its *glory*, the pride of this wonderous village, is now "*doused*." For about a week past, cracks have been observed in it, and yesterday they began to look "*squally*." Mr. Jackson, (the man who contracted to erect the building), [Probably Samuel Jackson, alderman in 1837,] ordered some of the bottom stones, which looked likely to fall, to be taken out. Yet he and his men assured people there was no danger of its falling. Jackson said, "You can't get it down," but there were others who were not so sure. My father, [Dr. Elijah D. Harmon], in the afternoon, told them it leaned to one side. They laughed at him, and so confident were some of its standing, that, but a few hours before it fell, they went upon the top of it; and amongst the rest, some women. Stones kept dropping from the hole in it; and, about nine o'clock in the evening, down tumbled the whole work with a terrible crash and a noise like the rattling of fifty claps of thunder. The walls were three feet thick, and it had been raised fifty feet in height; so you must know it made some stir when it fell. The first thing father said to the workmen when he went out was, "Does it lean any now." They were 'shorn of their locks,' and had nothing to say. Various reasons are assigned as the cause of its falling. Jackson wants to make it appear that it was owing to the quicksand under the building, which made it settle, and says that a light-house can not be made to stand here. It would be greatly for his interest to have this story believed; as, by this means he would probably get pay for what he has done; otherwise, he will not. People here, and those that are well qualified to judge, say there is no such thing as quicksand about it, and that it was all owing to the wretched manner in which it was built. I am inclined to believe them. Judging from the piece of wall now standing, the mortar looks like dry sand, and the wall is two-thirds filled up between with stones not bigger than a man's head. *Finis.*

CHARLES L. HARMON, Burlington, Vt.

Yours affectionately,
ISAAC D. HARMON.

Q.

COL. JOSEPH PLYMPTON.

Joseph Plympton was born Feb. 24th, 1787, at Sudbury, Mass. He was a direct descendant of Thomas Plympton, who was born in Sudbury, Suffolk County, England, landed in Massachusetts in 1633, founded the town of Sudbury, Mass., and was slain by the Indians on Boone's Plain, April 16, 1667. Joseph was appointed 2d-lieutenant, Jan. 3d, 1812, in the 4th U. S. Infantry; promoted to 1st-lieutenant, July 1st, 1813; to captain, June 1st, 1821, in the 5th U. S. Infantry, and brevetted major, June 1, 1831, "for ten year's faithful service." On March 15, 1824, he married Eliza Matilda Livingston, daughter of Peter William Livingston, of New-York City. Among the places commanded by Brevet-Maj. Plympton, before coming to Fort Dearborn, are St. Louis, Mo.; Fort Snelling, Minn.; Fort Armstrong, Mississippi River; Fort Howard, (Green Bay, Wis.); and Fort Winnebago, (Winnebago, Wis.) After his command of Fort Dearborn he was ordered to Florida, and distinguished himself in the Seminole war. On Sept. 22d, 1840, he was promoted to major in the 2d U. S. Infantry, and on Sept. 9th, 1846, to lieutenant-colonel in the 7th U. S. Infantry, and ordered to Mexico in command of that regiment. For "gallant and meritorious conduct" at the battle of Cerro Gordo, he was brevetted colonel. From 1851, for two years, he was in New-York City, as general superintendent of the recruiting-service, U. S. army. Feb. 9, 1854, he was promoted to colonel of the 1st U. S. Infantry, and ordered to Galveston, Texas. Col. Plympton died at Staten Island, N. Y., June 5, 1860. Among the many officers under his command during his long military service were Gens. U. S. Grant, Philip A. Sheridan, and Nathaniel Lyon. Mrs. Col. Plympton died, June 20th, 1873. Of their children, not elsewhere mentioned, are Cornelia De Peyster, born at Fort Howard, Green Bay, Wis., and married to Lieut. Henry M. Black, now colonel in the U. S. army; also, Gilbert M., of New-York City; also, Louisa E., born at Fort Snelling, and married to Lieut. John Pitman, Ordinance-Corps, U. S. army.

LITTLE TURTLE.

Drake's Book upon the Indians says: "Little Turtle died 14 July, 1812, aged 65 years, at his residence upon Eel River, near Fort Wayne, where the government had built him a house and provided him with the means of living. His portrait, by Stewart, is now in the War Department at Washington." [From this it appears that he had been dead over a month at the time of the Chicago massacre.]

AN INTERESTING RELIC.

A letter has been received from Charles P. Greenough, an attorney of Boston, a little yellow with age, which was among a collection of historical letters and papers the gentleman had, and deemed it appropriate to send to Mayor Harrison. It will prove interesting to old Chicagoans. It is addressed to "John Johnson, Esq., U. S. Factor, Fort Wayne. Per the express." On the outside margin is the name of the writer, Mr. Lalime. The letter reads as follows:

"CHICAGO, 7th July, 1811.

"Sir: Since my last to you we have news of other depredations and murders committed about the settlement of Cohokia. The first news we received was that the brothers-in-law of Mainpoe went down and stole a number of horses. Second, another party went down, stole some horses, killed a man, and took off a young woman, but they being pursued were obliged to leave her to save themselves. Third, they have been there and killed and destroyed a whole family. The cause of it, or in part, is from the little chief that came last fall to see Gov. Harrison under the feigned name of Wapewa. He told the Indians that he had told the Governor that the Americans were settling on their lands, and what should be done with them. He told the Indians that the Governor had told him they were bad people; that they must drive them off, kill their cattle, and steal their horses, etc.

"Being the quarter ending the 30th June I am busy with the Factory, and have a number of Indians here paying their visit to Capt. Heald. From those circumstances, I hope, sir, you will excuse my hurry. Please give my respects to Mrs. Johnston. I am with respect, sir, your obedient servant, J. LALIME."*

* THE KILLING OF LALIME EXPLAINED.

CHICAGO, June 25th, 1881.

HON. JOHN WENTWORTH,—*Dear Sir:* Your note of the 22d inst. I received yesterday. Thanks for the slip you enclosed.

In reply to your inquiries I have to say, that I think Mathew Irwin was not sub-agent at Fort Dearborn, but that he was United States factor, acting also as Indian-agent. His duties were principally confined to Indian affairs, under the direction of the commanding officer, when he was not specially instructed by the Department at Washington.

As regards the unfortunate killing of Mr. LaLime, by Mr. John Kinzie, I have heard the account of it related by Mrs. Kinzie, and her daughter, Mrs. Helm. Mr. Kinzie never, in my hearing, alluded to or spoke of it. He deeply regretted the act. Knowing his aversion to converse on the subject, I never spoke to him about it.

Mrs. Kinzie said that her husband and LaLime had been for several years on unfriendly terms, and had had frequent altercations; that at the time of the encounter, Mr. Kinzie had crossed the River alone, in a canoe, going to the Fort; and that LaLime met him outside of the garrison and shot him, the ball cutting the side of his neck. She supposed LaLime saw her husband crossing, and, taking his pistol, went through the gate purposely to meet him. Mr. Kinzie closing with LaLime stabbed him, and retreated to his house covered with blood. He told his wife what he had done, that he feared he had killed LaLime, that probably a squad would be sent for him, and that he must hide. She, in haste, took bandages, and with him retreated to the woods, where, as soon as possible, she dressed his wounds, returning just in time to meet an officer with a squad, with orders to seize her husband. He could not be found. For some days he was hid in the bush, and cared for by his wife.

LaLime was, I understood, an educated man, and quite a favorite with the officers, who were greatly excited. They decided he should be buried near Mr. Kinzie's house, and he was buried near the bank of the River, about the present terminus of Rush Street, and within about two hundred yards of Mr. Kinzie's house, in plain view from his front-door and piazza. The grave was enclosed by a picket-fence, which Mr. Kinzie, in his life-time, kept in perfect order. My impression has ever been that Mr. Kinzie acted, as he told his wife, in self-defence. This is borne out by the fact that, after a full investigation by the officers, whose friend the deceased was, they acquitted Mr. Kinzie, who then returned to his family.

In some of these details I may be in error, but the fact has ever been firm in my mind that LaLime made the attack, provoking the killing in self-defence. Most certainly Mr. Kinzie deeply regretted the result, and avoided any reference to it. Yours, G. S. HUBBARD.

THE FIRST LAKE-STEAMER.
THE OLD STEAMBOAT WALK-IN-THE-WATER.

Levi Bishop, of Detroit, in a series of articles, in the *Post and Tribune* of that City, on the early history of lake navigation, gives the following account of the old steamboat *Walk-in-the-Water*, the first steamer that plied Lake Erie:

"Capt. Newhall is doing good work as a historian of our lake marine. He has an old registry of the Custom-House of Detroit, of 1818, when William Woodbridge was the Collector of the Port. This record settles the point that the *Walk-in-the-Water*, being the first steamboat that ever navigated on Lake Erie, arrived at Detroit, August 27, 1818, and that she cleared for her return trip to Buffalo the next day. She was in general form a schooner, with an engine and two side-wheels, and she was named after an Indian chief, who found a local habitation and a name somewhere on the borders of the Detroit River, and probably in many other places too numerous to mention. She was doubtless a clumsy craft, but was a good experiment for the early days of steam navigation. The record referred to is in a good state of preservation, and it contains much valuable historical information. The pioneer steamboat went ashore and was wrecked on or near Long Point, in the year 1819 or 1820, and thus she ceased to walk in the water and found a grave therein. From that small beginning, the steamboats on the lakes went on increasing till they rivaled the sail vessels in number and far surpassed them in magnitude, accommodations, and attractions. Between 1830 and 1840, and on from the latter date till the railroads began to acquire the through carrying business, the lake steam marine was surpassed by but few, if any, in the world. The old *North America*, the *Commodore Perry*, the *Illinois*, and the *Michigan* are with others well remembered. Then the great steamboat line was from Buffalo to Chicago, about 1000 miles, and a Chicago boat, with such men as Capts. Blake and Appleby and others on deck, was looked upon as one of the great 'institutions' of the country. They were positively traveling luxuries. Of course it took longer to make the trip than it now does by rail, but those large steamboats presented attractions and comforts which no railroad-cars can afford. The old *Michigan* had two engines,—one on each side,—which, with the side-wheels, ran wholly independent of each other. This was all well in a smooth sea, but in rough weather one wheel would be deep in the water or in a swell, and would move slow, while the other at the same time would be all, or nearly all, out of the water, and would, consequently, fly like lightning. This had the effect to jerk the boat about in different directions, and make the navigation unpleasant and difficult. The double independent engines were, doubtless, an experiment, and, so far as I know, have never been imitated. It seems to be thought better to have the two wheels connected by a long shaft, so that when one does the work the other shall be kept in order and moderation by an inseparable attachment. It was sometimes positively thrilling to see old Capt. Blake on the upper deck in a storm, as he maintained his perfect self-possession and directed the ship beneath him, while the noble vessel

'Walked the water like a thing of life,
And seemed to dare the elements to strife.'

"Passengers had most perfect confidence in him, as they, no doubt, had in many other of our lake captains. The owner of the old *Illinois* was a well-known citizen. He was popularly known as the 'Commodore of the Lakes.' He was a Whig of the Henry Clay, Daniel Webster, and John J. Crittenden school. He was a patriotic citizen, and, as expressing his sentiments and the true spirit of the State and National Governments, he placed at the masthead of the *Illinois* a streamer, nearly or quite forty feet long, with the words

'State Sovereignty and National Union' boldly inscribed upon it in large and conspicuous letters.* That old steamboat and that National sentiment were the pride of Oliver Newberry (of Detroit), as well as the pride and boast of all beholders. When the railroads came into full operation, two grand floating palaces—the *Plymouth Rock* and the *Western World*—were put on Lake Erie, between Detroit and Buffalo, by the Michigan Central Railway Company. They were popular, and a great relief and comfort to the traveling public, but they were soon discontinued by railroad interests, since which our first-class steam navigation has disappeared, except on the Lake Superior lines."

CHICAGO'S FIRST PIANO.

To the Editor of The Chicago Tribune: CHICAGO, July 9, 1881.

In your issue of July 7, you published a letter from Charles Cleaver, Esq., one of our oldest and most honored citizens, whose reminiscences are in the main correct; he is, however, mistaken in some things, which I desire to correct:

1. The first piano brought to Chicago was by John B. Beaubien, about 1834, as Mr. Wentworth states, and not by Mr. Samuel Brooks. Mrs. Capt. J. B. F. Russell and Mrs. John H. Kinzie came here prior to Mr. Brooks, bringing their pianos.

2. He says, in speaking of the old residence of John Kinzie, that he was, at the time he came here, living in a "spacious log-house about opposite Dearborn Street." It was his son, John H. Kinzie, who was then living there; and the house was the United States Indian-Agency, the logs of which were put up by the Indian Agent, Jouett, and left without either roof or floors, and finished and occupied by his successor, Alexander Wolcott, and located where is now the S.-W. corner of North State and North Water Streets, now embraced in Wolcott's Addition. Mr. Wolcott married a sister of John H. Kinzie before there was any one authorized to perform the marriage ceremony nearer than Peoria, Ill., from which place, Mr. John Hamlin, a Justice of the Peace, was sent for and married them. Mrs. Wolcott, after the death of her husband, obtained a patent from the Government, under the preëmption law, for this eighty acres, now Wolcott's Addition to Chicago.

3. I differ with Mr. Cleaver in regard to the continued inundation of the prairie between the Chicago and Desplaines Rivers. It was only during spring and fall rains, or unusually heavy rains, that the roads were in the condition described by him. Generally in summer and early fall the road was perfectly dry, and very fine and smooth for horse and driver; there was an elasticity to our high or low prairie roads that made them far superior to macadamized ones; they were delightfully free from ruts or sloughs.

I trust Mr. Cleaver will continue to give us his valuable information, and that he will pardon me for this correction. We old settlers are making history for generations that may come after us, and we should be careful to make it correct. I will thank him to correct any misstatements that may come from me.   G. S. HUBBARD.

* The Steamer *Illinois*, Capt. Chelsey Blake, was presented with a suit of colors, on July 23, 1839, by the citizens of Chicago. Hon. Wm. B. Ogden made the presentation speech, and Walter L. Newberry, Esq., replied. Gen. Winfield Scott was present, and Mr. Ogden referred to him as the tried friend of Chicago.—See *Chicago Daily American*, July 24, 1839.

86 FORT DEARBORN.

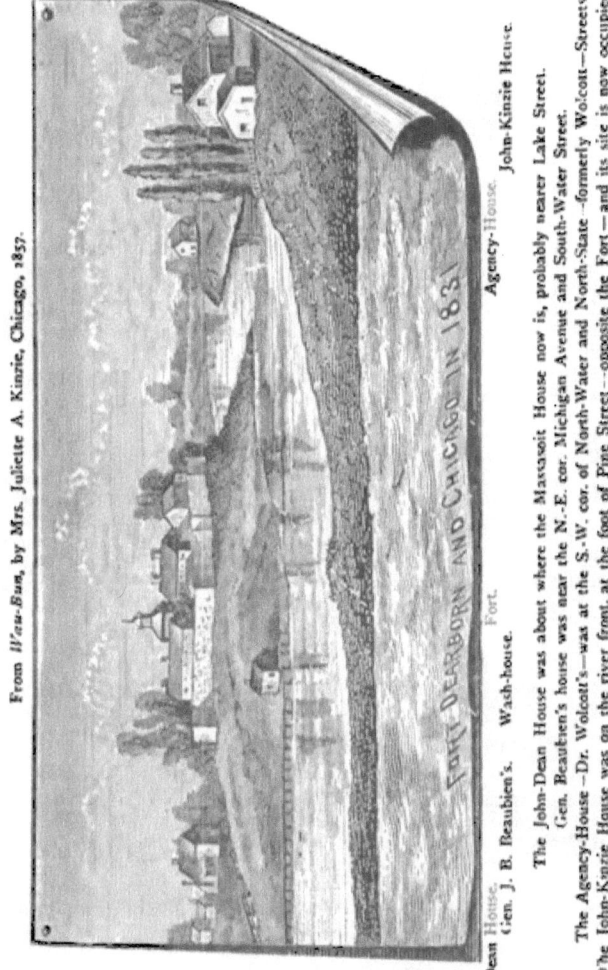

From *Wau-Bun*, by Mrs. Juliette A. Kinzie, Chicago, 1857.

FORT DEARBORN AND CHICAGO IN 1831

Dean House.
Gen. J. B. Beaubien's. Wash-house.
Fort.
Agency-House.
John-Kinzie House.

The John-Dean House was about where the Mascaroit House now is, probably nearer Lake Street.
Gen. Beaubien's house was near the N.-E. cor. Michigan Avenue and South-Water Street.
The Agency-House—Dr. Wolcott's—was at the S.-W. cor. of North-Water and North-State—formerly Wolcott—Streets.
The John-Kinzie House was on the river front, at the foot of Pine Street—opposite the Fort—and its site is now occupied by the Soap Manufactory of Mes-rs. Jas. S. Kirk & Co.
The dotted lines show the direction of the Government Piers, built in 1833-4.

Chicago, July 20, 1881.
HON. J. WENTWORTH; *Dear Sir:*—Referring to yours of the 15th inst., in which you submit, for my criticism, the cut representing "Fort Dearborn and Chicago in 1831," taken from *Wau-Bun*, by Mrs. Juliette A. Kinzie, published in 1857:

I can not believe that Mrs. Kinzie saw the picture until it appeared in her *Wau-Bun*. It was probably engraved from a sketch by her, and sent to her publishers, without an opportunity for her correction. It is certainly unlike the Fort and surroundings, as I recollect them.

The view appears to be from the north-east, as the enclosure of the Fort was nearly north and south, east and west. The River is intended to be shown inland probably not farther than Dearborn or Clark Streets, as the Agency house was at the corner of North-Water and North-State Streets.

Fort Dearborn is represented as located on a high elevation, much above the Kinzie House. This is incorrect, as the ground at the Fort was not over eight feet above the River at its lowest stage, while the Kinzie House was two or three feet higher than the Fort.

There was no sharp point in front of the Fort, north, as shown in the cut. The slope to the River was gradual. At no place fronting the north line of pickets was there over 80 feet to the water's edge; and at the narrowest point, opposite the north gate, from 50 to 60 feet.

The bend of the River, westerly from the Fort, was gradual. The direction of the River from the bend, westerly, was almost straight to Franklin Street. From Franklin Street it turned gradually southward to the junction of the north and south branches. The point of junction of the two streams was in sight from the Kinzie House. There was no sharp inlet in front of the Kinzie House, as represented in the cut, but there was a slight bend corresponding with the slight curve opposite. The direction of the cut through the sand-bar and the piers erected conformed to the general course of the River at the Kinzie House.

The cut shows the Block-House to be the highest building. It was considerably lower than the officers' or soldiers' quarters. The brick building, erected in about 1824 or '25, not shown in this cut, was the most prominent structure. It was located about 10 feet south of and parallel with the north picket, and about 10 or 15 feet west of the north gate. It was within the Fort enclosure, and would partially hide in this view the officers' original quarters. There was no fence along the River edge, east of the stockade.

The Kinzie House was about 200 feet from the River, with a piazza the whole length of its south front. The yard in front was enclosed by a split-picket fence. Inside and close to the east-and-west fence was a row of Lombardy poplar trees. From the piazza, the inside of the Fort was visible through to the south gate. G. S. HUBBARD.

FORT-DEARBORN MUSTER-ROLL,

THE LATEST ON FILE AT WASHINGTON BEFORE THE MASSACRE.

From a letter received from Hon. Robert T. Lincoln, Secretary of War, July 19, 1881, after most of this pamphlet had been printed, it appears that no Muster-Roll, giving the names of the garrison at Fort Dearborn in 1811 or '12, is on file in the War Department. But the general returns of the U. S. Army show that the Fort was garrisoned from June 4, 1804, to June, 1812, by a portion of the 1st Infantry. In these returns, the strength of the garrison, including commissioned and non-commissioned officers, musicians, and privates, is given at various times as follows: June 4, 1804, Capt. John Whistler, 69; Dec. 31, 1806, ————, 66; Sept. 30, 1809, Capt. John Whistler, 77; Sept. 30, 1810, Capt. Nathan Heald, 67; Sept. 30, 1811, Capt. Nathan Heald, 51; June —, 1812, Capt. Nathan Heald, 53.

The name of Fort Dearborn appears upon record as early as June 4, 1804.

The Muster-Roll of the garrison of Fort Dearborn, that is here given, was obtained from the Third Auditor's Office of the Treasury Department, where it is on file as a voucher. It is of the latest date that can be found. From the same office was obtained the affidavit of William Griffith and the letter by Capt. Nathan Heald.

88   FORT DEARBORN.

Muster-Roll of a Company of Infantry under the command of Captain Nathan Heald in the First Regiment of the United States, commanded by Colonel Jacob Kingsbury, from Nov. 30, when last Mustered, to Dec. 31, 1810:

NO.	NAMES.	RANK.	App'ed or Enlisted.	Remarks and Changes since last Muster.
1	Nathan Heald,	Captain,	31 Jan., 1807,	On furlough in Massachusetts.
2	Phillip O'Strander,	2d Lieu't,	1 May, 1808,	Present, of Capt. Rhea's Co., Act. asst.
3	Seth Thompson,	"	18 Aug., 1808,	" M'y agent. Sick.
4	John Cooper,	Surg. Mate,	13 June, 1808,	"
1	Joseph Glass,	Sergeant,	18 June, 1806,	" [Term of all enlisted men, 5 yrs.]
2	John Crozier,	"	2 July, 1808,	"
3	Richard Rickman,	"	10 May, 1806,	"
1	Thomas Forth,	Corporal,	6 July, 1807,	"
2	Asa Cambell,	"	26 Jan., 1810,	"
3	Rhodias Jones,	"	9 Dec., 1807,	"
4	Richard Garner,	"	2 Oct., 1810,	"
1	George Burnet,	Fifer,	1 Oct., 1806,	"
2	John Smith,	"	27 June, 1806,	"
3	John Hamilton,	Drummer,	5 July, 1808,	"
4	Hugh McPherson,	"	20 Oct., 1807,	"
1	John Allen,	Private,	27 Nov., 1810,	"
2	George Adams,	"	21 Aug., 1805,	"
3	Presley Andrews,	"	11 July, 1806,	" Sick.
4	Thomas Ashbrook,	"	29 Dec., 1805,	Term of service expired, 29 Dec., 1810.
5	Thomas Burnes,	"	8 June, 1806,	Present.
6	Patrick Burk,	"	27 May, 1806,	" Sick.
7	Redmond Berry,	"	2 July, 1806,	"
8	William Best,	"	22 April, 1806,	" Unfit for service.
9	James Chapman,	"	1 Dec., 1805,	Time expired, 1 December, 1810.
10	James Corbin,	"	2 Oct., 1810,	Present
11	Fielding Corbin,	"	7 Dec., 1805,	Time expired, 7 December, 1810.
12	Silas Clark,	"	15 Aug., 1806,	On command at Fort Wayne.
13	James Clark,	"	4 Dec., 1805,	Time expired, 4 December, 1810.
14	Dyson Dyer,	"	1 Oct., 1810,	Present. Sick.
15	Stephen Draper,	"	19 July, 1806,	"
16	Daniel Doryberry,	"	13 Aug., 1807,	"
17	Michijah Denison,	"	24 April, 1806,	"
18	Nathan Edson,	"	6 April, 1810,	"
19	John Fury,	"	29 Mch., 1808,	"
20	Paul Grummo,	"	1 Oct., 1810,	"
21	William N. Hunt,	"	8 Oct., 1810,	"
22	John Kelso,	"	17 Dec., 1805,	Time of service expired, 17 Dec., 1810.
23	David Kennison,	"	14 Mch., 1808,	Present.
24	Samuel Kilpatrick,	"	20 Dec., 1810,	" Re-enlisted, 20 Dec., 1810.
25	Jacob Laudon,	"	28 Nov., 1807,	" Unfit for service.
26	James Latta,	"	10 April, 1810,	"
27	Michael Lynch,	"	20 Dec., 1810,	" Re-enlisted, 20 Dec., 1810.
28	Michael Leonard,	"	13 April, 1810,	"
29	Hugh Logan,	"	5 May, 1806,	"
30	Frederick Locker,	"	13 April, 1810,	"
31	Andrew Loy,	"	6 July, 1807,	"
32	August Mortt,	"	9 July, 1806,	"
33	Ralph Miller,	"	19 Dec., 1805,	Time of service expired, 19 Dec., 1810.
34	Peter Miller,	"	13 June, 1806,	Present. Unfit for service.
35	Duncan McCarty,	"	31 Aug., 1807,	"
36	Patrick McGowen,	"	30 April, 1806,	"
37	James Mabury,	"	14 April, 1806,	"
38	William Moffitt,	"	23 April, 1806,	"
39	John Moyan,	"	28 June, 1806,	"
40	John Needs,	"	5 July, 1808,	"
41	Joseph Noles,	"	8 Sept., 1810,	"
42	Thomas Poindexter,	"	3 Sept., 1810,	"
43	William Prickitt,	"	6 June, 1806,	"
44	Frederick Peterson,	"	1 June, 1808,	"
45	David Sherror,	"	1 Oct., 1810,	"
46	John Suttonfield,	"	8 Sept., 1807,	"
47	John Smith,	"	2 April, 1808,	"
48	James Starr,	"	18 Nov., 1809,	"
49	Phillip Smith,	"	30 April, 1806,	"
50	John Simmons,	"	14 Mch., 1810,	" Pay due from 1 July, 1810; sick.
51	James Van Horne,	"	2 May, 1810,	" Sick.
52	Anthony L. Waggoner,	"	9 Jan., 1806,	"

RECAPITULATION:
Present, fit for duty, 50; sick, 6; unfit for service, 3. On command, 1. On furlough, 1. Discharged, 6. Total, 67.

We certify on honor that this Muster-Roll exhibits a true statement of the company commanded by Capt. Nathan Heald, and that the remarks set opposite their names are accurate and just

PH. O'STRANDER, Lieut.,
Commanding the Company,
J. COOPER, S.-Mate.

THE LAST PAYMENT TO THE GARRISON OF FORT DEARBORN BEFORE THE MASSACRE.

TERRITORY OF MICHIGAN, } to wit:
DISTRICT OF DETROIT. Personally appeared before me, the undersigned, a justice-of-the-peace in and for the district aforesaid, William Griffith, late lieutenant of the 28th United States Regiment of Infantry, who, being duly sworn, deposeth and saith that in the month of June, 1812, he, deponent, was orderly-sergeant of Capt. Heald's company of the 1st Regiment of U. S. Infantry, stationed at Fort Dearborn, Chicago, and well knows that said company was paid in the month of June, 1812, by Lieut. Eastman[*], through Capt. Heald, nine months' pay to the said month of June inclusive, and that the company at that time consisted of sixty-five rank and file, who, together with the officers, received nine months' pay as aforesaid; and deponent further saith that as he then understood and verily believes there was at the same time a deposit made and left in the hands of Capt. Heald of three months' additional pay, which, together with other public property, was taken by the Indians on the 15th of August, following, in consequence of the capture of the place.

WM. GRIFFITH.

Sworn to and subscribed before me,   THOMAS ROWLAND,
this 22d day of July, A.D. 1818.   Justice-of-the-Peace.

STATE OF NEW HAMPSHIRE, } Hollis, Sept. 25, 1819.
HILLSBOROUGH, ss. I, the undersigned, a justice-of-the-peace in and for the County aforesaid, do certify that I have carefully examined and compared the foregoing copy with the original, and find it true and correct.

BENJA. FARLEY, Justice-Peace.

ST. CHARLES, MISSOURI TERRITORY, May 18th, 1820.

SIR:—I had the honor of receiving your letter of the 30th of March, a few days since. The garrison at Chicago, commanded by me at the time Detroit was surrendered by Gen. Hull, were every man paid up to the 30th of June, 1812, inclusive, officers' subsistence and forage included.

The last payment embraced nine months, and was made by myself as the agent of Mr. Eastman, he having deposited the money with me for that purpose. After making the payment, there was a small balance remaining in my hands in favor of Mr. Eastman, but I can not say what the amount was. Every paper relative to that transaction was soon after lost. I am, however, confident there was no deposit with me to pay the garrison for the three months' subsequent to the 30th of June, 1812.

The receipt-rolls which I had taken for Mr. Eastman, together with the balance of money in my hands, fell into the hands of the Indians on the 15th of August, 1812, when the troops under my command were defeated near Chicago; what became of them afterwards, I know not. I have no papers in my possession relative to that garrison excepting one muster-roll for the month of May, 1812. By it I find the garrison then consisted of one captain; one 2d-lieutenant; one ensign; one surgeon's-mate; 4 sergeants; 2 corporals; 4 musicians; and 41 privates. I can not determine what the strength of the garrison was at any other time during the years 1811 and 1812, but it was on the decline. Monthly returns were regularly transmitted to the adjutant and inspector-general's office, at Washington City, which, I suppose, can be found at any time.   I am respectfully, sir, your most obed't serv't,

PETER HAGNER, Esq., 3d Auditor's Office,   NATHAN HEALD.
Treasury Department, Washington City.

[*] Jonathan Eastman, from Vermont, was appointed ensign, 1st Infantry, July, 18, 1803; 2d-lieutenant Artillery, March, 1805; District Paymaster, 1806; 1st-lieutenant, June, 1807; disbanded, May, 1814.

90   FORT DEARBORN.

Semi-Annual Muster-Roll of Capt. St. Clair Denny's Company, ("A") of the **Fifth Regiment of Infantry, Army of** the United States, (Col. Bvt. Brig.-Gen. **George M. Brooke,) from June 30,** 1836, when last **mustered, to Dec. 31, 1836.**

NO.	NAMES.	RANK.	ENLISTED. WHEN.	WHERE.	YRS.	REMARKS.
1	St. Clair Denny,	Capt.,	April 1, '36,	[Penn.]	–	Commanding Company.
2	E. K. Smith, - -	1st-Lt.,	March 4, '33,	[Conn.]	–	[joined since his promotion.
3	Samuel Whitehorn,	2d-Lt.,	Oct. 31, '36,	[R. I.]	–	At Ft. Winnebago, not having
1	Nathan'l Carpenter,	Sergt.,	April 13, '35,	Ft. Dearb'n,	3	Orderly Sergeant.
2	Michael Rothmon,	"	April 18, '34,	Albany,	3	Promoted to Sergt., Nov. 21, '36.
1	John Jack, - - -	Corpl.,	July 14, '36,	Ft. Dearb'n,	3	Appointed Corpl., Sept. 20, '36.
2	Daniel O'Connell,	"	Nov. 2, '36,	Ft. Dearb'n,	3	Appointed Corpl., Nov. 21, 1836.
1	Benjamin Yoemans,	Mus.,	May 1, '35,	Ft. Howard,	3	
2	Michael Walsh, -	"	Dec. 26, '36,	Ft. Dearb'n,	3	
1	Wm. R. Armstrong,	Pvt.,	April 30, '34,	Albany,	3	
2	John Aylward, -	"	June 26, '35,	Utica,	3	
3	David Barry, -	"	May 7, '34,	Utica.	3	
4	Thomas Brown, -	"	May 11, '35,	Ft. Dearb'n,	3	
5	Richard Clegg, -	"	April 23, '34,	Rochester,	3	On extra duty as Teamster, by
6	James M. Clemons,	"	Sept. 22, '36,	Ft. Dearb'n,	3	[order of Capt. Denny.
7	Thorndike Clary, -	"	Dec. 5, '36,	" "	3	
8	Hugh Donoly, -	"	May 6, '34,	Utica,	3	
9	Alvah Freeman, -	"	June 9, '35,	Albany,	3	
10	John Fisher, - -	"	Dec. 8, '35,	Ft. Dearb'n,	3	
11	John Gant, - - -	"	Oct. 22, '36,	" "	3	[by order of Capt. Denny.
12	Wm. S. Grames, -	"	May 11, '35,	" "	3	On extra duty Hospital Steward,
13	John Kane, - - -	"	April 26, '34,	Albany,	3	
14	Isaac Lane, - -	"	July 1, '35,	Ft. Dearb'n,	3	Deserted from Ft. Dearb'n, Sept. 22, appreh'd at Mackinac, Sept. 30, 1836.
15	Donold McKenzie,	"	July 6, '36,	" "	3	$10 paid for appreh'n, in confinement
16	George McGregor,	"	Feb. 5, '33,	Sacket's H.,	5	at Fort Mackinac.
17	Ezekiel Napton, -	"	April 10, '36,	Ft. Dearb'n,	3	On extra duty as Teamster, by
18	Hiram Persons, -	"	Feb. 19, '33,	Rochester,	5	[order of Capt. Denny.
19	William Pix, - -	"	July 25, '36,	Ft. Dearb'n,	3	
20	William Thompson,	"	Jan. 20, '36,	" "	3	
21	Marvin R. Wade,	"	May 9, '34,	Rochester,	3	
22	Edward Weever,	"	July 13, '36,	Ft. Dearb'n,	3	

DISCHARGED:

1	Sinclair Cree, - -	Pvt.,	Oct. 20, '33,	White Hall,	3	Term of enlistment expired.

DESERTED:

1	Henry Stark, - -	Corpl.,	March 1, '36,	Ft. Dearb'n,	3	July 17, '36, from Ft. Dearborn.
2	Lorin Bingham, -	Pvt.,	June 22, '35,	Utica,	3	Aug. 25, '36, " "
3	James Clark, - -	"	Jan. 12, '33,	Sacket's H.,	3	July 25, '36, " "
4	John G. Doherty,	"	May 27, '35,	Syracuse,	3	June 26, '36, " Jefferson Bar.
5	Lorenzo Downing,	"	Feb. 21, '35,	Ft. Dearb'n,	3	July 8, '36, his furlough expired.
6	Hiram Lyon, - -	"	April 23, '34,	Albany,	3	July 29, '36, from Ft. Dearborn.
7	Franklin Mills, -	"	June 25, '35,	Syracuse,	3	July 25, '36, " "
8	John Shehan, - -	"	June 23, '35,	Utica,	3	Aug. 2, '36, " "
9	Thomas Cassidy, -	"	Feb. 15, '33,	Sacket's H.,	5	Aug. 28, '36, " "
10	Donold McKenzie,	"	July 6, '36,	Ft. Dearb'n,	3	Sept. 22, '36, " "
11	John Bryson, - -	Corpl.,	June 10, '35,	Rochester,	3	Oct. 6, '36, " "
12	James Youngs, -	Pvt.,	June 24, '35,	Albany,	3	Oct. 16, '36, " "
13	James A. Lynch, -	"	Nov. 22, '33,	Ft. Dearb'n,	3	Oct. 22, '36, " "
14	Alvarado Burt, -	Mus.,	July 25, '36,	" "	3	Dec. 14, '36, " "
15	Peter Shepperd, -	Pvt.,	June 23, '35,	Utica,	3	Dec. 15, '36, " "
16	Thomas Brady, -	"	Oct. 25, '36,	Ft. Dearb'n,	3	Dec. 22, '36, " "
17	George Gardiner, -	"	June 17, '35,	Syracuse,	3	Dec. 23, '36, " "
18	William Brady, -	"	June 17, '35,	Rochester,	3	Dec. 25, '36, " "
19	David H. Pierson,	"	Oct. 21, '36,	Ft Dearb'n,	3	Dec. 26, '36, " "

RESIGNED:

1	T. Stockton, - -	2d-Lt.,	July 1, '34,	[Del.]	–	Resigned, Oct. 31, 1836.

RECAPITULATION:—Present, fit for duty, 26; on extra duty, 3. Absent on detached service, 1; in confinement, 1. Total, 37. Alterations since last muster: enlisted in 12; transferred, 1; desertion, 1; total, 14. Discharged by expiration of service, 2; deserted, 19.

[Certificates signed by]   ST. CLAIR DENNY, Captain 5th Infantry.
[Dated at] Camp Brady, Wisconsin Terr'y, Dec. 31, '36. Received at A.-G. O., Feb. 25, '37.
Left Ft. Dearb'n, Chicago, Ill., on Dec. 29, '36, and arr'd at C'p Brady, W. T., Dec. 30, '36.

APPENDIX—ADDITIONAL EARLY RECORDS.

Semi-Annual Muster-Roll of Capt. and Bvt.-Maj. **Wilcox's Company, ("B,")** of the Fifth Regiment of Infantry, Army of the United States, (Col. Bvt. Brig.-Gen. George M. Brooke,) from June 30, 1836, when last mustered, to Dec. 31, 1836.

NO.	NAMES.	RANK.	ENLISTED. WHEN.	WHERE.	YRS.	REMARKS.
1	D. Wilcox, Capt.	& Bt. Mj.	April 1, '22,	—	—	On Detached Serivce, Recruting.
2	J. H. Whipple,	2d-Lt.	Oct. 31, '36,	[Mass.]		At Fort Winnebago, not having
1	Dudley Johnson, Or. Serg.		Aug. 17, '34,	Ft. Dearb'n,	3	[joined since promotion.
2	Conrad Schopfer,	Sergt.,	Feb. 23, '33,	Buffalo,	5	
3	Hiram Bogert,	"	May 9, '35,	Rochester,	3	Promoted to Sergt., Nov. 21, '36.
1	Arnold Reynolds,	Corpl.	April 18, '36,	Ft. Dearb'n.	3	Des'd 15, app'd Aug. 20, '36, pard.
2	Richard Vennor,	"	June 27, '35,	Albany,	3	Appointed Corpl., Nov. 21, '36.
1	Henry I. Ostrom,	Mus.,	Aug. 29, '36,	Ft. Dearb'n,	3	
1	Edward Burrows,	Priv'te,	Dec. 7, '36,	" "	3	
2	William Bell,	"	Oct. 3, '36,	"	3	Reënlisted, Oct. 3, 1836.
3	Luke Brennan,	"	May 29, '35,	Rochester,	3	
4	Michael Enghart,	"	April 17, '36,	Ft. Dearb'n,	3	
5	John Foss,	"	June 30, '35,	Albany,	3	
6	Samuel Granger,	"	May 25, '35,		3	Left sick at Chicago.
7	John Guy,	"	Sept. 28, '36,	Ft. Dearb'n,	3	Reënlisted, Sept. 28, 1836.
8	Peter Johnson,	"	June 29, '37,	Philadelp'a,	5	
9	John King,	"	Dec. 24, '36,	Ft. Dearb'n,	3	
10	John B. LaFontine,	"	Dec. 28, '35,	" "	3	
11	John F. Mapes,	"	June 24, '35,	Syracuse,	3	
12	Wesley B. Porter,	"	Nov. 13, '36,	Ft. Dearb'n,	3	
13	William Reed,	"	Feb. 12, '35,	New York,	3	
14	John Summers,	"	June 27, '35,	Albany,	3	
15	John Smith,	"	May 1, '34,	Utica,	3	[joined since transfer.
16	Peter Sang,	"	June 18, '35,	Albany,	3	At Fort Winnebago, not having
17	Robert Wiliston,	"	Dec. 28, '32,	Buffalo,	5	["E," at Ft. Winnebago.

TRANSFERRED:

1	A. H. Tappen, Bvt. 2d-Lt.,		July 1, '35,	[Ohio.]		Prom'd and transf'd to Company
2	L. T. Jamison,	1st-Lt.,	April 30, '36,	[Virginia.]		Prom'd to Capt. of Comp'y "F."
3	J. L. Thompson,	2d-Lt.,	July 1, '28,	[Tennessee,]		Prom'd to 1st-Lt. of Comp'y "F."
4	Joseph Adams, Or. Sergt.,		May 1, '34,	Ft. Dearb'n,	3	Left at Chicago.

DISCHARGED:

1	Robert Lingard,	Priv'te,	Aug. 14, '33,	Chicago,	3	Term expired, Aug. 14, 1836.
2	William Bell,	"	Oct. 10, '33,	Ft. Dearb'n,	3	" " Oct. 10, 1836.
3	John Guy,	"	Oct. 23, '33,	"	3	" " Oct. 23, 1836.
4	Antonie Ritchner,	"	Oct. 30, '33,	New York,	3	" " Oct. 30, 1836.
5	Hugh Livingston,	"	Oct. 20, '36,	Ft. Dearb'n,	3	Disch'g'd, Nov. 29, '36; Disable.
6	William Adams,	"	Dec. 28, '33,	Chicago,	3	Term expired, Dec. 28, 1836.

DESERTED:

1	Robert Rand,	Priv'te,	April 25, '34,	Rochester,	3	July 18, '36, from Ft. Dearborn,
2	Moulton Bartlett,	"	July 1, '35,	Rochester,	3	July 22, '36, " "
3	Otto Miller,	"	Feb. 17, '32,	Buffalo,	5	July 25, '36, " "
4	Rich. VanVraukin,	"	June 6, '35,	Utica,	3	July 26, '36, " "
5	George B. Mack,	"	June 16, '35,	Rochester,	3	July 30, '36, " "
6	William Tripp,	"	April 29, '34,	Albany,	3	Aug. 6, '36, " "
7	Arnold Reynolds,	Corpl.,	April 18, '36,	Ft. Dearb'n,	3	Aug. 15, '36, " "
8	David Sherman,	Priv'te,	April 17, '34,	Rochester,	3	Aug. 30, '36, " "
9	Daniel W. Johnson,	Corpl,	June 6, '35,	"	3	Oct. 6, '36, " "
10	John P. Bennett,	Priv'te,	June 2, '35,	"	3	Oct. 12, '36, " "
11	Martin Redding,	"	June 16, '35,	Albany,	3	Oct. 12, '36, " "
12	Thomas D. Vault,	"	May 8, '36,	Ft. Dearb'n,	3	Nov. 17, '36, " "
13	Palmer Robinson,	Mus.,	May 25, '35,	Syracuse,	3	Dec. 15, '36, " "
14	Joseph C. M. Cole,	Priv'te,	June 27, '35,	Rochester,	3	Dec. 15, '36, " "
15	Horace H. Wheeler,	"	April 18, '35,	"	3	Dec. 15, '36, " "
16	Horatio Feebe,	"	Sept. 12, '36,	Ft. Dearb'n,	3	Dec. 19, '36, " "
17	Patrick McMullen,	"	June 10, '35,	Baltimore,	3	Dec. 21, '36, " "
18	Patrick Welch,	"	April 2, '35,	Frederk't'n,	3	Dec. 25, '36, " "
19	Richard Parker,	"	May 16, '34,	Utica,	3	Dec. 27, '36, " "

RECAPITULATION:—Present for duty, 21; absent on detached service, 3; sick, 1; Total, 25. Alterations since last muster: recruits from depots, 7; reënlisted, 2; by transfer, 1: desertion, 1; total, 11. Discharged, 6; transferred, 5; deserted, 19.

[C'tif's signed by] J. H. WHIPPLE, Lt. Com'd'g Co., [and] ST. CLAIR DENNY, Capt. 5th Infy.
[Dated at] Camp Brady, Wisconsin Terr'y. Dec. 31, 1836.

Left Ft. Dearb'n, Chicago, Ill., Dec. 29, '36, and arr'd at Camp Brady, W. T., Dec. 30, '36.

APPENDIX—FORT DEARBORN, ETC. 93

The cut on above page, from a photo. taken in 1855, by Alex. Hester, from the U. S. Marine Hospital, looking north-west, correctly represents two of the principal buildings of the Fort —the Commandant's Quarters, A (brick, about 25 x 50 ft.), and the Officers' Quarters, B (wood, about 30 x 60 ft.), occupying the north-west corner of the enclosure. C is the parade-ground (80 x 250 ft.); D is the Sutler's; E the north gate. The figure in the foreground, in uniform, represents Col. J. D. Graham, U. S. Engineer, in charge of Govt. Works, and residing in the Fort, and, to his right, Mr. and Mrs. John H. Kinzie. The vessel in the river on the right is the brig *Maria Hilliard*. The Rush-St. Ferry was used to cross the river here, and landed on the South-side at a point, indicated in this view, under the west chimney of the Commandant's quarters; the direction of the ferry from this point to the North-side was nearly north-west; width of the channel, 225 feet.

1. St. James Church, Cass St., S. of Illinois, E. front, brick, about 40 x 80 ft.; on S. 70 ft. of lots 1 and 2, blk 12, Kinzie's Add'n. 2. Residence of John H. Kinzie, N.-E. cor. Cass and Mich. Sts., 2½-story, brick, S. front. 3. Mrs. Robert Barr's Young Ladies' Boarding School, Mich. St., E. of Cass, N. front, 2-story and basement, brick. 4. Residence of Hon. John V. LeMoyne, N.-E. cor. Cass and Ill. Sts., cottage, S. front; 150 ft. west were those of C. R. Larrabee, 2-story, frame; Jas. J. Richards, 2-story, frame; and Wm. M. Larrabee, on N.-E. cor. N. State, 2-story, frame, all S. front. 5. Residence of Michael Mullin, waterman, Mich. St., N. front, 1½-story. 6. Residence of Henry Brown, S.-W. cor. N. State and Ontario Sts., E. front, 2-story, frame, with 1-story wings; just S. of this on Ohio St., S. front, was John B. Turner's, 2-story, frame. 7. Residence of John C. Dodge, Ontario St., 75 ft. W. of N. State, S. front, 2-story, frame. 8. House built by Govt. for Billy Caldwell, 1-story, frame, 20 x 45 ft. (was built on S. side Chicago Ave., bet. Cass and N. State, and removed by Gurdon S. Hubbard to Indiana St., 50 ft. W. of Cass, N. front. 9. Residence of Col. Richard J. Hamilton, Mich. St., bet. Rush and Cass, N. front, 2-story, frame. 10. Shakespeare Hotel (Edmund Gill, proprietor in 1839), 2-story, frame, N.-E. cor. Rush and Kinzie Sts. 11. Residence of Haines H. Magie, in blk. bounded by N. State, Ontario, Cass, and Ohio Sts., showing the E. front, 2½-story, brick. 12. Residence of Eli S. Prescott, N.-E. cor. Ill. and Cass Sts., W. front, brick cottage. 13. Residence of Col. Gurdon S. Hubbard, later of Samuel Lisle Smith, on S.-W. cor. Mich. and Rush Sts., 2½-story, brick, N. front. 14. Residence of Justin Butterfield, N.-W. cor. Mich. and Rush Sts., frame cottage, stone foundations, S. front (originally Robert A. Kinzie's), veranda on S. and E. fronts. 15. Residence of Judge Grant Goodrich, Ill. St., 80 ft. W. of Rush, S. front, 2-story, frame. 16. Church of the Holy Name, S.-E. cor. N. State and Superior Sts., W. front, brick and stone. 17. Coal Yard of C. H. Dyer, S.-E. cor Rush and Kinzie Sts., which was the site of Newberry & Dole's warehouse, destroyed by fire; immediately east and adjoining was Kinzie & Hunter's warehouse. 18 to 21 were formerly business houses, on N. side of Kinzie St., bet. Rush and Cass, but at this date were sailors' boarding-houses.

The Lake House was built in 1835, for a company of Northside business men, among whom were: Col. Gurdon S. Hubbard, Gen. David Hunter, John H. Kinzie, Dr. William B. Egan, and Maj. James B. Campbell; was opened in the fall of 1836, by Jacob Russell, was originally 3 stories and basement of brick, and cost nearly $100,000; was sold, some years later, under a mortgage held by Arthur Bronson, by Hon. Isaac N. Arnold, Att'y, to Hon. Thos. Dyer, for $10,000. In 1854, an additional story and cupola were added and was re-opened in 1855, by Geo. F. Boardman. For its foundations, 3 pieces of 8 x 8 pine timber were used, across these were nailed 2-inch pine plank, and upon this substitute for stone was laid the brickwork; in 1875, this timber was taken out perfectly sound.

East of and adjoining the Lake House on Kinzie St., S. front, was the residence of Dr. Edmund S. Kimberly, 2-story, brick, N. of the Lake House, on Mich. St., near Rush, was the residence of Geo. W. Dole; next E. Col. Thos. J. V. Owen's; and immediately N. of these, on Ill. St., was that of Gen. David Hunter; opposite, on the N.-W. cor. of Ill. and Pine, was that of Hon. Wm. H. Brown, and diagonally opposite, S. of the S.-W. cor. of Ill. and Pine Sts., Alex. Brand's.—F.

CHICAGO'S EARLY HARBOR.

MENOMINEE, MICH., April 13, 1881.

This morning, I saw a notice of the death of David McKee and Mark Beaubien. My mind is carried back to the time when my brother, wife, and two children, on the second day of October, 1836, landed off the little topsail-schooner *White Pigeon*, on about one hundred feet of dock—all there was at that time. Then young, but now an old man in my 73d year, it scarcely seems possible, yet all the little incidents and occurrences of that time are fresh in my mind. In Lake Huron our little craft was cast on her beam-ends in a terrible squall, but, after half an hour, righted, and managed to get into Presque Isle, ninety miles below Mackinaw, where we found six other schooners. The wind finally lulled and hauled round in the east, and we all came out and had a splendid run through the Straits, and up to the Manitous, when the wind hauled around to the northwest and gave us "Hail Columbia." We were three or four days in making the west shore, and then under close-reefed sails ran up to Chicago to find that we could not get into the harbor. They had got it dredged across the breadth of the peninsula, and timbers in sufficient to let small vessels through, but the terrible storm had torn up the timbers to such an extent, as to obstruct the passage entirely, and we were obliged to lie off till the obstruction was removed, when our schooner was warped in, but not one of the other six vessels got in. Two of them lost their masts and drove across the lake and beached. Two others, the *Erie* and *Cedes*, beached about three miles above the harbor. The *Martin Van Buren* attempted to enter the harbor, but the *Wm. Henry Harrison*, a larger vessel, coming in close behind, struck her in the stern, breaking a hole in her, when she sank, while the *Harrison* bounded off and glided around the pier and sunk on the south side. Many thought at the time it was portentious, and it looked something like it, as Gen. Harrison, in the pending presidential election, succeeded over Van Buren, and then died in thirty days. After the election of 1840 it was often spoken of. There was an immense quantity of dry-goods spoiled, or nearly so; the prairie was covered with prints, the house-tops with cloths and finer goods, and all were sold at auction that could be, and it was gay times and money was plenty. But before next spring the whole scene changed, and what a change! Wild-cat Banks first showed their eyes, then their claws, and then their teeth, and the crash came.

I really thought I would write an article, but being old and not very well I shall have to give it up, as it will be too long. At some future time, if I am well, I will give you a little touch of early times and scenes. [Died May 18, 1881.] THOMAS Q. GAGE.

INDEX.

A.

Abbott, *Dr.* Lucius, 16.
Ackerman, William K., 5.
Adair, John, 21.
Adams, George, 88.
Adams, Henry, 70.
Adams, Joseph, 32, 36, 70, 71, 91.
Adams, Ralph, 70.
Adams, William, 91.
Adams, William H., 65.
Adams, Sybel, 14.
Adams, Sarah H., married *Dr.* Allen W. Gray, 70.
Ah-mah-quau-zah-quuah, *or* Mary Wells, 45, 46.
Ah-pez-zah-quah, *or* Ann Wells, 45, 46.
Allen, B. F., 33.
Allen, James, 33-6, 38, 48, 71.
Allen, John, 88.
Ament, Anson, 66, 79.
Ament, Calvin, 66, 79.
Ament, Edward, 79.
Ament, Hiram, 79.
Ament, John, 79.
Ament, John, jr., 79.
Ament, Justus, 79.
Anderson, *Capt.* Thomas, 55, 57.
Andrews, Presley, 18, 88.
Anthony Wayne (steamboat), 75.
Appleby, *Capt.* Gilman, 84.
Archer, Robert H., 69.
Armstrong, Wm. R., 90.
Arnold, Isaac N., 3-6, 8, 23, 93.
Ashbrook, Thomas, 88.
Atwater, *Major*, 50.
Ayer, Benjamin F., 5.
Aylward, John, 90.

B.

Bailey, Daniel, 64.
Bailey, Jacob W., 69.
Bailey, Esther, 12.
Baker, Daniel, 23, 47.
Barber, William, 66.
Barclay, *Capt.*, 61.
Barr, *Mrs.* Robert, 93.
Barry, David, 90.
Bartlett, Moulton, 91.
Bates, George C., 26.
Bates, John, 4.
Bates, Kinzie, 26.
Bauer, Lawrence, 4.
Baxley, Joseph, 35, 48.
Beach, John, 69.
Beach, Samuel S., 5.
Beard, Henry S., 24.
Beard, *Mrs.* Henry S., 24.
Beaubien, Alexander, 5, 21, 26, 27, 79.
Beaubien, Charles, 44, 79.
Beaubien, David, 5.
Beaubien, Edward, 5.
Beaubien, Frank, 5.
Beaubien, Frank Gordon, 5, 79.
Beaubien, George, 5.
Beaubien, Henry, 5.
Beaubien, Isadore, 5.
Beaubien, *Gen.* John B., 5, 12, 15, 21, 24, 33, 38-42, 44, 55, 68, 71, 79, 85, 86.
Beaubien, John, 5.
Beaubien, Josette (Lafromboise), 24.
Beaubien, Maurice D.P., 5.
Beaubien, Mark, 5, 15, 34, 42, 44, 55, 66, 67, 68, 76, 77, 79, 94.
Beaubien, Mark, jr., 55.
Beaubien, Medore B., 21, 23, 24, 68.
Beaubien, Philip, 5.
Beaubien, Saliston, 5.
Beaubien, Slidell, 5.
Beaubien, Therese (Lafromboise) (Watkins), 24.
Beaubien, William R., 5.
Beaubien, William S., 5.
Beauregard, *Gen* P. G. T., 62.
Beebe, Horatio, 91.

Beeson, J. S. W., 25.
Bell, William, 91.
Bender, George, 34, 35, 48.
Benham, Henry W., 24.
Bennett, John P., 91.
Bennett, Reuben J., 4.
Bennett, Robert J., 3, 4, 5, 6.
Berry, Redmond, 88.
Best, William, 88.
Bishop, Levi, 84.
Bingham, Lorin, 90.
Black Bird (Indian chief), 52.
Black Hawk (Indian chief), 12, 31, 34, 37, 55, 65, 72, 73.
Black, Henry M., 82.
Black Snake, or *Capt.* William Wells, 45.
Blake, *Capt.* Chelsey, 75, 84, 85.
Blanchard, Rufus, 17.
Blodgett, *Judge* Henry W., 66.
Blodgett, I. P., 66.
Boardman, George E., 93.
Bogert, Hiram V., 91.
Bomford, James V., 69.
Bond, Ezra, 65.
Bond, Heman S., 65.
Bond, William, 65.
Boone, *Dr.* Levi D., 39.
Bouché, Henry, 65.
Bouché, Joseph, 25.
Housha, *or* Bouché, Henry, 65.
Bowen, James (or Joseph), 17, 53.
Bowman, James M., 69.
Brackett, John E., 69.
Brady, *Gen.* Hugh, 35, 71.
Brady, Thomas, 90.
Brady, William, 90.
Bradley, Hezekiah, 22, 23, 47.
Bradley, H., 73.
Brand, Alexander, 93.
Brennan, Luke, 91.
Brewster, Hogan & Co. (firm), 25.
Brewster, Theron D., 77.
Brice, Wallace A., 17.
Bristol, Robert C., 72, 75.
Bristol & Porter (firm), 76.
Brock, *Gen.* Isaac, 15, 59.
Bronson, Arthur, 93.
Brooke, George M., 90, 91.
Brooks, Samuel, 85.
Bross, William, 4, 67.
Brown, Adam, 61.
Brown, Henry, 17, 93.
Brown, *Gen.* Jacob, 27, 47.
Brown, Jacob, 69.

Brown, Jesse B., 65.
Brown, Rufus, 65.
Brown, Thomas, 90.
Brown, *Hon.* William H., 93.
Brush, Alfred, 69.
Bryson, John, 90.
Buchanan, *Pres.* James, 44.
Buckner, Simon B., 32.
Bunker Hill (steamboat), 75.
Burchard, Mathew, 39, 40, 42.
Burgoyne, *Gen.* John, 14, 44.
Burk, Patrick, 88.
Burley, Arthur G., 5.
Burnam, ———, 18.
Burnes, Thomas, 88.
Burnett, Ward Benjamin, 38, 69.
Burnett, George, 18, 88.
Burnham, ———, 74.
Burrows, Edward, 91.
Burt, Alvarado, 90.
Bushy, Joseph, 25.
Butterfield, Justin, 93.
Butterfield, Lyman, 66.

C.

Caldwell, Billy, *or* Sauganash (Indian Chief), 25–28, 31, 33, 60, 61, 68, 93.
Caldwell, Susan, 28.
Calhoun, John, 25.
Calhoun, John C., 22.
Calumet Club, 32, 44, 67, 68, 76, 77, 78, 79.
Cambell, Asa, 88.
Campbell, *Major* James B., 93.
Carey Mission, 25.
Carpenter, Philo, 33.
Carpenter, Nathaniel, 90.
Carter, Thomas B., 5.
Cass, George W., 69.
Cass, *Gen.* Lewis, 58, 59, 60, 71.
Cassidy, Thomas, 90.
Caton, John Dean, 22, 67, 70.
Cedes (schooner), 94.
Chamberlain, *Dr.*, 74.
Chamblee, *or* Shabonee (Indian ch'f), 27, 28, 31, 33, 58, 60, 61.
Chandonais, Jean Baptiste (Indian chief), 19, 20.
Chapman, James, 88.
Che-che-pin-gua, *or* Alexander Robinson (Indian chief), 26–8, 31, 33, 41.
Chetlain, A. L., 5, 15.
Clark, Denis, 66.
Clark, James, 88.

INDEX. 97

Clark, James, 90.
Clark, John M., 57.
Clark, *Mrs.* Robert, 57.
Clark, Silas, 88.
Clark, *Gen.* William, 49, 50.
Clary, Thorndike, 90.
Clay, Henry, 84.
Cleaver, Charles, 85.
Clegg, Richard, 90.
Clemons, James M., 90.
Clybourn, Archibald, 77.
Cocke, Philip St. George, 69.
Cole, Josephus C. M., 91.
Collins, James H., 40, 41.
Collinsworth, John T., 33, 48.
Columbus (steamboat), 75.
Commodore Perry (steamboat), 84.
Conrad, Charles M., 41.
Cooper, Isabella, 56.
Cooper, John, 18, 55, 56, 88.
Corbin, Fielding [or Phelim], 18, 53, 88.
Corbin, James, 18, 53, 88.
Corbin, Phelim [or Fielding], 18, 53, 88.
Corbin, *Mrs.* Phelim, 18, 53.
Corinthian Lodge (Free Mason), 14.
Cornwallis, *Lord*, 44.
Couch, James, 4.
Cree, Sinclair, 90.
Crittenden, George B., 69.
Crittenden, John J., 84.
Croghan, George, 58.
Crosby, Charles, 5.
Crozier, John, 88.
Cummings, Alexander, 23, 30, 47, 49.
Currin, John, 25.

D.

Daniel Webster (steamboat), 75.
Davis, Jefferson, 28, 29.
Day, Hannibal, 32, 48.
Dean, John, 27, 41, 86.
Dearborn, *Gen.* Henry, 9, 10, 14, 22, 59.
Dearborn, *Gen.* Henry A. S., 10.
Dearborn, Henry G. R., 10.
Deas, Edward, 69.
Debaif, Samuel, 65.
De Camp, *Dr.* Samuel G. I., 30, 31, 48, 49.
Denison, Michijah, 18, 88.
Denny, St. Clair, 35, 48, 90, 91.
Dewey, George, 80.

Dix, Robert S., 69.
Dodge, John C., 93.
Doe, John, 71.
Dole, George W., 25, 64, 93.
Doherty, John G., 90.
Donoly, Hugh, 90.
Dorr, ——— (Master of Schooner Tracy), 13.
Doryherty, Daniel, 88.
Douglas, Charles, 44.
Douglas, Stephen A., 23, 77.
Downing, Lorenzo, 90.
Downs, Oscar, 5.
Doyle, Alexander, 26.
Drake, Samuel G., 82.
Draper, Stephen, 88.
Dulanty, Michael, 4.
Dyer, C. H., 93.
Dyer, Dyson, 18, 53, 88.
Dyer, Thomas, 93.

E.

Eastman, *Lieut.* J. I., 50.
Eastman, Jonathan, 89.
Edson, Nathan, 17, 53, 88.
Edwards, Aaron, 59.
Edwards, *Dr.* Abraham, 55-60.
Edwards, Albert G., 69.
Edwards, A. H., 55-60.
Edwards, *Mrs.* Maria (Heald), 15.
Edwards, *Mrs.* Ruthy (Hunt), 59.
Edwards, T. A. H., 55, 57.
Egan, *Dr.* William B., 93.
Ellis, Samuel, 65.
Ellis & Fergus (firm), 17.
Enghart, Michael, 91.
Engle, James, 30, 48.
Engle, *Mrs.* James, 30.
Erie (schooner), 94.
Ewell, Benjamin S., 69.

F.

Fair, Richard G., 69.
Farley, Benjamin, 89.
Farnum, *Mrs.* Isabella (Cooper), 56.
Fearson, John, 13.
Fearson, Julia, 13.
Fearson, Mary (La Dake), 13.
Fergus, Robert, 17, 57, 58.
Findly, James, 59.
Finley, Clement A., 30, 48.
Fisher, John, 90.
Ford, *Judge* Thomas, 39.
Forth, Thomas, 88.

Foss, John, 91.
Foster, Amos, 30, 48.
Foster, Caleb, 66.
Foster, *Dr.* John H., 30.
Fowle, John, jr., 30, 33, 48.
Fox, George, 66.
Fox, John, 66.
Freeman, Alvah, 90.
Fuller, Henry, 43, 44.
Furman, John G., 30, 48.
Fury, John, 18, 88.

G.

Gage, S. T., 65.
Gage, Thomas Q., 94.
Galloway, Andrew J., 4.
Gant, John, 90.
Gardner, C. K., 14, 20, 45.
Gardner, George, 90.
Garner, Richard, 88.
Gatlin, Richard C., 69.
Gault, William, 66.
Gibson, John C., 44.
Giddings, Josiah H., 66.
Gilbert, *Mrs.* Mary Ann (Wolcott), 46.
Gill, Edmund, 93.
Ginsday, James, 65.
Glass, Joseph, 88.
Goodrich, Grant, 93.
Gordon, *Mrs.* Nellie (Kinzie), 23.
Graham, *Col.* J. D., 93.
Grames, Wm. S., 90.
Granger Samuel, 91.
Grant, *Gen.* Ulysses S., 82.
Graves, Dexter, 25.
Gray, *Dr.* Allen W., 70.
Gray, John, 70.
Gray, Wm. B. H., 5.
Great Western (steamboat), 75, 76.
Greene, John, 23, 35, 47, 48.
Greenough, Charles P., 82.
Griffin, George H., 69.
Griffith, William, 87, 89.
Griggs, Mathew, 46.
Griggs, Samuel, 46.
Gromet, *see* Grummon, 17, 18, 53.
Grummo, Paul, 17, 18, 53, 88.
Grummon, or Grummond, or Grummow, or Gromet, Paul, 17, 18, 53.
Guy, John, 91.

H.

Hackley, Ann, 45.
Hackley, John, 45.
Hackley, Rebecca (Wells), 46.
Hackley, *Capt.* ———, 45.
Hackley, *Mrs. Capt.* ———, 46.
Hadduck, Edward H., 25, 70.
Hager, Albert D., 4.
Hagnar, Peter, 89.
Haines, Elijah M., 4.
Hall, Eugene J., 3, 7.
Hamilton, Richard J., 64, 65.
Hamilton, John, 18, 88.
Hamlin, John, 26, 85.
Hardin, James P., 69.
Harmar, *Gen.* Josiah, 45.
Harmon, Charles L., 81.
Harmon, *Dr.* Elijah Dewey, 25, 65, 81.
Harmon, Isaac, 25, 65.
Harmon, Isaac D., 65, 81.
Harris, Benjamin, 65.
Harrison, Carter H., 4, 82.
Harrison, Edmund, 66.
Harrison, *Gen.* William H., 22, 28, 44, 46, 51, 57, 61, 82, 94.
Hays, *Sergeant*, 18.
Hawley, Perez, 66.
Heald, Darius, 5, 20-22.
Heald, Eliza, 15.
Heald, Jonas, 15.
Heald, Margaret, 20.
Heald, Maria, 15.
Heald, Mary, 20.
Heald, Nathan, 3, 14-6, 18-21, 45-7, 50-1, 53-5, 57, 83, 87, 88, 89.
Heald, *Mrs.* Rebekah (Wells), 14, 16, 18-20, 47, 53.
Heald, *Mrs.* Sybel (Adams), 14.
Heald, Thomas, 14.
Heald, *Judge* Thomas, 15.
Helm, Charles J., 16.
Helm, Francis T., 16.
Helm, Linai T., 16, 52, 53.
Helm, *Mrs.* Louise (Whistler), 16.
Helm, *Mrs.* Margaret (McKillup), 16, 52, 53, 83.
Helm, William Edwin, 16.
Helm, William Willis, 16.
Henry Clay (steamboat), 37, 38, 72.
Hernandez, *General* Joseph, 24.
Herndon, John F., 65.
Hesler, Alexander, 93.
Hickling, William, 27.
Hill, Thomas M., 69.
Hilliard, Maria (vessel), 93.
Hobson, Basley, 66.

INDEX.

Hogan, John S. C., 25, 64.
Holden, Charles C. P., 5.
Holt, *Sergeant*, 18.
Holt, wife of *Sergeant*, 18.
Hooke, Moses, 11.
Hotchkiss, Miles, 26.
Howell, George, 76.
Howell, Lewis, 69.
Hoyne, Frank, 5.
Hoyne, Thomas, 3, 4, 6.
Hoyt, William M., 3, 5, 6.
Hubbard, Gurdon S., 4, 6, 31, 76, 83, 85, 87, 93.
Hull, *Gen.* William, 15, 18, 42, 51, 53, 55, 59, 60, 67, 79, 89.
Humphreys, *Gen.* A. A., 34, 36.
Hunt, Alexander, 59.
Hunt, *Gen.* Henry J., 56, 59.
Hunt, *Gen.* Lewis C., 56.
Hunt, Ruthy, 55, 59.
Hunt, Samuel W., 56.
Hunt, Thomas, 54, 56, 57, 59.
Hunt, Thomas, jr., 56, 57, 59.
Hunt, William N., 88.
Hunter, *Gen.* David, 28, 30, 48, 93.
Hurlbut, H. H., 12.

I.

Illinois (steamboat), 75, 84, 85.
Irwin, Mathew, 25, 49, 83.
Irvine, Mathew, 49.

J.

Jack, John, 90.
Jackson, *Pres.* Andrew, 38, 60, 63.
Jackson, John, 39.
Jackson, Samuel, 81.
James Allen (steamboat), 34.
James Madison (steamboat), 75.
Jameson, *Judge* John A., 4.
Jamison, Lewis T., 33, 36, 48, 70, 71, 91.
Jefferson, *Pres.* Thomas, 9, 59, 62.
Jewett or Jouett, Charles, 25, 85.
Jocelyn & Chamberlin (firm), 76.
Johnson, Daniel W., 91.
Johnson, Dudley, 91.
Johnson, Harriet, 32.
Johnson, Peter, 91.
Johnson, Richard M., 58.
Johnson, Seth, 32, 37, 48, 74.
Johnston, John, 49, 82, 83.
Johnston, *Mrs.* John, 83.

Jones, Rhodias, 88.
Jones, *Gen.* Roger, 47, 49.
Jordon, Walter, 50, 51.
Jouett, Charles, 25, 85.
Joy, James F., 42.

K.

Kane, Elias K., 26.
Kane, John, 90.
Keamble, ——, 18.
Kello, William O., 69.
Kelso, John, 88.
Kenney, T. B., 35.
Kennison, David, 88.
Kerchival, Gholson, 25, 64.
Keyes, Erasmus D., 69.
Kilpatrick, Samuel, 88.
Kimball, Mark, 5.
Kimball, Walter, 4.
Kimball, ——, 18.
Kimberly, *Dr.* Edmund S., 93.
King, John, 91.
King, Sherman, 66.
King, W. H., 5.
King, *Vice-Pres.* William R., 60.
Kingsbury, Gaines P., 69.
Kingsbury, Jacob, 88.
Kingsbury, Julius J. B., 32, 48.
Kinzie, *Mrs.* Eleanor (McKillup), 26, 83.
Kinzie, Ellen M., 26, 54.
Kinzie, James, 65, 71.
Kinzie, John, 16, 21, 25, 26, 30, 54, 83, 85, 86.
Kinzie, John H., 10, 11, 16, 17, 23, 54, 85, 93.
Kinzie, *Mrs.* Juliette A., 11, 14, 17, 27, 50, 85, 86, 93.
Kinzie, *Mrs.* Louise (Whistler), 16.
Kinzie, Maria H., 30, 54.
Kinzie, Nellie (Gordon), 23.
Kinzie, Robert A., 12, 16, 25, 54, 55, 67, 93.
Kinzie, *Mrs.* Robert A., 12, 16.
Kinzie & Hunter (firm), 76, 93.
Kirk & Co., James S. (firm), 86.
Klokke, E. F. C., 4.
Knapp, H. S., 17, 57.
Knickerbocker, A. V., 34.
Knowles, Joseph [or Noles], 17, 53, 88.

L.

Labaque, Francis, 65.

INDEX.

LaDake, Mary, 13.
Lafayette, *Marquis de*, 56.
LaFontine, John B., 91.
Lafromboise, Claude, 24, 65.
Lafromboise, Francis, 24.
Lafromboise, Francis, jr., 24.
Lafromboise, Joseph, sen., 24.
Lafromboise, Joseph, 24, 65.
Lafromboise, Josette, married Benj. K. Pierce, 24.
Lafromboise, Josette, married John B. Beaubien, 24.
Lafromboise, Madeline (Marcotte), 24.
Lafromboise, Therese (Schindler), 24.
Lafromboise, Therese (Watkins), 24.
Lalime, J., 82, 83.
Landon N., 4.
Lane, Isaac, 90.
Lane, James, 4.
Langdon, Daniel, 66.
Larrabee, C. Rolin, 93.
Larrabee, Wm. M., 93.
Lasby, Samuel C., 44, 80.
Latta, James, 88.
Laudon, Jacob, 88.
Leavenworth, *Gen.* Henry, 70.
Leavenworth, Jesse H., 36, 78.
Leavenworth, *Mrs.* Jesse H., 36.
Le Clerc, Peresh, 26.
Lee, or See, ———, 50.
Leonard Michael, 88.
LeMoyne, John V., 93.
Lincoln, *Pres.* Abraham, 29.
Lincoln, Robert T., 87.
Lindsley, A. B., 26.
Lingard, Robert, 91.
Little Turtle, or Me-che-kau-nah-qua (Indian chief), 45, 46, 54, 82.
Livingston, Eliza Matilda, 36, 81.
Livingston, Hugh, 91.
Livingston, Peter William, 81.
Locker, Frederick, 18, 88.
Logan, Hugh, 18, 53, 88.
Long, Edwin R., 33, 48.
Long, James, 44.
Lossing, Benson J., 17.
Lovell, Mansfield, 36.
Loy, Andrew, 88.
Lynch, James A., 90.
Lynch, Michael, 18, 88.
Lyon, Hiram, 90.
Lyon, Nathaniel, 82.

M.

Mabury, James, 88.
Mack, George B., 91.
Macomb, *Gen.* Alexander, 27, 30, 35, 47, 49.
Macomb, John M., 37, 69.
Madison, *Pres.* James, 46, 59, 62.
Magie, Haines H., 93.
Mainpoe (Indian chief), 82.
Mapes, John F., 91.
Manning, John, 66.
Marcotte, Jean Baptiste, 24.
Marcotte, Madeline, 24.
Marcy, Randolph B., 69.
Marfitt, ———, 18.
Maria Hilliard (vessel), 93.
Martin Van Buren (schooner), 94.
Marquette, Jacques, 6.
Marshall, Humphrey, 31, 69.
Marshall, James A., 77.
Mathews, Elizabeth, 68, 79.
Mathews, George, 68, 79.
Maxwell, *Dr.* Philip, 31, 32, 48.
McArthur, *Gen.* Duncan, 59.
McBride, ———, 17.
McCarty, Duncan, 88.
McCausland, David, 20.
McCausland, *Mrs.* Mary (Heald), 20.
McChesney, ———, 5.
McClellan, John, 36.
McClellan, Robert, 36.
McClure, *Gen.* George W., 33.
McClure, *Mrs.* Harriet (Johnson), 32.
McClure, Josiah E., 32.
McConnell, Murray, 39.
McCoy, *Rev. Mr.*, 46.
McDuffie, Franklin, 31, 69.
McFadyen, *Capt.* John, 75.
McGowan, Patrick, 88.
McGregor, George, 90.
McKee, David, 25, 64, 65, 68, 94.
McKeever, Chauncey, 49.
McKillup, Eleanor, 26.
McKillup, Margaret, 16.
McKillup, *Capt.* ———, 16.
McKenzie, Donold, 90.
McMullen, Patrick, 91.
McNeil, *Gen.* John, 23, 24, 47.
McNeil, J. W. S., 24.
McPherson, Hugh, 18, 88.
Meacham, Silas, 44.
Me-che-kau-nah-qua, or Little Turtle (Indian chief), 45, 46, 54, 82.

Michigan (steamboat), 75, 84.
Miller, *Gen.* James, 59.
Miller, Otto, 91.
Miller, Peter, 88.
Miller, Ralph, 88.
Miller, Samuel, 65.
Milliken, Isaac L., 5.
Mills, Elias, 17, 18, 53.
Mills, ———, 18.
Mills, Franklin, 90.
Miranda, Victoria, 25.
Moffitt, William, 88.
Monroe, *Pres.* James, 22, 60.
Monroe (steamboat), 75.
Morfit, ———, 18.
Mooris, H. V., 76.
Mortt, August [or Motte], 18, 53, 88.
Moselle, Charles, 65.
Motte, August [or Mortt], 18, 53 88.
Moyan, John, 88.
Murray, Robert N., 66.

N.

Naper, John, 66.
Naper, Joseph, 65, 66.
Napton, Ezekiel, 90.
Nash, Frederick A., 77.
Neads, John [or Needs], 18, 53, 88.
Nelson, ———, 18, 53.
Newberry, Oliver, 73, 75, 85.
Newberry Walter L., 85.
Newberry & Dole (firm), 76, 93.
Newby, E. W. B., 35.
Newcastle, *Duke of*, 29.
Newhall, *Capt.* ———, 84.
Nichols, Luther, 31.
Noles, Joseph [or Knowles], 17, 53, 88.
North American (steamboat), 84.
Nourse, Charles J., 47.

O.

O'Connell, Daniel, 90.
O'Fallon, John, 20.
Ogden, William B., 76, 85.
Ogilvie, P. H., 76, 77.
Ogee, *Mrs.* Sophia (Beaubien), 44, 79.
"Old Tempest," *i.e.*, Anthony Wayne, 28, 61.
Ostrom, Henry J., 91.
Osborn, James T., 65.
O'Strander, Philip, 88.
Ouilmette, *or* Wilmette, Michael, 65.

Owen, Thomas J. V., 25, 26, 64, 93.

P.

Paine, Christopher, 66.
Paine, Uriah, 66.
Parker, Richard, 91.
Parsons, T., 66.
Parsons, T. E., 66.
Peck, Philip F. W., 66.
Pearsons, Daniel K., 5.
Pe-me-sah-quah, *or* Rebekah Wells, 45.
Peneton, David, 65.
Penrose, James W., 32, 48.
Persons, Hiram, 90.
Peterson, Frederick, 18, 88.
Pettis, William H., 69.
Pickering, *Capt.*, 34.
Pierce, Benjamin K., 24.
Pierce, *Pres.* Franklin, 24, 44, 60.
Pierce, Harriet, 24.
Pierce, John Sullivan, 24.
Pierce, Josette (Lafromboise), 24.
Pierson, David, 90.
Pitman, John, 82.
Pix, William, 90.
Plymouth Rock (steamboat), 85.
Plympton, Cornelia De Puyster, 82.
Plympton, *Mrs.* Eliza Matilda (Livingston), 36, 81, 82.
Plympton, Emily, 36.
Plympton, Gilbert M., 82.
Plympton, Joseph, 35, 36, 48, 70, 71, 81, 82.
Plympton, Joseph R., 36.
Plympton, Louisa E., 82.
Plympton, Peter W. L., 36.
Plympton, Thomas, 81.
Poindexter, Thomas, 88.
Poinsett, Joel R., 39.
Polk, *Pres.* James K., 44.
Pope, Nathaniel, 14, 45.
Porter, *Rev.* Jeremiah, 5, 71.
Porter, Wesley B., 91.
Pothier, Joseph, 25.
Potter, Chandler E., 24.
Prescott, Eli S., 93.
Prickett, William, 88.
Prince of Wales, 29.
Proctor, *Gen.* Henry A., 52, 53, 58.
Prophet (Indian chief), 49, 50, 58.
Pruyne, Peter, 25.
Puthuff, Harriet, married John S. Pierce, 24.

INDEX

Puthuff, William H., 24.

Q.

Queen Charlotte (vessel), 50.

R.

Rand, Robert, 91.
Rapp, Thomas, 4.
Red Bird (Indian chief), 27.
Red Jacket (Indian chief), 58, 59.
Redding, Martin, 91.
Reed, Charles M., 75.
Reed, William, 91.
Reynolds, Arnold, 91.
Reynolds, *Gov.* John, 64.
Rhea, James, 88.
Richards, James J., 4, 93.
Ritchner, Antonie, 91.
Ricketts, Harriet (Pierce), 24.
Ricketts, James B., 24.
Rickman, Richard, 88.
Roberts, *Captain*, 52.
Robinson, Alexander, *or* Che-che-pin-qua (Indian chief), 26-8, 31, 33, 41.
Robinson, Palmer, 91.
Ronan, George, 15, 16, 18, 46, 52.
Rothmon, Michael, 90.
Round Head (Indian chief), 61.
Rowland, Thomas, 89.
Russell, Jacob, 93.
Russell, John B. F., 23, 70.
Russell, *Mrs.* John B. F., 85.
Russell, ———, 50.

S.

Salienne (Indian interpreter), 49.
Salisbury, Stephen M., 66.
Sang, Peter, 91.
Sauganash, *or* Billy Caldwell (Indian chief), 25-8, 31, 33, 60, 61, 68, 93.
Schien, ———, 58.
Schindler, Therese (Lafromboise), 24.
Schneidau, Polycarpus von, 43.
Schopfer, Conrad, 91.
Scott, Martin, 30, 48.
Scott, Williard, 66.
Scott, *Gen.* Winfield, 3, 24, 31, 34, 36, 37, 65, 72, 74, 85.
See, or Lee, 50.
See, *Rev.* William, 25.
Seybold, Ferdinand, 25.
Seymour, James, 76.
Seymour, W. H., 76.

Shabonee, *or* Chamblee (Indian chief), 27, 28, 31, 33, 58, 60, 61.
Shapley, Morgan L., 34.
Shaw-nee-aw-kee, *or* John Kinzie, 16.
Shedaker, Christopher, 65.
Sheldon Thompson (steamboat), 37, 72, 73, 75.
Shehan, John, 90.
Shepperd, Peter, 90.
Sheridan, *Gen.* Philip H., 5, 29, 82.
Sheridan, *Mrs. Gen.* P. H., 14.
Sherman, David, 91.
Sherror, David, 88.
Sill, Henry G., 69.
Simpson, James H., 69.
Simmons, John, 88.
Sitgreaves, Lorenzo, 69.
Smallwood, James, 25.
Smith, Ephraim Kirby, 35, 48.
Smith, George, 76.
Smith, Jeremiah, 65.
Smith, John, 88.
Smith, John, 88.
Smith, John, 91.
Smith, Philip, 88.
Smith, Robert P., 69.
Smith, S. Lisle, 93.
Smith, *Judge* Theophilus W., 39.
Smith, William, 65.
Smith, ———, 18.
Spaulding & Merrick (firm), 43.
Sprague, John T., 22, 23.
Stark, Henry, 90.
Starr, James, 88.
St. Clair, *Gen.* Anthony, 45.
Stevens, John, 66.
Stevens, John, jr., 66.
Stevens, William M., 44.
Stewart, Hart L., 55.
Stewart, James, 25.
St. Joseph Mission, 25.
Stockton, T., 90.
Stone, *Mrs.* Eliza (Heald), 15.
Storer, William H., 69.
Stose, Clemens, 25.
Stowell, Augustine, 66.
Stowell, Calvin M., 66.
Stowell, Walter, 66.
Strong, Henry, 67.
Stuart, Gilbert, 82.
Stuart, John T., 23.
Summers, John, 91.
Superior (steamboat), 21, 37, 58, 72, 73.

Suttonfield, John, 88.
Swartwout, Henry, 69.
Swearengen, James S., 13.
Sweet, Alanson, 66.
Sweet, Richard M., 66.
Swing, *Rev.* David, 4.

T.

Taliafero, ———, married William W. Helm, 16.
Tappan, Alexander H., 35, 48, 91.
Taylor, Augustine Deodat, 4.
Taylor, A. W., 65.
Taylor, Edmund D., 39, 76.
Taylor, *Pres.* Zachary, 30, 44, 60.
Tecumseh (Indian chief), 28, 58, 61.
Thompson, James L., 33, 35, 48, 71, 91.
Thompson, Robert, 65.
Thompson, Seth, 88.
Thompson, William, 90.
Thompson, W. H., 5.
Thurston, Henry, 10.
Thurston, Sarah M., 10.
Tilghman, Tench, 69.
Tracy (schooner), 13.
Tripp, William, 91.
Tuley, *Judge* Murray F., 64.
Turner, John B., 93.
Turner, *Mrs.* Ann (Wells), 46.
Turner, William, 45.
Tyler, *Pres.* John, 22.

U.

Ury, Ashburn, 69.
Usher, I. L., 31.

V.

Vallandigham, Clement L., 29, 61-3.
Van Buren, Abram, 30, 48.
Van Buren, *Pres.* Martin, 30, 40, 94.
Vance, Joseph C., 69.
VanHorn, James [or Horne], 17, 18, 53, 88.
Van Voorhis, *Dr.* Isaac V., 15, 16, 46, 52.
VanVraukin, Richard, 91.
Varnum, A. B., 26, 27.
Vault, Thomas D., 91.
Vennor, Richard, 91.
Von Schneidau, Polycarpus, 43.

W.

Wade, David, 65.
Wade, Marvin R., 90.
Waggoner, Anthony L., 88.
Wales, Prince of, 29.
Walker, *Capt.* Augustus, 37, 72, 76.
Walker, Charles H., 76.
Walker, George H., 65.
Walker, *Rev.* Jesse, 71.
Walker, Smith and others, 76.
Walk-in-the-Water (Indian chief), 61.
Walk-in-the-Water (steamboat), 58, 84.
Wall, William, 69.
Wallace, *Ensign*, 55.
Walsh, Michael, 90.
Walter, Joel C., 5, 32.
Wa-nan-go-path, first wife of *Capt.* William Wells, 45.
Wa-pe-mong-gah, or William Wayne Wells, 46.
Wapewa (Indian chief), 82.
Ward, Bernard, or Barney, 70.
Ward, George W., 69.
Ward, Henry A., 70.
Ward, Samuel D., 4.
Ward, ———, married Ralph Adams.
Washburne, Elihu B., 5.
Washington, *Pres.* George, 62, 63.
Watkins, John, 33.
Watkins, Thomas, 24.
Watson, George, 69.
Wayne, *Gen.* Anthony, 10, 11, 21, 28, 45, 55, 56, 61.
Weah, second wife of *Capt.* William Wells, 45.
Webster Daniel, 55, 77, 84.
Webster, Fletcher, 77.
Webster, Joseph Dana, 36.
Weever, Edward, 90.
Welch, John, 25.
Welch, Patrick, 91.
Wellmaker, John, 65.
Wells, Ann, *or* Ar-pez-zah-quah, 45, 46.
Wells, Jane, 46.
Wells, Juliana, 46.
Wells, Mary, *or* Ah-mah-quaw-zah-quuah, 45, 46.
Wells, Rebekah, married *Capt.* Nathan Heald, 14, 16, 18, 55.
Wells, Rebekah, *or* Pe-me-sah-quah, 45, 46.

Wells, Samuel, 14, 16, 18, 20, 21, 22, 45.
Wells, Samuel G., 46.
Wells, William, 14, 15, 16, 18, 19, 20, 21, 22, 45, 46, 50-8.
Wells, William Wayne, 21, 46.
Wells, Yelberton P., 46.
Wentworth, John, 3, 8, 9, 21, 28, 29, 54, 61, 64, 65, 67, 68, 70, 71, 76, 77, 79, 80, 83, 85, 86.
Wentworth, Moses J., 5.
Wescott, Seth, 66.
Western World (steamboat), 85.
Wheeler, *Dr.* Hiram, 4.
Wheeler, Horace H., 91.
Whipple, J. H., 91.
Whistler, George W., 13.
Whistler, John, 10, 13, 14, 87.
Whistler, John H., 12.
Whistler, J. N. G., 13.
Whistler, *Mrs.* Julia (Ferson), 12, 13.
Whistler, Louise, 16.
Whistler, William, 10, 12, 13, 14, 16, 30-3, 37, 48, 49, 55, 74.
White, Liberty, 50.
White Pigeon (schooner), 94.
White Raccoon (Indian chief), 51.
Whitehorn, Samuel, 90.
Whiting, Daniel P., 69.
Wicoffe, Peter, 66.
Wilcox, D. Lafayette, 33, 39, 48, 70, 71, 91.
Wilkinson, *Gen.* James, 9, 10.
Wilkinson, Theophilus F. J., 69.
William H. Harrison (schooner), 92.
William Penn (steamboat), 37, 72, 75.
Williams, J. L., 46.
Williston, Robert, 91.
Wilmette *or* Ouilmette, Michael, 65.
Wilson, Henry (*or* Harry) T., 66.
Winchester, *Gen.* James, 58, 59.
Winslow & Beeson (firm), 25.
Wolcott, Alexander, 25, 26, 45, 85, 86.
Wolcott, *Mrs.* Ellen M. (Kinzie), 26, 85.
Wolcott, Frederick Allen, 46.
Wolcott, Henry Clay, 46.
Wolcott, *Judge* James, 45, 46.
Wolcott, *Mrs.* James, 46.
Wolcott, James Madison, 46.
Wolcott, Mary Ann, 46.
Wolcott, William Wells, 46.
Woodbridge, William, 84.
Woodworth, Hiram P., 77.
Wool, *Gen.* John E., 16.
Woolley, Jeddiah, 65.
Worth, *Gen.* William J., 23.

Y.

Yoakum, Henderson K., 69.
Yoemans, Benjamin, 90.
Youngs, James, 90.

Z.

Zarley, J. W., 65.

FERGUS PRINTING COMPANY CHICAGO

OLD SETTLERS DECEASED SINCE MAY 27, 1879.

BARNES, JOSEPH A.
BEAUBIEN, MARK.
BICKERDIKE, GEORGE.
CLARKE, WILLIAM H.
CORRIGAN, WILLIAM.
CROCKER, OLIVER C.
CUNNINGHAM, HENRY.
DEWEY, DENNIS S.
DUCK, CHARLES H.
FULLER, HENRY.
FULLERTON, ALEX. N.
GAGE, JARED.
GILBERT, SAMUEL H.
HADDOCK, EDWARD H.
HAMLIN, ALONZO.
HASTINGS, HIRAM.
HUNTOON, GEORGE M.
JOHNSON, LATHROP.
LARRABEE, WILLIAM M.
MCKEE, DAVID.
MILLAR, ROBERT M.

MILTIMORE, IRA.
MORRIS, BUCKNER S.
MORRISON, EPHRAIM.
NICHOLS, LUTHER.
OGDEN, WILLIAM B.
OGDEN, MAHLON D.
PAGE, PETER.
PECK, EBENEZER.
PORTER, HIBBARD.
REES, JAMES H.
REIS, JR., JOHN P.
RUMSEY, GEORGE F.
RYAN, EDWARD G.
SHERMAN, EZRA L.
SMITH, ELIJAH.
SPEER, ISAAC.
STOW, WILLIAM H.
TUTTLE, LUCIUS G.
WATERS, BENJAMIN.
WILCOX, SEXTUS N.
WILLIAMS, ELI B.

August 24th, 1881.

INDEX

TO

"Early Chicago:"—First Lecture,

(No. 8 of Fergus' Historical Series.)

BY

HON. JOHN WENTWORTH, LL.D.,

Delivered Sunday, April 11, 1875.

[This Index was prepared by Mr. Wentworth, August, 1881.]

A.

Adams, James, 43.
Adams, John, 12.
Adams, John Q., 5, 17.
Ahert, William, 35, 40.
Allen, Archibald, 48.
Allouez, Claude, 8.
Alscomb, E. Antoine, 48.
Archer, William B., 43.
AuSable, Jean Baptiste Point, 14, 15.
Avery, Elias P., 48.

B.

Bancroft, George, 4.
Bane, Sarah, 34.
Banks, Thomas, 48.
Barney, Sarah, 36.
Baresford, Robert, 48.
Barker, Andrew, 48.
Barker, John, 48.
Bates, George C., 24.
Bauskey, Joseph, 36.
Beabor, Louis, 48.
Beaubien, Alexander, 24.
Beaubien, John Baptiste, 15, 24, 28, 34, 36, 40, 41, 42, 46, 47, 48.
Beaubien, Mark, 21, 26, 41.
Beauchamp, Noah, sr., 48.
Beauchamp, Noah, jr., 48.
Bethard, Elza, 48.
Bismark, *Prince*, 6.
Black Hawk (Indian chief), 22, 25, 26, 27, 30, 34, 38, 43.
Blake, *Capt.* Chelsey, 47.
Blanchard, William, 48.
Bogardus, John I., 44, 48.
Bonaparte, Napoleon, 7, 9, 23.
Bonaparte, Louis Napoleon, 9, 13, 23.
Bond, Shadrack, 24.
Bourbonne, Francis, sr., 48.
Bourbonne, Francis, jr., 48.
Braddock, *Gen.*, 12.
Bratton, Reuben, 48.
Brierly, Thomas, 48.
Brown, Cornelius, 48.
Brown, Henry, 4.
Brown, *Gen.* Jacob, 22.
Brown, Stephen, 34.
Bryant, Joseph, 48.
Bull, John, 10.

C.

Caldwell, Archibald, 33, 34, 39, 40, 41, 42, 46.
Caldwell, Billy (Sauganash, Indian chief), 38, 39, 41.
Caldwell, Lovisa B., 36, 40, 46.
Caldwell, Alexander, 40.
Caldwell, Susan, (only child), 38.
Calhoun, John C., 40.
Camlin, Thomas, 48.
Carroll, Stephen, 48.
Casey, Zadoc, 28.
Cass, Lewis, 6, 14, 25.
Caton, John Dean, 34.

Chamblee (Shabonee, Indian chief), 22, 23, 38, 39.
Che-che-pin-qua (Alexander Robinson, Indian chief), 40, 41, 48.
Clarissa (sloop), 47.
Clark, ———, 35.
Clark, Elizabeth, 35, 40.
Clark, *Gen.* George Rogers, 7, 9, 13, 20.
Clark, Hadassah, 36.
Clark, John K., 33, 35, 36, 40, 46, 48.
Clark, William, 48.
Clay, Henry, 17.
Clermont, Jerry, 48.
Cline, George, 48.
Cline, John, 48.
Clybourn, Archibald, 25, 33, 34, 35, 40, 42, 43, 44.
Clybourn, Henly, 33, 35, 42.
Clybourn, Jonas, 33, 35, 40, 48.
Clybourn, Thomas, 34.
Coles, Edward, 24.
Columbus, Christopher, 4.
Cooper, Abner, 48.
Countraman, Frederick, 48.
Coutra, Louis, 48.
Crafts, John, 48.
Crocker, Austin, 48.
Cromwell, Nathan, 48.
Curry, Hiram M., 48.

D.

Daniel, ———, *widow*, 34.
Daniel, Aramosa, 34.
Daniel, Harmon, 34.
Darling, Lucius R., 37.
Davis, Jefferson, 17, 18.
Davis, William, 48.
Dearborn, Henry, 14.
DeJoinville, *Prince*, 12.
Deroshee, John, 37.
DeSoto, Fernando, 4.
Dillon, Absalom, 48.
Dillon, Jesse, 48.
Dillon, John, 48.
Dillon, Nathan, 48.
Dillon, Thomas, 48.
Dillon, Walter, 48.
Dixon, John, 47, 48.
Dodge, Henry, 46.
Dodge, Augustus C., 46.
Donahoue, *Major*, 48.
Dougherty, Allen S., 48.

Douglas, Stephen A., 30.
DuMont, Peter, 48.
Duncan, Joseph, 43.

E.

Eads, Abner, 42, 48.
Eads, William, 48.
Economy (fire-engine), 3.
Edwards, Ninian, 15.
Egan, William B., 28, 29.
Egman, Isaac, 39.
Egman, Jesse, 48.
Ellis, Levi, 48.
Eustis, *Col.* Abraham, 46.
Evans, James, 43.
Everett, David, 37.

F.

Fassett, Samuel M., 2.
Fergus, Robert, 2, 32.
F. [Fergus], 2.
Fergus Printing Company, 33.
Field, Gilbert, 48.
Fish, Elisha, 41, 48.
Fish, Josiah, 41.
Fisk, Elisha, 41.
Fisk, Josiah, 41.
Forbes, Stephen, 41–43.
French, Stephen, 48.
Frontenac, *Gen.* Louis DeBuade, 10.
Fulton, James, 48.
Fulton, Josiah, 48.
Fulton, Samuel, 48.
Fulton, Seth, 48.
Funk, Isaac, 48.
Funk, Jacob, 48.

G.

Garibaldi, Giuseppe, 6.
Garrett, Augustus, 17.
Gay, J. M., 43.
Gilbert, Levi, 48.
Griffin, John, 48.
Griffin (schooner), 8.

H.

Hale, Isaiah, 45.
Hale, Virginia, 45.
Hall, Benjamin, 33, 34, 35, 39.
Hall, Charles, 34.
Hall, David, sr., 34, 35.

INDEX.

Hall, David, jr., 33, 34.
Hall, Edward B., 34.
Hall, J. R., 34.
Hallock, Lewis, 48.
Hamlin, John, 48.
Hanson, *Rev.* ——, 12.
Harlin, George, 48.
Harlin, Joshua, 48.
Harrison, Jesse, 48.
Harrison, William H., 14, 19, 21, 22.
Hawley, Aaron, 46, 48.
Hawley, Caroline, 36, 46.
Hawley, Pierce, 46, 48.
Heacock, Russell E., 36, 40, 41.
Heald, Nathan, 16.
Henley, Geo. P. A., 2.
Henry Clay (steamer), 26.
Hennepin, Louis, 8, 9.
Henry, Patrick, 12.
Hickling, William, 38.
Hoge, Joseph P., 16, 32.
Hogan, John S. C., 41.
Holland, William, 48.
Hubbard, Gurdon S., 3, 24, 25, 28.
Hull, William, 16, 21.
Hunter, *Gen.* David, 25.
Hunter, Jacob M., 48.
Huntington, Alonzo, 29.
Hyde, E. & N. (firm), 48.

I.
Ish, George, 48.

J.
Jackson, Andrew, 16, 17, 26.
Jefferson, Thomas, 40.
Jenkins, Alexander M., 43.
Johnson, Andrew, 31.
Johnson, Richard M., 22, 23.
Joliet, *Rev.* Louis, 8.
Joinville, *Prince de*, 12.

K.
Keating, William H., 25.
Kimball, Walter, 28.
Kinney, William, 43.
Kinzie, Ellen Marion, 24.
Kinzie, Elizabeth, 35.
Kinzie, James, 34, 35, 40, 43, 45.
Kinzie, John, 15, 21, 22, 24, 34, 35, 41, 46, 48.
Kinzie, John H., 15.
Kinzie, Juliette A., 37, 42.

Kinzie, Maria H., 25.
Kinzie, Robert A., 15.
Kinzie, William, 34, 35.

L.
Lafayette, *Marquis de*, 12, 13.
Lafromboise, Claude, 48.
Lafromboise, Joseph, 15, 48.
Lafromboise, Josette, 15.
Langworthy, Augustus, 48.
LaSalle, Robert C., 8, 9.
Latham, J., 48.
Latham, Philip, 48.
Latta, James, 48.
Laughton, Barney H., 28, 36, 40, 47.
Laughton, David, 40.
LeClerc, Peresh, 46.
LeClair, Peter, 46.
Liberty (fire-engine), 3.
Like, Daniel, 48.
Lincoln, Abraham, 14, 26, 27.
Long John (fire-engine), 3.
Louis XIV, 8.
Louis XVI, 12.
Louis XVII, 12.
Love, Charles, 48.
Love, George, 48.

M.
Madison, James, 9.
Mann, John, 37.
Maranda, Victoria, 46.
Marquette, James, 6, 7, 8, 9.
Marshall, Humphrey, 27.
Mather, David, 48.
Maury, W. F., 18.
Maximillian, *Emperor*, 9.
McCormick, Levi, 48.
McKee, David, 33, 35, 36, 48.
McKee, Stephen J. S., 36.
McKinzie, Elizabeth, 34, 35.
McKinzie, Margaret, 34, 35.
McLaree, Jesse, 48.
McLaughlin, Robert K., 43.
McNaughton, Alexander, 48.
McNeil, John, 24.
Michigan (steamboat), 47.
Millen, Walter, 36.
Miller, Jacob, 33, 34.
Miller, John, 33, 34, 35.
Miller, Samuel, 33, 34, 35, 40, 41, 42, 44.
Mills, Benjamin, 43.

Moffatt, Alva, 48.
Moffatt, Aquilla, 48.
Montgomery, Hugh, 48.
Murphy, John, 26.

N.

Neeley, Henry, 48.
Newberry, Oliver, 47.
Nicollet, Sieur Jean, 8.
Norton, Nelson R., 47.

O.

Ogden, William B., 3, 32.
Ogee, Joseph, 48.
Ouilmette (Wilmette), Antoine, 24, 37, 48.

P.

Pakenham, *Gen.* E., 16.
Patterson, John, 48.
Pearsons, Hiram, 47.
Pearson, John, 29.
Pee-he-que-ta-rou-ri, Margaretta, 46.
Perkins, Isaac, 48.
Perry, *Commodore* Oliver H., 22.
Phillippe, Louis, 12.
Phillips, John, 48.
Phillips, William, 48.
Piche, Peter, 48.
Polk, James K., 17.
Porter, Martin, 48.
Pothier, Joseph, 46.
Powell, George N., 34.
Prince, Daniel, 48.
Proctor, *Gen.* Henry A., 21.
Pugh, Jonathan H., 43.
Putnam's *Magazine*, 12.

R.

Ramsay, John L., 48.
Ransom (or Rousser), Amherst C., 41, 42, 48.
Redman, Eli, 48.
Redman, Henry, 48.
Reed Charles H., 29.
Reed, William, 45.
Reynolds, John, 46.
Ridgeway, John, 48.
Robinson, Alexander (Che-che-pinqua, Indian chief), 40, 41, 48.
Rousser (or Ransom), A. C., 48.

S.

Sambli, Arkash, 37.
Sauganash (Billy Caldwell, Indian chief), 38, 39, 41.
Scarrett, *Rev.* Isaac, 46.
Scott, Alice Lovisa, 36.
Scott, Alvin, 36.
Scott, Deborah, 36.
Scott, Peter, 48.
Scott, Permelia, 36, 46.
Scott, Stephen J., 36, 46 -47.
Scott, Thaddeus, 36.
Scott, Wealthy, 36.
Scott, Williard, 36-46.
Scott, Williard, jr., 36.
Scott, Willis, 36, 40, 46.
Scott, William H., 36.
Scott, *Gen.* Winfield, 26, 27, 34, 46, 47.
See, *Rev.* William, 44, 45, 46.
Shabonee (Chamblee, Indian chief), 22, 23, 38, 39.
Sharp, George, 39, 48.
Sheldon (schooner), 36.
Sheldon Thompson (steamboat), 27, 46.
Sherwood, *Capt.* ———, 36.
Smith, Joseph, 48.
Smith, William, 48.
Sommers, John, 48.
Stevensen, James W., 43.
Stephenson, John, 48.
Stewart, William, 29.
Storey, Wilbur F., 29.
Stout, Ephriam, 48.
Strode, James M., 43.
Stuart, John T., 30.

T.

Taylor, Edmund D., 25, 28.
Tecumapeance, sister to Tecumseh, 38.
Tecumseh (Indian chief), 22, 23, 25, 38, 39.
Thomas, Francis, 39.
Thompkins, L. M., 43.
Thorp, Jonathan, 48.
Tonti, Henry de, 8, 9.
Trask, Hadassah, 36.
Turner, Ezekiel, 48.

V.

VanBuren, Martin, 22.

Vance, Moses, B., 45.
VanScoyk, Joseph, 48.
Vermit, Vital, 46.

W.

Walker, Alfred, 37.
Walker, *Capt.* A., 27.
Walker, Cornelia, 46.
Walker, David, 37, 46.
Walker, George E., 38.
Walker, Hugh, 48.
Walker, *Capt.* James, 37-41.
Walker, James, 37.
Walker, Jesse, 25, 33, 32, 38, 46, 48.
Walker, John, 37.
Walk-in-the-Water (steamboat), 24.
Warrington, Arthur, 36.
Wasegoboah (Indian chief), 38.
Washington, George, 9, 12, 13.
Waters, Isaac, 48.
Watkins, Munson, 36.
Wayne, Anthony, 9, 13.
Weed, Edmond, 41, 48.
Weeks, Cole, 39, 40.
Welch, Michael, 37.
Welch, Mary Ann, 37.

Wells, William, 19.
Wentworth, Elijah, sr., 26.
Wentworth, Elijah, jr., 43.
Wentworth, John, 2, 3, 17, 20.
Whistler, William, 24.
Williams, Eleazer, 11.
Williams, Eli B., 30.
Williams, Erastus S., 29.
Wilmette (Ouilmette), Antoine, 24, 37, 48.
Wilmette, Elizabeth, 37.
Wilmette, Francis, 37.
Wilmette, Joseph, 37.
Wilmette, Josette, 37.
Wilmette, Louis, 37.
Wilmette, Mitchell, 37.
Wilmette, Sophia, 37.
Wilson, Jacob, 48.
Wilson, Seth, 48.
Wolcott, Alexander, 24, 40, 41, 48.
Woodrow, Hugh, 48.
Woodrow, Samuel, 48.

Y.

Yellow Head (Indian chief), 38.

INDEX

TO

"Early Chicago:"—Second Lecture,

(No. 7 of Fergus' Historical Series.)

BY

HON. JOHN WENTWORTH, LL.D.,

Delivered Sunday, May 7, 1876.

[This Index was prepared by Mr. Wentworth, August, 1881.]

A.

Abel, Sidney, 53, 55.
Acay, Gabriel, 54.
Adams, John, 9.
Adams, John Quincy, 6, 7, 8, 17.
Ament, Edward, 16, 53.
Anderson, Joseph, 16, 53.
Aruwaiskie, Theotis, 56.
Aurora (schooner), 24.
Ayers, Thomas, 54.

B.

Bailey, Jonathan A., 16, 53, 54.
Banny, [Barry or Bannot;] Augustine, 16, 52, 54.
Bates, George C., 51.
Bates, Sophia, 56.
Bauskey, Joseph, 17, 54, 56.
Beaubien, John B., 15, 16, 18, 22, 24, 51, 52, 54, 55, 56.
Beaubien, Mark, 17, 24, 25, 54.
Beaubien, Medore B. [Medard B.], 16, 18, 22, 33, 35, 52, 54, 55.
Benedict, Sarah, 52.
Benton, Thomas H., 8.
Black Hawk (Indian chief), 4, 10, 44.
Blow, Lewis, 54.
Bogardus, John L., 15.
Bourassea, Daniel, 16, 56.
Bourassea, Leon, 16, 54.
Bradain [Beaubien], John B., 55.
Breese, Sidney, 12, 14.
Brown, James, 16, 54.
Brown, Jesse, 19.
Brown, Thomas C., 19.
Brown, William H., 11.
Buchanan, James, 8.
Buell, E., 24.
Burr, Aaron, 9.

C.

Caldwell, Archibald, 52, 53.
Caldwell, Billy, (Sauganash, Indian chief), 14, 16, 17, 18, 25, 33, 54, 55.
Calhoun, John, 3.
Calhoun, John C., 7, 17.
Caldwell, Lovisa B., 56.
Cass, *Gen.* Lewis, 8, 22.
Catie, Joseph, 16.
Chamblee (Shabonee, Indian chief), 33.
Charlevoix, Pierre François Xavir de, 10—13.
Chavellea, John Baptiste, 16.
Chavellie, Peter, 16.
Che-che-pin-qua (Alexander Robinson, Indian chief), 15, 16, 33, 54, 56.
Chevalier, Catherine, 56.
Chi-ka-gou (Indian chief), 12.
Clairmore [Clermont?], Jeremiah, 16.
Clark, John K., 15, 16, 17, 18, 52, 54, 55.
Clay, Henry, 7, 17.
Clermont [Clairmore?], Jeremiah, 15, 16, 52.
Clybourn, Archibald, 16, 17, 18, 52, 53, 54, 55, 56.

Clybourn, Henly, 52.
Clybourn, Jonas, 15, 16, 17, 51, 54, 55.
Cobb, Silas B., 44.
Conant, , 52.
Cook, Daniel P., 17, 25.
Coutra, Louis, 15.
Crafts, John, 15, 16, 51, 52.
Crittenden, John J., 8.

D.

Davis, Jefferson, 7, 26.
Davis, John L., 16, 53, 54.
Dearborn, *Gen.* Henry, 7.
Debigie, Simon, 54.
Displattes, Basile, 16.
Dodge, *Gen.* Henry, 8.
Dorr, *Capt.* of Schooner Tracy, 8.

E.

Eads, Abner, 15, 50.
Edwards, *Gov.* Ninian, 17, 25.
Engle, *Lt.* James, 54, 55.

F.

Fair Play (revenue cutter), 24.
Fergus, Robert, 26.
Ferrel, John, 51.
Field, Darby, 19.
Fillmore, Millard, 7, 8.
Forbes, Stephen, 53, 55.
Forbes, *Mrs.* Stephen, 55.
Ford, *Gov.* Thomas, 38, 39, 40, 56.
Foster, *Lt.* Amos, 54, 55.
Fridley, John, 56.
Frique, Peter, 16, 54, 55.
Fulton, Samuel, 50.

G.

Gage, *Gen.* Thomas, 11.
Gale, James V., 56.
Galloway, James, 54.
Galloway, *Miss*, married Archibald Clybourn, 52.
Ganday, Lewis, 17, 54.
Gardner, Alvin Noyes, 56.
Garie, , 12.
Garow, James, 54.
Garrett, Augustus, 33.
Griffin, Ann, 51.

H.

Hale, Artimas, 9.
Haley, Julia, 56.
Hall, Benjamin, 52.
Hallam, *Rev.* Isaac W., 33.
Hamilton, *Mrs. Gen.* Alexander, 9.
Hamilton, William S., 51.
Hamlin, John, 50, 51.
Harrison, *Gen.* William H., 8.
Heacock, Russell E., 16, 18, 53, 54, 55.
Heartless (schooner), 24.
Henry Clay (steamboat), 5.
Hinton, *Rev.* Isaac T., 42, 43, 45.
Hogan, John S. C., 16, 53, 54, 55.
Holcomb, John, 51.
Hoyne, Thomas, 43.
Hubbard, Gurdon S., 12.
Hull, *Gen.* William, 25.
Hunter, *Gen.* David, 54, 55.

J.

Jackson, *Gen.* Andrew, 8, 17, 28, 32, 44.
Jamboe, Paul, 16.
Jefferson, Thomas, 9, 12.
Jewett, William P., 54.
Jewett, William, 55.
Johnston, Samuel, 16.
Jowett [or Jewett], Charles, 51.
Joyal, John, 54.
Junio, Peter, 16.

K.

Kearney, *Gen.* Stephen W., 19.
Keating, William H., 22.
Kelley, Henry, 16, 52, 54.
Kennison, David, 9.
Kerchival, Benjamin B., 22.
Kimball, Walter, 3.
Kingsbury, Julius J. B., 42.
Kinzie, Elizabeth, 53, 56.
Kinzie, Ellen M., 51.
Kinzie, James, 16, 18, 26, 53, 54, 55, 56.
Kinzie, John, 15, 16, 17, 18, 23, 50, 51, 52, 53, 54, 55, 56.
Kinzie, *Mrs.* Juliette A., 52, 55.
Kinzie, Maria H., 55.

L.

Laducier, Francis, 16, 17, 53.

Laducier, John Baptiste, 54.
Lafortune, John Baptiste, 16.
Lafromboise, Claude, 15, 16, 52.
Lafromboise, Francis, sr., 16.
Lafromboise, Francis, jr., 16.
Lafromboise, Joseph, 15, 16, 17, 33, 51, 52, 54.
Larant, Alexander, 16.
Laughton, Barney H., 16, 53, 55, 56.
LeClerc, Peresh (LeClair, Peter), 17, 54.
Lincoln, Abraham, 8.
Littleton, Samuel, 54.
Long, Stephen H., 22.

M.

Mack, *Major*, 53.
Mack, Stephen, 16, 53, 54.
Madison, James, 8, 9.
Madison, *Mrs.* James, 8, 9.
Malast, John Baptiste, 16.
Mann, John, 16, 54, 55, 56.
Martin, Laurant, 17.
Marquette, *Rev.* James, 13.
Maximillian, *Emperor*, 20.
McDole, Alexander, 16, 54.
McKee, David, 15, 16, 22, 23, 24, 53, 54, 55.
McNeil, John, 24.
Miller, Samuel, 53, 54, 55, 56.
Mills, Benjamin, 26.
Miner, Horace, 55.
Miranda, Victoria, 53.
Monroe, James, 8.
Muller, Peter, 55.
Murphy, John, 25, 44.

O.

Orleans, *Duchess of*, 13.
Ouilmette (Willmette), Antoine, 15, 16, 52, 54, 56.
Ouilmette, Elizabeth, 52, 56.
Owen, Thomas J. V., 51.

P.

Papan, Joseph, 54.
Pepot, Joseph, 16.
Perrot, Nicholas, 13.
Phelps, John, 56.
Piche, Peter, 15, 52.
Pierce, Franklin, 8.
Polk, James K., 7, 8, 20.

Pothier, Joseph, 16, 23, 33, 53, 54.

R.

Ransom, *Capt.*, 50.
Rausom, Amherst C., 15, 50.
Reynolds, *Gov.* John, 17.
Robinson, Alexander, (Che-che-pin-qua, Indian chief), 15, 16, 33, 54, 56.
Rose, Russell, 54, 55.
Roussain, Eustache, 50.
Rousser (Rausam), Amherst C., 15, 50.
Russell, Benjamin, 16.

S.

Sambli, Arkash, 56.
Sauganash (Billy Caldwell, Indian chief), 14, 16, 17, 18, 25, 33, 54, 55.
Scott, Deborah, 56.
Scott, Permelia, 52.
Scott, Stephen J., 16, 52, 53, 54, 55, 56.
Scott, Wealthy, 53.
Scott, Willard, 53, 54, 55.
Scott, Willis, 52, 53, 56.
Schuyler, *Gen.* Philip, 9.
Secor, John Baptist, 16, 17, 54.
See, *Rev.* William, 16, 53, 55, 56.
Shabonee (Chamblee, Indian chief), 33.
Shedaker, John, 55.
Sheldon Thompson (steamboat), 5.
Smith, Horatio G., 54.
Smith, Joseph, 41.
Smith, Mary Ann, 56.
Smith, Matthias, 54, 55.
St.Clair, *Gen.* Arthur, 11.
Strode, James M., 26.
Sullivan, Jeremiah, 20.
Sullivan, *Lt.* ———, 20, 21.
Superior (steamboat), 5.
Swing, *Rev.* David, 37.

T.

Tappan, Benjamin, 6.
Taylor, Augustine D., 3.
Taylor, Zachary, 8.
Tecumseh (Indian chief), 13, 14, 17.
Thibeaut, Joseph, 16, 54.
Thompson, *Lt.* J. L., 55.
Thompson, Enoch, 55.

Thompson, Samuel, 11, 17.
Titus, *Capt.* ———, 24.
Todd, John, 11.
Tombien (or Toubien), Jean Baptiste, 54.
Tracy (schooner), 8.
Tyler, John, 8.

V.

VanBuren, Martin, 8, 55.
VanEaton, David, 16, 54, 55.
VanHorn, John, 16, 54.
VanOsdell, John M., 43.
VanSicle, Martin, 16, 53.
VanSicle, Almira, 53.
VanStow, David, 54.
Vivier, *Rev.* Louis, 12.

W.

Wales, *Prince of*, 22.
Walker, *Capt.* A., 5.
Walker, *Rev.* Jesse, 16, 18, 53, 55.
Washington, *Gen.* George, 6, 9.
Watkins, Deborah (Scott), 56.
Watkins, Samuel, 56.
Wayne, *Gen.* Anthony, 8, 12, 22.

Webster, Daniel, 8.
Weeks, Cole, 16, 52.
Welch, Michael, 17, 19, 52, 54, 56.
Wellmaker, John, 54, 55.
Wentworth, Elijah, sr., 26, 51.
Wentworth, Elijah, jr., 26, 51.
Wentworth, George P., 54.
Wentworth, Hiram, 51.
Wentworth, John, 50.
Whistler, John, 7, 8, 10.
Whistler, William, 8.
Wilkins, William, 8.
William Penn (steamboat), 5.
Wilmette [Ouilmette], Antoine, 15, 16, 52, 54, 56.
Wilmette [Ouilmette], Elizabeth, 56.
Winthrop, *Gov.* John, 19.
Wolcott, Alexander, 15, 18, 23, 50, 51, 54, 55.
Woodbridge, William, 8.
Woodbury, Levi, 8.
Woodville, N. D., 51.
Wright, Silas, 47.
Wycoff, Peter, 54, 55.

Y.

Young Tiger (schooner), 24.

INDEX

TO

The Proceedings of the First "Reception to the Settlers of Chicago prior to 1840, [as compiled by Hon. John Wentworth], by the Calumet Club, May 27, 1879."

[This Index was prepared by Mr. Wentworth, August, 1881.]

A.

Adams, Charles, 11.
Adams, John Quincy, 58.
Adams, Joseph, 11.
Adams, William H., 11, 51, 57, 84.
Adsit, James M., 11, 84.
Adsit, James M., jr., 5.
Aldrich, William, 5.
Alexander, G. M., 5.
Allen, Edward R., 11
Allen, Thomas, 11.
Allerton, Samuel W., 5.
Allison, Thomas, 11.
Anderson, T. W., 5.
Andrews, Joseph H., 5.
Angell, William A., 5.
Archer, William B., 53.
Areadne (vessel), 38.
Armour, George, 54.
Armour, George A., 5.
Armour, Joseph F., 5.
Arnold, Isaac N., 11, 31, 50, 56, 57, 59, 84.
Asay, E. G., 5.
Asay, J. F., 5.
Ashwell, W. C., 5.
Averill, A. J., 5.
Ayers, Enos, 5.

B.

Bacon, Henry M., 5.
Bacon, Roswell B., 5.
Baker, William T., 5.
Baker, W. Vincent, 5.
Bailey, Amos, 11, 52.
Bailey, Bennett, 11, 84.
Balcom, Uri, 5.
Ballard, D. P., 5.
Baker, Franklin, 11, 84.
Baldwin, W. A., 11, 84.
Balestier, Joseph N., 11, 50, 84.
Balsley, John, 11, 84.
Barnes, Charles J., 5, 6, 9.
Barnes, R. B., 11.
Barrett, O. W., 6.
Bartlett, A. C., 6.
Bartlett, Charles S., 6.
Bascom, Flavel, 11, 52, 76.
Batchelor, Ezra, 12, 84.
Bates, John, 12, 36, 84.
Baumgarten, Chris, 12.
Baumgarten, John, 12.
Beach, James S., 12.
Beaubien, Alexander, 74.
Beaubien, Henry, 74.
Beaubien, John Baptiste, 35, 74.
Beaubien, Mark, 12, 31, 36, 37, 39, 40, 42, 43, 48, 49, 60, 61, 70, 71, 74, 81, 82, 84.
Beaubien, Medore B., 12, 49, 51, 74.
Beaubien, Philip, 74.
Beecher, Jerome, 12, 31, 58, 84.
Beggs, Stephen R., 12, 23, 24, 47, 74, 84.
Berdel, Nicholas, 12, 78.
Berg, Anton, 12.
Bigelow, A. A., 6.
Billings, Charles A., 6.
Billings, H. F., 6.

Birch, Hugh T., 6.
Bishop, Henry W., 6.
Bishop, James E., 12, 51, 75, 78.
Bismarck, *Prince*, 29.
Black, Francis, 12, 78.
Black Hawk (Indian chief), 50, 60.
Blackstone, T. B., 6.
Blackman, Edwin, 12, 51, 59.
Blair, Chauncey B., 6.
Blair, Chauncey J., 6.
Blair, Watson F. 5, 6.
Blake, *Capt.* Chelsey, 54.
Blake, E. Sanford, 12.
Blake, L. S., 12.
Blake, S. Sanford, 84.
Blasy, Barnhard, 12, 78.
Blatchford, E. W., 78.
Blodgett, Henry W., 12, 31, 43, 44, 57, 58, 59, 63, 84.
Boggs, Charles T., 78.
Bonaparte, Napoleon, 27.
Boone, Levi D., 12, 31, 51, 56, 57, 84.
Borland, J. J., 6.
Botsford, Jabez K., 12, 31, 51, 52, 84.
Botsford, Moss, 12.
Bowen, Erastus S., 12.
Boyer, Valentine A., 12, 49, 51, 78.
Bradley, Asa F., 12, 52.
Bradley, Timothy M., 12, 57.
Bradwell, James B., 12, 84.
Brainard, *Dr.* Daniel, 34.
Bridges, T. B., 12.
Briggs, Clinton, 6.
Brooks, Henry, 12.
Brooks, Joshua, 12.
Brooks, Samuel M., 12.
Bross, William, 70.
Brown, Andrew, 6.
Brown, Andrew J., 12, 51, 55.
Brown, Henry, 55.
Brown, Lemuel, 12.
Brown, J. M., 6.
Brown, Nathaniel J., 12, 60.
Brown, William H., 34, 75.
Bryan, Fred. A., 12, 84.
Bryant, J. Ogden, 6.
Buchanan, James, 59.
Buckingham, C., 6.
Burgess, Wm. T., 54.
Burley, Arthur G., 13, 31, 51, 58, 75, 84.
Burley, Augustus H., 13, 31, 57, 75, 84.
Burley, Charles, 13, 75, 78.
Burnham, D. H., 6.
Butler, John H., 13.
Butterfield, Justin, 34.
Byford, Henry T., 6.

C.

Cæsar, Augustus, 45.
Caldwell, Archibald, 13, 30, 47.
Caldwell, Billy (Indian chief), 48, 49, 73, 74.
Calhoun, Alvin, 34, 68, 69.
Calhoun, John, 34, 68.
Campbell, Augustus S., 6.
Campbell, B. H., jr., 6.
Campbell, James, 13, 84.
Canda, Florimond, 13.
Carpenter, Abel E., 13, 85.
Carpenter, Philo, 13, 31, 49, 50, 51, 59, 74, 77, 85.
Carroll, Edward, 13.
Carver, W. S., 6.
Carter, Thomas B., 13, 31, 51, 85.
Casey, Edward, 40, 70.
Cassidy, J. A., 6.
Caton, Arthur J., 6.
Caton, John Dean, 13, 31, 34, 35, 40, 47, 50, 51, 56, 58, 67, 69, 85.
Chacksfield, George, 13, 51, 85.
Chamberlain, *Rev.* J. S., 13, 78.
Chamblee (or Shabonee, Indian chief) 48.
Chapin, John P., 30, 66, 67, 69.
Che-che-pin-qua (or Alexander Robinson, Indian chief), 48.
Chisholm, William, 5, 6, 9.
Chumasero, John T., 6.
Church, William L., 13, 57, 85.
Clarissa (sloop), 54.
Clark, John K., 48.
Clark, John L., 13, 78.
Clark, John M., 6.
Clark, Stewart, 6.
Clark, T. B., 25.
Clarke, Abram F., 13.
Clarke, Henry B., 34.
Clarke, Henry W., 13, 51, 54, 85.
Clarke, L. J., 13, 85.
Clarke, Norman, 13, 85.
Clarke, Samuel C., 13.
Cleaveland, James O., 6.
Cleaver, Charles, 13, 52, 85.
Cleaver, Edward C., 13, 78.
Clybourn, Archibald, 34, 48.

INDEX.

Clybourn, Henly, 34, 48.
Clybourn, Jonas, 34, 48.
Cobb, Calvin, 6.
Cobb, Silas B., 6, 9, 11, 13, 23, 24, 25, 31, 34, 36, 52, 59, 60, 71, 73, 75, 77, 79, 80, 81, 85.
Coburn, Charles E., 6.
Coburn, Joseph G., 6.
Coburn, Lewis L., 6.
Collier, Z. Clinton, 6.
Collins, James H., 40.
Collins & Caton (firm), 40.
Comes, Charles W., 6.
Connell, Charles J., 6.
Cook, Isaac, 13, 51, 52, 57, 59, 85.
Cook, Thomas, 13.
Cooper, E. M., 6.
Corrigan, William, 13, 78.
Corwith, Gurden, 6.
Corwith, Henry, 6.
Corwith, Nathan, 6.
Couch, Ira, 34.
Couch, James, 13, 85.
Counselman, Charles, 6.
Cowles, Alfred, 6.
Cox, R. W., 6.
Crane, Albert, 6.
Crane, Charles A., 6.
Crerar, John, 6.
Critchell, R. S., 6.
Crocker, Hans, 13, 54.
Culbertson, C. M., jr., 6.
Curtiss, James, 34.

D.

Davidson, O., 13.
Davis, Jefferson, 53.
Davlin, John, 13, 57, 78.
Densmore, Eleazer W., 13, 58, 85.
Derby, W. M., 6.
Dewey, A. A., 6.
Dewey, Dennis S., 13, 78, 85.
DeWolf, Calvin, 13, 85.
Dexter, A. A., 13.
Dickey, Hugh T., 14, 31, 51, 54, 57, 58, 85.
Dickinson, Augustus, 14, 78.
Doane, J. W., 6.
Dodge, George E. P., 6.
Dodge, Martin, 14.
Dodge, Usual S., 14.
Dodson, Christian B., 14, 53, 85.
Dole, George W., 39, 74, 75.
Doty, Theodorus, 14, 85.

Douglas, Stephen A., 51.
Drake, John B., 6.
Drew, Charles W., 5, 6,
Drummond, Thomas, 14, 31, 57, 58, 85.
Duck, Charles H., 14.
Dwight, J. H. 6.
Dyer, Charles V., 34.
Dyer, George R., 14.
Dyer, Thomas, 34.

E.

Eddy, Augustus N., 5, 6, 9.
Eddy, Devotion C., 51, 85.
Edgell, Stephen M., 14.
Egan, William B., 34.
Egan, Wiley M., 14, 85.
Eldridge, John W., 14, 31, 51.
Ellis, Joel, 14.
Elliot, James F. D., 14, 85.
Ellithorpe, Albert C., 14, 85.
Estes, Mrs. Elijah, 25.

F.

Fairbank, N. K., 6.
Fake, Henry, 14.
Fargo, Charles, 6.
Fauntleroy, T. S., 6.
Fergus, Robert, 14, 85.
Field, Marshall, 6.
Filer, Alanson, 14.
Filmore, Millard, 59.
Fisher, Fred P., 6.
Fleetwood, Charles, 6.
Fleetwood, Stanley, 6.
Fleming, Robert H., 6.
Flood, Peter F., 14, 78.
Follansbee, Charles, 14, 31, 57, 85.
Foss, Robert H., 57.
Foster, John H., 30.
Freeman, Robert, 14, 85.
Freer, L. C. Paine, 14, 31, 85.
Fuller, George W., 6.
Fuller, William A., 6.
Fullerton, Alexander N., 14, 50.

G.

Gage, Albert S., 6.
Gage, Jared, 14.
Gage, John, 14, 56.
Gale, Abram, 14, 86.
Gale, Stephen F., 14, 31, 51, 52, 75, 86.

Gardner, C. S., 7.
Garrett, Augustus, 31, 34, 60, 66, 67, 69.
Garrett, Brown & Co. (firm), 60.
Gates, Philetus W., 14, 86.
Germaine, George H., 14, 86.
Getchell, E. F., 7.
Gilbert, Samuel H., 14, 86.
Glover, Samuel J., 7.
Goodhue, Josiah C., 66, 67, 69.
Goodman, James B., 5, 7.
Goodrich, Grant, 14, 31, 49, 50, 51, 52, 54, 56, 62, 70, 86.
Goodrich, Thomas Watson, 14, 86.
Goodwin, Jonathan, 7.
Goold, Nathaniel, 14.
Gore, George P., 7.
Gorton, Anson, 7.
Gould, M. B., 7.
Graff, Peter, 14, 86.
Granger, Elihu, 14, 57, 86.
Grannis, Amos, 15, 57, 86.
Grannis, S. W., 15.
Grannis, W. C. D., 7.
Grant, James, 15, 31, 44, 45, 51, 58, 86.
Grant, W. S., 59.
Graves, Henry, 15.
Graves, Dexter, 39.
Gray, Charles M., 15, 57.
Gray, Franklin D., 7, 9, 11, 15, 31, 73, 77, 79, 86.
Gray, George M., 15, 31, 86.
Gray, John, 15, 31, 57, 86.
Gray, Joseph H., 15, 31, 86.
Gray, William B. H., 15, 31, 86.
Green, Russell, 15.
Grey, William, L., 7.
Gurnee, Walter S., 15, 57.

H.

Hackett, John, 15.
Hackney, H. C., 7.
Hackney, John J., 7.
Hadduck, Edward H., 15, 39, 56, 59, 68, 86.
Haines, Elijah M., 15, 57.
Haines, John C., 15, 57, 78.
Hall, Amos T., 7.
Hall, Benjamin, 15, 47, 86.
Hall, David, 48.
Hall, Phillip A., 86.
Hall, William S., 7.
Hallam, *Rev.* Isaac W., 15, 34, 74.
Hamill, Charles D., 7.
Hamill, Ernest A., 7.
Hamilton, Polemus D., 15, 86.
Hamilton, Richard J., 30, 34, 73, 74.
Hanchett, John L., 15, 86.
Hanford, P. C., 7.
Hardin, S. H., 7.
Harmon, Elijah Dewey, 25, 34, 35.
Harmon, Isaac D., 15, 34.
Harmon, Isaac N., 15, 74, 86.
Harmon, Edwin R., 15.
Harrington Augustus M., 15.
Harrington, James C., 15.
Harrison, *Gen.* William H., 48, 59.
Haskell, Fred T., 7.
Hastings, Hiram, 15.
Hawley, John S., 15, 86.
Hayes, Rutherford B., 59.
Heacock, Russell E., 31, 34.
Heald, Hamilton, 15.
Heaton, E. S., 7.
Henderson, E. F., 7.
Henry, R. L., 7.
Hibbard, William G., 7
Hickling, William, 15, 86.
Higgins, Van H., 15, 31, 87.
Hilliard, Lorin P., 15, 87.
Hitchcock, *Rev.* Luke, 15, 52.
Hoard, Samuel, 15, 57, 59, 87.
Hodges, L., 7.
Hogan, John S. C., 34, 37, 74.
Holden, Charles N., 15, 59, 87.
Holbrook, John, 51.
Holliday, John M., 7.
Horton, Dennison, 15, 58, 87.
Howe, Fredrick A., 16, 87.
Hoyne, F. G., 7.
Hoyne, T. M., 7.
Hoyne, Thomas, 16, 31, 51, 56, 57, 58, 87.
Hubbard, Elijah K., 34.
Hubbard, Gurdon S., 16, 31, 37, 46, 51, 52, 53, 59, 64, 71, 75, 87.
Hubbard, Thomas H., 16.
Hughes, John B., 7.
Hugunin, James R., 16.
Hugunin, Lemuel C., 16.
Hull, *Gen.* William, 48, 71.
Humphreys, *Gen.* A. A., 16, 53.
Hunter, David, 16, 75, 76.
Hunter, George W., 16.
Huntington, Alonzo, 16, 51, 58, 87.
Huntoon, George M., 16.
Husted, H. H., 58.

Hutchings, Charles S., 7, 9.
Hyman, R. W., jr., 7.

I.

Isham, Henry P., 7.

J.

Jackson, Andrew, 47, 59.
Jackson, Carding, 58.
Jansen, E. L., 7.
Jefferson, **Joseph**, 55.
Jefferson, **Thomas**, 47.
Jenkins, T. R., 7.
Johnson, **Andrew**, 57, 59.
Johnston, **William J.**, 7.
Jones, Fernando, 16.
Jones, Nathaniel A., 16, 87.
Jones, S. J., 7.
Jones, William, 31.
Judah, Noble B., 7.

K.

Keep, Albert, 7.
Keep, Chauncey, 7.
Keep, Fred A., 7.
Keep, Henry, 7.
Kehoe, Michael, 16, 87.
Keith, Edson, 5, 7.
Keith, O. R., 7.
Kelley, David, 7.
Kellogg, A. N., 7.
Kennicott, Jonathan A., 16, 87.
Kennicott, Joseph E., 16.
Kettlestrings, Joseph, 16.
Kimball, C. Fred, 7.
Kimball, C. P., 7.
Kimball, Harlow, 16.
Kimball, Mark, 7, 9, 11, 16, 31, 73, 77, 80, 87.
Kimball, Martin N., 16, 87.
Kimball, Walter, 16, 31, 51, 52, 53, 57, 59, 87.
Kimball, W. W., 7.
Kimbark, S. D., 7.
King, Tuthill, 16, 31, 50, 51, 52, 87.
Kinzie, James, 34, 48, 74.
Kinzie, John, 47, 64.
Kinzie, John H., 30, 34, 64, 74, 75.
Kinzie, Robert A., 36, 64, 74.
Kinzie, William, 48.
Kirkpatrick, W. E., 7.
Knickerbocker, Abram V., 53.
Knickerbocker, Joshua C., 7.
Knickerbocker, H. W., 16, 87.

Knight, Darius, 16.
Knight, W. S., 7.
Kuhl, John, 16.

L.

Laflin, George H., 16.
Laflin, Mathew, 16, 31.
Lafromboise, Joseph, 49.
Lane, Elisha B., 16, 87.
Lane, George W., 16, 87.
Lane, James, 57, 87.
Larrabee, William M., 16, 56, 59.
Lathrop, Samuel, 16.
Law, Robert, 7.
Lay, A. Tracy, 7.
Leavenworth, Jesse H., 16, 53.
Leiter, Levi Z., 7.
Lester, John T., 7.
Lincoln, Abraham, 57, 59.
Lind, Sylvester, 16, 58, 78.
Lineburger, *Rev.* Isaac, 25.
Lock, William, 16, 58, 87.
Logan, John A., 7.
Loomis, Henry, 16, 78.
Loomis, Horatio G., 17, 51, 58, 87.
Loomis, John M., 7.
Loyd, Alexander, 34.
Ludington, Nelson, 7.

M.

'Magill, Julian, 17.
Maher, Hugh, 17.
Marlborough, *Duke of*, 27.
Malony, Mathew S., 17.
Manierre, Edward, 17, 87.
Manierre, George, 34.
Markoe, Hartman, 17.
Marsh, Sylvester, 17.
Marshall, George E., 7.
Marshall, James A., 17, 58, 61, 87.
Martineau, Harriet, 29.
May, Edward, 7.
McCarthy, Owen, 17.
McClelland, H. W., 7.
McClure, Josiah E., 17, 78.
McDaniels, Alexander, 17, 87.
McDonnell, Charles, 17, 56.
McKee, David, 17, 47.
McIntosh, David, 17.
Meeker, George W., 68, 69.
Metz, Christopher, 17, 79.
Michigan (steamer), 54.
Miller, Jacob, 34, 48.
Miller, DeLaskie, 7.

Miller, John, 34, 48.
Miller, R. B., 7.
Miller, Samuel, 34, 48.
Milliken, Isaac L., 17, 57, 88.
Mills, John R., 17, 88.
Miltimore, Ira, 17, 56, 88.
Mitchell, Arthur, 78.
Mitchell, John J., 7.
Molony, Mathew S., 51.
Moore, Henry, 34, 58.
Moore, John, 54.
Moore, Robert, 17.
Morgan, Patrick R., 17.
Morley, E. W., 7.
Morris, Buckner S., 17, 31, 51, 56, 58, 70, 79.
Morrison, Daniel, 17, 88.
Morrison, Ephraim, 17, 88.
Morrison, Ezekiel, 17, 88.
Morse, T. E., 7.
Murphy, James K , 17, 88.
Murphy, John, 34.
Murray, Robert N., 17, 50, 54, 88.
Myrick, Willard F., 17, 88.

N.

Newberry, Walter L., 34, 55, 75.
Nichols, Luther, 17, 52.
Noble, John, 17, 88.
Norris, Joseph F., 58.
Norton, Nelson R., 17, 54.

O.

Oakley, J W., 7.
Ogden, J. W., 7.
Ogden, Mahlon D., 17, 51, 57, 69, 88.
Ogden, William B., 34, 56, 69, 75.
Oliver, John A., 88.
Olmstead, Edward, 8.
Osborn, Andrew L., 17, 88.
Osborn, William, 17, 51, 88.
Otis, George L., 8.
Otis, Joseph E., 8.
Otis, Philo A., 8.
Otis, X. L., 8.
Owen, George, 74.
Owen, Thomas, 74.
Owen, Thomas J. V., 74.
Owen, William, 74.

P.

Packard, Edward A., 8.

Page, Peter, 17, 57, 88.
Page, William R., 8.
Pardee, Theron, 17.
Parker, John, 18.
Parker, Thomas L., 18.
Peacock, Elijah, 18.
Peacock, Charles D., 8.
Peacock, Joseph, 18, 88.
Peck, Clarence I., 8.
Peck, Ebenezer, 18, 77.
Peck, Ferdinand W., 8.
Peck, John L., 8.
Peck, Philip F. W., 34, 74.
Perry, Robert L., 5, 8.
Peters, George, 18.
Phelps, Erskine M., 8.
Pickering, *Capt.*-——, 38.
Pierce, Asahel, 18, 54, 56, 88.
Pierce, Franklin, 59.
Pierce, Smith D., 18.
Pitkin, Nathaniel, 18.
Plum, William B., 18.
Polk, James K., 59.
Pool, *Capt.* J. W., 18, 88.
Porter, Hibbard, 18, 88.
Porter, *Rev.* Jeremiah, 18, 52, 77, 78.
Porter, *Mrs.* Jeremiah, 77.
Porter, *Rev.* J. G., 18.
Powell, Samuel, 8.
Powers, William G., 88.
Price, Cornelius, 88.
Prindeville, John, 18, 88.
Prindeville, Redmond, 18, 88.
Pullman, George M., 8.

Q.

Quick, John H. S., 8.

R.

Ralston, R. W., 8.
Rand, Socrates, 18.
Raymond, Benjamin W., 18, 31, 51, 52, 56, 59, 89.
Rees, James H., 9, 11, 18, 31, 52, 73, 80, 89.
Reis, John M., 18.
Reis, Jacob, 18.
Reis, John P., 18.
Rexford, Norman, 18.
Rexford, Stephen, 18, 89.
Richards, James J., 18, 89.
Robinson, Alexander (or Che-che-pinqua, Indian chief), 48.

INDEX.

Rockwell, A. L., 8.
Roe, John, 8.
Rogers, Edward K., 18, 51, 59, 89.
Rogers, John G., 8.
Root, J. S., 18.
Root, John W., 8.
Rue, John C., 18.
Rumsey, George F., 18, 31, 89.
Rumsey, Julien S., 18, 31, 57, 89.
Russell, Jacob, 34.
Russell, John B. F., 34.
Ryan, Edward G., 18.

S.

Saltonstall, F. G., 18.
Sare, William H., 8.
Satterlee, Merritt L., 18, 51, 89.
Sauganash (or Billy Caldwell, Indian chief), 48, 49, 74.
Sawyer, E. T., 8.
Sawyer, Nathaniel, 18.
Sawyer, Sidney, 18, 51, 89.
Scammon, J. Young, 19, 30, 31, 50, 57, 65, 68, 89.
Schneider, George, 8.
Scott, Willard, 19, 47, 89.
Scott, Willis, 19, 47, 50, 89.
Scott, *Gen.* Winfield, 50.
Scoville, William H., 19, 89.
See, *Rev.* William, 25.
Seeberger, A. F., 8.
Seeberger, C. D., 8.
Shabonee (or Chamblee, Indian chief), 48.
Shapley, Morgan L., 19, 53.
Shay, M. D., 8.
Shepard, J. H., 8.
Sheridan, *Gen.* Philip H., 8, 54, 76.
Sherman, Alanson S., 19, 52, 56, 58, 89.
Sherman, Ezra I., 19, 59, 89.
Sherman, Francis C., 34.
Sherman, Frank T., 19.
Sherman, J. S., 19.
Sherman, Oren, 19, 51, 89.
Shipman, Daniel B., 8.
Skeele, J. H., 8.
Skinner, Mark, 19, 31, 51, 57, 58, 59, 89.
Smith, Byron L., 8.
Smith, *Dr.* David S., 19, 51, 89.
Smith, Elijah, 19.
Smith, Fred I., 8.
Smith, George, 19.

Smith, Joseph F., 19.
Snowhook, William B., 19, 54, 57, 59, 89.
Sollett, John, 19, 89.
Soules, Rufus, 19.
Spaulding, S. F., 19.
Speer, Isaac, 19.
Spring, Giles, 34, 40.
Stager, Anson, 5, 8, 25.
Stanton, Daniel D., 19.
Stearns, Marcus C., 8, 9, 11, 19, 31, 73, 80, 89.
Steele, James W., 19, 89.
Stevens, George E., 8.
Stevens, Thomas H., 19.
Stewart, Hart L., 19, 31, 54, 57, 59, 89.
Stone, Joseph A., 8.
Stone, John, 58.
Stone, Lewis W., 19.
Storrs, Emory A., 8.
Stow, Henry M., 19.
Stow, William H., 19, 56.
Strail, J. Milo, 19, 51.
Strong, Henry, 8, 26, 34, 40.
Stubbs, S. A., 89.
Stuart, John T., 51.
Sturtevant, Austin D., 19, 90.
Surdam, Samuel J., 19, 51, 58, 90.
Sweeney, John, 19.
Sweet, *Mrs.* Charles, 25.
Swift, Richard K., 19.

T.

Talcott, Edward B., 19, 52, 53, 59.
Taylor, Augustine Deodat, 19, 31, 52.
Taylor, *Mrs.* Charles, 77.
Taylor, Edmund D., 20, 31, 46, 47, 51, 53, 57, 59, 90.
Taylor, Ezra, 20.
Taylor, Reuben, 20.
Taylor, William H., 20, 51, 52, 79.
Taylor, *Gen.* Zachary, 58, 59.
Tecumseh (Indian chief), 48, 49.
Temple, Peter, 20, 79.
Tenney, D. K., 8.
Thacher, J. M., 8.
Thompson, John L., 8.
Throop, Amos G., 57.
Toner, John, 20.
Towner, Norman K., 74, 75.
Tripp, Robinson, 20, 58, 90.
Tucker, W. F., jr., 8.

Turner, John, 20, 79.
Turner, John B., 34, 75.
Turner, John M., 20, 52.
Turner, Leighton, 20.
Tuttle, Frederick, 8, 9, **11, 20, 73,** 80, 90.
Tuttle, Frederick B., **5, 8, 9.**
Tuttle, Lucius G., 20.
Tyler, John, 57, 59.

U.

Underwood, John M., **20, 75.**

V.

Vail, H. S., **S.**
Vail, Walter, 20, 79, 90.
Vallette, Henry F., 20.
VanBuren, Martin, 51, 59.
Vandercook, Charles R., 20.
VanNortwick, John, 20, 90.
VanOsdell, John M., 20, 52, **90.**
VanSchaack, Peter, 8.
VanSchaick, A. G., **5, 8, 9.**

W.

Wadhams, Carlton, **20.**
Wadhams, Seth, 20, **90.**
Wadsworth, Elisha S., **20, 31, 51, 79.**
Wadsworth, Julius, **20, 31, 56.**
Waite, George W., **20, 90.**
Walker, *Rev.* Jesse, **24, 48, 73, 74.**
Walker, Lucy, 25.
Walker, Samuel B., **58.**
Walker, William B., **8.**
Walter, Joel C., 8, 9, **11, 20, 31, 51, 73, 79, 80, 90.**
Walton, Nelson **C., 20.**
Warner, Seth P., **20.**
Warner, **Spencer, 20.**
Warren, **Julius** M., **54, 60, 61, 63, 71.**
Waters, Benjamin, 20.
Watkins, John, 20, 50, **74.**
Watkins, Thomas, 49.
Watson, William, jr., **8.**

Wattles, William **W.,** 39.
Wellington, *Duke of,* 27.
Wells, M. D., **8.**
Wentworth, Elijah, sr., 34.
Wentworth, Elijah, jr., 25, **34.**
Wentworth, Moses J., 8.
Wentworth, John, 20, 31, 45, 71, **81,** 90.
Wentworth, Lucy (Walker), 25.
Wetmore, C. L., 8.
Wheaton, George D., 8.
Wheeler, C. T., 8.
Wheeler, Ezra J., 8.
Wheeler, H. N., 8.
White, George, 36, 64.
Whitehead, *Rev.* Henry, 20, **90.**
Whitney, J. C., 8.
Wicker, Charles G., 20.
Wicker, Joel H., 20.
Wight, Thomas, 8.
Wilbor, Philo A., 8.
Wilcox, Sextus N., 21, **90.**
Wilde, George W., 21.
Williams, Abram, 8.
Williams, Clifford, 8.
Williams, Norman, 8.
Willard, Alonzo J., 21, 90.
Willard, Elisha W., 21.
Williams, Eli B., 21, 31, 51, 54, 56, 59, 90.
Williams, **Giles, 21.**
Wilson, Hugh **R., 8.**
Wilson, John L., **21, 34, 52, 57, 90.**
Winship, James, 21, 90.
Wolcott, Alexander, 21, **52, 90.**
Wood, Alonzo C., 21.
Woodruft, Charles W., 8.
Woodworth, James H., 34.
Woodworth, Robert P., 34.
Wright, George S., **21.**
Wright, John, 31, 35, **74.**
Wright, John S., 31.
Wright, Truman G., **21, 79.**

Y.

Yates, Horace H., **21, 90.**

FERGUS PRINTING COMPANY, CHICAGO.

THE MARTYRDOM OF LOVEJOY.

An **account of the Life**, Trials, and Perils **of** Rev. Elijah P. Lovejoy, killed by a Pro-Slavery Mob, at Alton, Ill., on the night of Nov. 7, 1837. By HENRY TANNER, of Buffalo, N.Y., an Eye-Witness. Cloth boards; Gilt-top; Side and bottom uncut; Illustrated; Pp. 233; 8vo, 1881. Price, $2.

An exceedingly interesting and fully authentic narrative of one of the most thrilling episodes in the history of the great anti-slavery movement which culminated in the War of the Rebellion and the emancipation of the slaves by President Lincoln. But for such books as this, it would be difficult for us, in this day, **to** realize what heroic courage, what patience **in** suffering and self-sacrifice it required to stand up against the bitter opposition which the publication of anti-slavery sentiments elicited in the dark days of 1837, when Lovejoy published the Alton *Observer*. There is no doubt but that Lovejoy's name **will go into** history as the first American martyr **for** the right of free speech and a free press. He was a brave, great-souled, clear-headed **man, and, like** Samson of old, it may be said of him **that he** slew more Philistines at his death than in all his life. The publishers **of** this and other **valuable** documents relating to the early history **of our** State, are doing a good work for the **general** public and for posterity. They rank among the oldest printing companies of the City, and **it** seems peculiarly appropriate **that** they should seek to rescue from fast-approaching oblivion all accessible facts relating **to** early pioneer life within the bounds of our glorious Commonwealth. The "Martyrdom of Lovejoy" is not the **only** valuable work which has already issued from **their** press, and which they keep constantly **on hand** for sale.—*Chicago Journal*, Feb. 5, 1881.

The story is deeply interesting, **and now seems** almost incredible, so far have we **risen beyond** the stagnant condition in which **Lovejoy's death** found us. The book is handsomely **printed and** contains a few engravings and fac-similes,—one, a head of Lovejoy himself, who does not look like a great man, but like a good one, as in fact he was,—brave and earnest and well fitted to be a martyr.—*Springfield Republi'n*, Mass., March 24th, 1881.

Not only to those who at the time were personally interested in the career and heroic death of the Rev Elijah Parrish Lovejoy, nor to those who now warmly sympathize with the noble purposes which prompted the martyr to the pursuit of ends apparently chimerical in the extent of their nobility; but to all students of the germs and first budding of a mighty reformation in the history of morals, and to all lovers of mysterious natural development this book will be valuable. Here is vividly portrayed the first blood-letting for outspoken antagonism to the villainies of slave-traffic and slave-holding, **and** the wonderful persistence in aim, as well as the power of thought and pen that prepared Lovejoy for his glorious end. From the early articles on transubstantiation and nunneries to the last fiery denunciation of negro subjection, the hero shows the same outspoken boldness of conviction, combined with a continual increase in ability of expression. That any pledge was violated in the **assumption** of an anti-slavery tone in the **leaders of the** *St. Louis Observer*, Mr. Tanner has clearly proved groundless: and that the life of Elijah Parrish Lovejoy is worthy **to** be ranked among the highest and purest, no **candid** reader can pretend to doubt. "So shines **a good** deed in a naughty world."—*Buffalo Express*, May 18, 1881.

Probably no single event in the early history **of** the progress of the anti-slavery sentiment in the United States, produced a more profound impression at the time than the successive destruction, by mobs, of the four printing-presses which belonged to Mr. Lovejoy, and in the defence of the last of which, under the sanction of civil authority, he sacrificed his life. These early annals of the anti-slavery agitation can well be perused by many who lived at the time, while **to** the student of American history, who has **been** born since those years, they are invaluable.—*Iowa State Register*, May 14, 1881.

The "Martyrdom of Lovejoy" is the title of a well-printed octavo volume, published by the Fergus Printing Company, of Chicago, which contains an account of the life, trials, and perils of Rev. Elijah P. Lovejoy. * * * The author, Henry Tanner, of Buffalo, N.Y., who assisted Mr. Lovejoy in the defence of his property and **his** rights, and was by his side when he died, **has** done a valuable service in gathering, from the records of the past, so many items of historic interest to combine with his **own** recollections of the tragic event which shook the whole country like an earthquake.—*Sunday Herald*, Boston, March 6, 1881.

This is a plain, unvarnished history of **the** life and perils of the Rev. Elijah P. Lovejoy. * * * So rapid has been the march of public sentiment that the generation of young men and women of to-day can not realize the bitter and deadly antagonism of slavery forty-three years ago. The book will give an insight into the bitter and unrelenting spirit which held sway even in the old North. It is not written to keep alive old antagonisms, but as history, which all should know, that they may better appreciate all that has been accomplished in the past, and appreciate the present. The story is told without any effort at embellishment, and wonderfully free from every vindictive expression. If the friends of human **slavery** object to anything in the volume, it will be the honest facts of the history, which need **no** embellishment or sharp phrase to make them abhorrent to every lover of the right and free institutions.—*Inter Ocean*, Chicago, Feb. 5, 1881

As the narrative has **reference to events long** since past, connected with the early days of the anti-slavery contest, we had no idea until we began reading the book that we **should find it** so deeply interesting **and well calculated to give** an insight into the **struggle for the liberty of** the press which led to the abolition of slavery.—*Messiah's Herald*, Boston, March 30, 1881.

Reception **to the** Settlers of Chicago, prior to 1840, by the CALUMET CLUB, May 27, 1879. Containing Club Members' Names; Origin of Reception: Record of Old Settlers invited; Reception: Speeches of Rev. Stephen R. Beggs, Gen Henry Strong, Ex.-Chief-Justice John Dean Caton, Judge Henry W. Blodgett, **Judge** James Grant, Hon. John Wentworth, Judge Grant Goodrich, Hon. J. Young Scammon, and Hon. Wm. Bross; Tables showing places of birth, year of arrival, **and age** of those who attended and signed Register; Appendix with letters from John Watkins, Norman K. Towner, Rev. Flavel Bascom, Maj.-Gen. David Hunter, Judge Ebenezer Peck, Rev, Jeremiah Porter, and the names from whom brief letters of regret were received; Extracts from *Chicago Tribune* and *Evening Journal*; and Register of Old Settlers: with name, date of arrival, birthplace, age, and present address. Compiled by Hon. JOHN WENTWORTH. Pp 90; 8vo, 1879.

Sent by mail, post-paid,

FERGUS' HISTORICAL SERIES:

1.

Annals of Chicago: A Lecture read before the Chicago Lyceum, Jan. 21, 1840. By JOSEPH N. BALESTIER, Esq. Republished from the original edition of 1840, with an Introduction, written by the Author in 1876; and, also, a Review of the Lecture, published in the *Chicago Tribune*, in 1872. Pp. 48; 8vo. 1876. Price, 25 cents.

2.

Fergus' Directory of the City of Chicago, 1839; with City and County Officers, Churches, Public Buildings, Hotels, etc.; also, list of Sheriffs of Cook County and Mayors of the City since their organization; together with the Poll-list of the First City Election (Tuesday, May 2, 1837). List of Purchasers of Lots in Fort-Dearborn Addition, the No. of the Lots and the prices paid, etc., etc. (Historical Sketch of City compiled for Directory of 1843, etc.) Compiled by ROBERT FERGUS. Pp. 68; 8vo. 1876. Price, 50 cents.

3.

The Last of the Illinois, and a Sketch of the Pottawatomies: A Lecture read before the Chicago Historical Society, Dec. 13, 1870. Also, Origin of the Prairies: A Lecture read before the Ottawa Academy of Natural Sciences, Dec. 30, 1869. By Hon. JOHN DEAN CATON, LL.D., late Chief-Justice of Illinois. Pp. 56; 8vo. 1876. Price, 25 cts.

4.

Early Movement in Illinois for the Legalization of Slavery: An Historical Sketch read at the Annual Meeting of the Chicago Historical Society, Dec. 5, 1864. By Hon. WM. H. BROWN. Pp. 32; 8vo. 1876. Price, 25 cents.

5.

Biographical Sketches of Early Settlers of Chicago. Part I:—Hon. S. Lisle Smith, Geo. Davis, Dr. Philip Maxwell, John J. Brown, Richard L. Wilson, Col. Lewis C. Kerchival, Uriah P. Harris, Henry B. Clarke, and Sheriff Samuel J. Lowe. By W. H. BUSHNELL. Pp. 48; 8vo. 1876. Price, 25 cts.

6.

Biographical Sketches of Early Settlers of Chicago. Part II:—Hon. Wm. H. Brown, with Portrait, B. W. Raymond, Esq., with Portrait, Hon. J. Y. Scammon, Chas. Walker, Esq., Thos. Church, Esq. Pp. 48; 8vo. 1876. Price, 25 cents.

7.

Early Chicago: A Sunday Lecture read in McCormick's Hall, May 7th, 1876. With Supplemental Notes. 2d Lecture. By Hon. JOHN WENTWORTH. Portrait. Pp. 56; 8vo. 1876. Price, 35 cts.

8.

Early Chicago: A Sunday Lecture read in McCormick's Hall, April 11, 1875. With Supplemental Notes. 1st Lecture. By Hon. JOHN WENTWORTH. Portrait. Pp. 48; 8vo. 1876. Price, 35 cts.

9.

Present and Future Prospects of Chicago: An Address read before the Chicago Lyceum, Jan. 20, 1846. By Judge HENRY BROWN, author of "History of Illinois."

Rise and Progress of Chicago: An Address read before the Centennial Library Association, March 21, 1876. By JAMES A. MARSHALL, Esq.

Chicago in 1836: "Strange Early Days." By HARRIET MARTINEAU, author of "Society in America," etc. Pp. 48; 8vo. 1876. Price, 25 cents.

10.

Addresses Read before Chicago Historical Society, by Hon. J. Y. SCAMMON, Hon. I. N. ARNOLD, WM. HICKLING, Esq., Col. G. S. HUBBARD, and HIRAM W. BECKWITH, Esq.; Sketches of Col. John H. Kinzie, by his wife, JULIETTE A. KINZIE; Judge Geo. Manierre, Luther Haven, E. Q. and other Early Settlers; also, of Billy Caldwell and Shabonee, and the "Winnebago Scare," of July, 1827, and other important original matter connected with "Early Chicago." Pp. 52; 8vo. 1877. Price, 35¢.

11.

Early Medical Chicago: An Historical Sketch of the First Practitioners of Medicine; with the Present Faculties, and Graduates since their Organization of the Medical Colleges of Chicago. By JAMES NEVINS HYDE, A.M., M.D. Illustrated with numerous Wood Engravings and Steel Engravings of Professors J. Adams Allen, N. S. Davis, and the late Daniel Brainard. Pp. 84; 8vo. 1879. Price, 50 cts.

12.

Illinois in the 18th Century.—Kaskaskia and its Parish Records. A Paper read before the Chicago Historical Society, Dec. 16, 1879.

Old Fort Chartres. A Paper read before the Chicago Historical Society, June 16, 1880. With Diagram of Fort.

Col. John Todd's Record Book. A Paper read before the Chicago Historical Society, Feb. 15, 1881. By EDWARD G. MASON. Pp. 68; 8vo. 1881. (In Press.) Price, 50 cents.

13.

Recollections of Early Illinois and her Noted Men. By Hon. JOSEPH GILLESPIE, Edwardsville. Read before the Chicago Historical Society, March 16, 1880. With Portraits of Author, Govs. Reynolds and Bissell, and Henry Gratiot. Pp. 52; 8vo. 1880. Price, 50 cents.

14.

The Earliest Religious History of Chicago. By Rev. JEREMIAH PORTER, its 1st Resident Pastor. An Address read before the Chicago Hist. Soc., 1859.

Early History of Illinois. By Hon. WILLIAM H. BROWN. A Lecture read before the Chicago Lyceum, Dec. 8, 1840.

Early Society in Southern Illinois. By Rev. ROBERT W. PATTERSON, D.D. An Address read before the Chicago Historical Society, Oct. 19, 1880.

Reminiscences of the Illinois-Bar Forty Years Ago: Lincoln and Douglas as Orators and Lawyers. By Hon. ISAAC N. ARNOLD. Read before the State Bar Association, Springfield, Jan. 7, 1881.

The First Murder-Trial in Iroquois County for the First Murder in Cook County. Pp. 112; 8vo. 1881. Price, 50 cents.

15.

Abraham Lincoln: A Paper read before the Royal Historical Society, London, June 16, 1881. By Hon. ISAAC N. ARNOLD, of Chicago.

Stephen Arnold Douglas, An Eulogy. Delivered before the Chicago University, in Bryan Hall, July 3, 1861. By Hon. JAMES W. SHEAHAN, of *The Chicago Tribune*, 1881. 8vo. 48 pp.; paper. Price, 25 cents.

16.

Early Chicago—Fort Dearborn: An Address read at the unveiling of a tablet on the Fort site, under the auspices of the Chicago Historical Society, Chicago, May 21, 1881. 3d Paper. By Hon. JOHN WENTWORTH, LL.D. With an Appendix, etc., etc. Portraits of Capt. Wm. Wells and Mrs. C pt. Heald. Also, Indexes to 1st and 2d Lectures and "Calumet Club Reception." 8vo. 112 pp. 75¢

Any of the above books sent by mail on receipt of price, postpaid, to any part of the U. S., by the Publishers.

August 15, 1881. **Fergus Printing Company, Chicago.**

www.ingramcontent.com/pod-product-compliance
Lightning Source LLC
Chambersburg PA
CBHW021936160426
43195CB00011B/1112